The Wings of Democracy

TEXAS A&M UNIVERSITY
MILITARY HISTORY SERIES
22

The Wings of Democracy

THE INFLUENCE OF AIR POWER

ON THE ROOSEVELT ADMINISTRATION, 1933–1941

Jeffery S. Underwood

TEXAS A&M UNIVERSITY PRESS

COLLEGE STATION

The paper used in this book meets the minimum requirements of the
American National Standard for Permanence of Paper for Printed Library
Materials, Z39.48-1984. Binding materials have been chosen for durability.
∞

Library of Congress Cataloging-in-Publication Data
Underwood, Jeffery S., 1954–   *64t 5/99*
    The wings of democracy : the influence of air power on the
Roosevelt Administration, 1933–1941 / Jeffery S. Underwood. — 1st
ed.,
        p.   cm. — (Texas A&M University military history series ;
22)
    Includes bibliographical references and index.
    ISBN 0-89096-388-6
    1. Air power—United States—History.   2. United States. Army.
Air Corps—History.   I. Title.   II. Series.
  UG633.U46   1991
    358.4'03'0973—dc20   91-15653
                                                                      CIP

To my mother, *Mary B. Underwood*

Contents

Illustrations

Acknowledgments

Without the patient assistance of Charles Royster, this book would not have been written. For his help, I will always be grateful.

To Randall Rogers, John L. Loos, Gaines Foster, Karl A. Roider, Patricia Lawrence, John Tew, and Brady Banta at Louisiana State University, I would also like to express my appreciation. Frank Freidel, Jr., John F. Shinner, Joseph Dawson, and Betty Kennedy gave insights, suggestions, and corrections that helped change this work from a manuscript to a book. My research was ably furthered through the kind assistance of George C. Chalou, Wilbert B. Mahoney, and the staff of the Military Reference Branch of the National Archives and Records Administration; James H. Hutson, Fred Bauman, Chuck Kelly, and the staff of the Manuscript Division of the Library of Congress; and Raymond Teichman and the staff of the Franklin D. Roosevelt Library.

To Larry, Steve, Deborah, Valerie, and Trooper, a special thanks.

The Wings of Democracy

Introduction

In writing about an air force not at war, I tried to step outside the traditional boundaries of military history. Avoiding a detailed discussion of tactics, organization, and weapons development, I have emphasized the political growth of the officers who built the air force with which the United States fought the Second World War.

While researching this book, I held a belief similar to John F. Shiner, who wrote: "When Roosevelt did concern himself with defense issues, his interest focused on his old love—the Navy. As Billy Mitchell said in 1935 after seeing the President's desk covered with naval mementos: 'I wish I could have seen one airplane in that collection.' Those who believed FDR would intervene in the Army air arm's behalf were victims of their own wishful thinking."[1]

To my surprise and pleasure, I discovered that Roosevelt possessed an appreciation for the *potential* of air power as early as 1919 when he served as President Woodrow Wilson's assistant secretary of the navy. Also, I learned that in the early 1930s Billy Mitchell influenced FDR's view of air power. However, Roosevelt took a pragmatic view toward air power. He saw the potential of air power but demanded proof of its feasibility. Once the Army Air Corps proved the value of air power, Roosevelt quickly turned to it as a solution for diplomatic and military problems. Furthermore, I discovered the reason behind Roosevelt's change from a man wanting to ban bombers and aerial bombardment into a man willing to bomb civilian populations.

When Franklin D. Roosevelt became president of the United States of America in 1933, he inherited a factious group of airmen in the United States Army Air Corps. These aviators had claimed incessantly throughout the 1920s that their airplanes held the key to modern warfare. Boasting that airplanes could sink any battleship, they stated that the nation needed only airplanes for protection against foreign invasion. Their planes, furthermore, could ensure a quick battlefield victory. However, they believed that armies should never need to meet in combat. Through strategic bombing campaigns, the army fliers argued, an enemy nation could be defeated before its armies reached the field. But when the army failed to heed their claims, they, led by General William "Billy" Mitchell, openly advocated separating the air force from the army. Hoping to rally public opinion and force the government to respond, these men created problems for the three Republican administrations preceding Roosevelt.

By using public confrontations, constantly bemoaning the poor condition of the air arm, and making unproven pronouncements about air power, Mitchell and his followers only antagonized the General Staff of the United States Army, the very men who could grant them independence. As this antagonism turned to distrust, the General Staff started to ignore anything the army airmen said. After Mitchell's court-martial and retirement from the army in 1926, other air officers continued using his tactics, even after Roosevelt took office.

In April of 1941, Hanson W. Baldwin, a military affairs writer for the *New York Times,* published *United We Stand! Defense of the Western Hemisphere.* In this assessment of America's defensive needs, Baldwin wrote that "the Army Air Corps has been hampered unquestionably, in past years, by the conservatives of the general staff. But there is equal certainty that the Air Corps has contributed to the stunting of its own growth because of the boastful egotism of too many of its members, the undisciplined and exaggerated claims of others, the lack of a leader like [Rear Admiral William A.] Moffett, a leader who combined tact with zeal and quiet firmness and an abiding faith in the plane."[2] Baldwin correctly interpreted the damage done by the army fliers, but he failed to notice that the Army Air Corps had produced officers equal to Admiral Moffett, the navy's advocate of air power. During Roosevelt's first term, a change had occurred in the Army Air Corps. Men, convinced of the importance of air power but also endowed with extraordinary political acumen, took command of the army's air arm. Once in positions of authority, Oscar Westover, Henry H. "Hap" Arnold, and Frank M. Andrews launched a concerted effort to persuade the General Staff and the Roosevelt administration that the Army Air Corps had given up the caustic, separatist attitudes of Billy Mitchell. By presenting themselves as "team players," these officers reduced the animosity of their superiors, and no longer blinded by rage, the General Staff started listening to what the Army

Air Corps had to say. With spectacular, long-range flights and other examples of efficiency, these airmen proved that the Army Air Corps could deliver what it promised. As a result, the Roosevelt administration and the General Staff more readily accepted the claims of the air power advocates.

Then, beginning in 1939, the war in Europe appeared to further substantiate many of the prophecies about air power, especially that land-based airplanes could force unprotected naval forces to withdraw. The Roosevelt administration, persuaded of their reliability, entrusted the Army Air Corps officers with implementing America's foreign policy in the Far East. For twenty years, army planners had considered the Philippines indefensible, but on the eve of American entry into World War II, the Army Air Corps was given the critical task of defending the islands with its long-range, B-17 bombers. Confident in the Army Air Corps, Roosevelt and his advisors believed the long-range bombers could effectively blockade Japan. Almost as an afterthought, the bombers were expected to deter further Japanese expansion by playing upon Japan's long-standing and well-known fear of having its cities burned by enemy bombers. However, this would not have been an idle threat.

With both the United States and Japan intent upon establishing economic hegemony in the Far East after World War I, a test of wills grew. Throughout the 1930s, the Japanese won. The Japanese Imperial Navy dominated the Far East, and the United States lacked the military and naval might to force its will upon the Japanese. Presidents Hoover and Roosevelt could do little more than threaten nonrecognition of Japanese conquests, impose trade embargoes, or move the United States' only naval fleet closer to Japan. But by 1941, American technology in the form of air power promised to change the balance of power in the Pacific. Five years before the United States exploded its first atomic bomb at Alamogordo, New Mexico, the strategy of using superior technology to deter an enemy had taken root in American foreign policy. The atomic diplomacy practiced by the United States after World War II was only an updated version of a foreign policy based on the application of air power.

I. The Billy Mitchell Years

"Join the Army Air Service—Be an American Eagle!" Thus exhorted a 1918 recruiting poster. The illustration showed a sleek, powerful American bald eagle subduing a mangy eagle of Imperial Germany. Behind them, American planes on their way to fight the Huns darkened a brilliant sunrise.[1]

Using a bald eagle to represent the air force became common, but the poster was significant because it appealed to a number of assumptions held by Americans during the First World War. Its clashing eagles symbolized the superiority of American democracy over German autocracy, and the image of skies blackened by a vast fleet of American-built aircraft reflected Americans' belief in their industrial capabilities. Yet, the poster also displayed what would become a dominant theme in twentieth-century American military planning: fighting a war with machines rather than great numbers of troops.

The American preference for fighting with machines became apparent immediately. In June, 1917, the Aircraft Production Board created an ambitious plan for placing 4,500 airplanes, 5,000 pilots, and 50,000 mechanics on the western front within a year. The board said that its plan would allow the United States to win air superiority, "and with that we hope to become an immediate, decisive factor in ending the war." Congress enthusiastically appropriated $640 million on July 24, 1917, for the army air arm to implement the production plan.

Ironically, Americans' conceptions of how they would fight to make the world safe for democracy were just the opposite of how they actually fought the war. Although many Americans flew over the western front, American-built planes never filled the skies over the western front. Beset by a wide variety of problems, the American aircraft industry failed to fulfill the Aircraft Production Board's expectations, and only 696 American-built airplanes reached the front before the armistice. The American fliers had to use French or British airplanes. In contrast, millions of American doughboys reached the western front. American manpower, not American technology or industrial power, made the difference in 1918.[2]

Even if the skies over Europe had been darkened by American planes, disagreements over how to use the new weapons would have hindered their use. Pres. Woodrow Wilson would have objected to using American planes to attack civilians. When the war broke out in 1914, Wilson tried to convince the Germans not to bomb Allied cities; but, as with his attempts to stop the Germans from using submarines, he failed. Desperately seeking a way to win the war, the Germans refused to let either their submarines or aircraft go unused. They launched air raids against England with zeppelins and Gotha bombers. Although the air raids did little real damage, they frightened the British people. Public opinion forced the government to withdraw aircraft from the western front to defend England from the German air raiders. To coordinate aerial defenses, the government separated the air arms from the army and navy. The Royal Flying Corps and the Royal Naval Air Service were joined together into the Royal Air Force in April of 1918. To retaliate for the German air raids, the RAF placed Gen. Hugh Trenchard in command of a strategic bombing force—the Inter-Allied Independent Air Force—to carry the air war deep into Germany. Hoping to coordinate the aerial assault on Germany, the British convinced the French to join an Independent Air Force, and the American Army Air Service planned to participate also. Once the Germans learned of the IAF, they tried to forestall the Allied bombing campaign by announcing that future bombing would be limited to the battle zone, but the Allies refused to recognize the de-escalation and continued their preparations.[3]

Early contact with the British helped shape the way American airmen prepared to fight. Maj. William "Billy" Mitchell visited Trenchard in May, 1917, and the British commander's ideas on strategic bombing influenced him. When promoted to brigadier general and placed in command of the Army Air Service for the First Army Group in France, Mitchell put into practice Trenchard's teachings and used his airplanes as an offensive weapon behind the German lines. During the attack on the Saint-Mihiel salient in September of 1918, General Mitchell successfully led a combined force of 1,500 American, British, French, Italian, and Portuguese aircraft against the Germans.

1. Brig. Gen. William Mitchell. *Courtesy U.S.A.F*

Later, with fewer planes at his disposal, Mitchell commanded the American air assault during the Meuse-Argonne offensive with equal success. On October 9, 1918, Mitchell concentrated over 350 American and French aircraft to attack German troops massing for a counterattack. In the Army Air Service's most significant attack of the war, Mitchell's planes overwhelmed the German air defenses and disrupted the counterattack. Although Mitchell had used his airplanes as tactical forces rather than strategic forces, he had followed Trenchard's teachings and had taken the offensive. The Associated Press, reporting on the attack of October 9, claimed that the bombing squadrons of "this air fleet probably represent the first definite American unit of major importance in the independent air forces which are being built up by the Entente powers. This navy of the air is to be expanded until no part of Germany is safe from the rain of bombs. . . . The work of the independent force is bombing munitions works, factories, cities, and other important centers far behind the German lines. It has been promised that eventually Berlin itself will know what an air raid means, and the whole great project is a direct answer to the German air attacks on helpless and unfortified British, French, and Belgian cities."[4]

Political leaders in the United States, however, opposed the use of aerial bombardment. On November 8, Secretary of War Newton D. Baker ordered Chief of Staff Gen. Peyton March to inform the Army Air Service that the United States would not take part in any plans for the "promiscuous bombing upon industry, commerce, or population, in enemy countries disassociated from obvious military needs to be served by such action."[5] Baker showed that the United States government remained consistent in its views on the conduct of war. Refusing to condone unrestricted submarine warfare, the U.S. government also refused to approve the aerial bombardment of civilian populations. The armistice ended the Inter-Allied Independent Air Force and prevented an open breach between the American military leaders in France and the political leaders at home over the tactical conduct of the war. Throughout the 1920s and 1930s, America's political leaders continued to reject the idea of bombing civilian targets, but many Americans came to believe that the threat of strategic bombing would prevent any future war or end it quickly.

While playing an important role, air power did not decide the outcome of World War I. The inability of airplanes to take or hold ground caused military leaders to adhere to one of two different ideas on how to employ air power in warfare. One group wanted airplanes to provide support for the ground forces and control the airspace above the armies. The other group believed that using airplanes to bomb strategic targets would cripple an enemy's ability to wage war. During the interwar years, the European nations developed their air forces to perform one of these two missions. France, Russia, and Nazi Germany shaped their air forces to support their traditionally large armies, but the Italians and British adopted the doctrine of strategic bombing. The terrible casualties of the World War made politicians in Italy and Great Britain receptive to the strategic bombing doctrine. Realizing that modern industrial systems made possible the recent war of attrition, the proponents of strategic bombing concluded that bombing an enemy's cities and factories could disrupt the production of war materiel needed to sustain a war of attrition. Furthermore, they believed that bombing the capital of an enemy nation would paralyze that nation and make it incapable of conducting a war. Advocates of strategic bombing explained that the resulting deaths of many civilians would be justified in the long run. A quick, successful air campaign would mean fewer casualties than a drawn-out war of attrition. Also, they argued that the threat of air attacks on cities and industry would deter any future wars. Taking great comfort in these assurances, the politicians in Italy and Great Britain readily accepted the concept of strategic bombing.[6] Underlying the theories of those advocating air raids on an enemy's capital was the experience of 1918, when Kaiser William II abdicated in the face of street disorders and a naval mutiny. This experience apparently influenced American and British planning during the Second World War. The Allies expected the German people to force Adolf Hitler to abdicate and create a liberal government as they had in 1918.

In the United States, different political considerations hindered the acceptance of strategic bombing as a doctrine. Disillusioned by the world war, the United States returned to its traditional defenses—the Atlantic and Pacific oceans—and reduced its army and navy to a size just large enough to repel an invasion. Choosing to stay out of European affairs, America refused to join the collective security of the League of Nations. But Americans willingly participated in international disarmament efforts at the Washington Arms Conference of 1921–22, the disarmament talks at Geneva and London, and signed the Briand-Kellogg Pact of 1928. Since strategic bombing is offensive in nature, the adoption of strategic bombing as a military doctrine met resistance from government officials preferring defense and disarmament.

Within the U.S. Army, two views on the employment of air power emerged. The General Staff viewed the air service as a servant of the ground forces, and they opposed the adoption of an air force based on a doctrine of strategic bombing. With Billy Mitchell as their spokesman, the supporters of strategic bombing looked to the wartime, long-range flights made by Italian Caproni bombers and Maj. Gen. Hugh Trenchard's planned raids on Germany with bombers of the Independent Air Force as examples to follow. Because the General Staff had the final say as to which doctrine would be adopted, the supporters of strategic bombing started seeking independence in order to implement their ideas. The movement to create a separate air force similar to the RAF gained momentum when Mitchell and the other fliers returned home.

Mitchell expected to be given command of the air service upon his return from France in 1919, but Maj. Gen. C. T. Menoher, who had no aviation experience, was named the chief of the air service. Mitchell became the assistant chief, and undaunted, he launched a campaign to promote the cause of air power. Ignoring the prevailing antiwar sentiment, he advised the nation to put its "defense money and effort into active offensive equipment designed directly to defeat the enemy." Then, to the displeasure of the navy, he claimed that surface ships were helpless against aircraft. He urged the nation to stop wasting its money on battleships and spend it wisely for airplanes. Like his European counterparts, Mitchell asserted that airplanes could end wars of attrition. By using air power to attack what he called "vital centers," Mitchell claimed that an enemy could be paralyzed and defeated without having to destroy his army first.[7]

Mitchell expected people to adopt his ideas and became upset when they did not. The navy exacerbated his anger by refusing to let him use surrendered German battleships for bombing tests. When Henry H. "Hap" Arnold met with Mitchell in El Paso on July 4, 1919, he noticed an "undercurrent of angry impatience" in Mitchell. Arnold later wrote that "he seemed to brush aside the possibility that a lot of people still might not understand his theories, and he could not be convinced that air power was not being blocked by deliberate and well-organized enemies." Mitchell blamed admirals "unable to face the fact that sea power was done for," old-fashioned generals, and profiteers building battleships. Mitchell's main concern that summer, Arnold recalled, seemed "to be to show them—with activities like the transcontinental air race, the Border Patrol, the Forest Fire Patrol, and now a mass flight to Alaska and a mass flight around the world—and above all, to sink those damned battleships!" Statements by Adm. William S. Benson, Chief of Naval Operations, finally goaded Mitchell into action. Assistant Secretary of War Benedict Crowell headed a board studying the various forms of air forces, and Admiral Benson told one of the board members that he could not "conceive of any use the fleet will ever have for aircraft." He also told Crowell that the navy "doesn't

2. Maj. Gen. Henry H. "Hap" Arnold, who would later become a five-star general and commander of the United States Army Air Forces during World War II. *Courtesy U.S.A.F*

need airplanes." Then on August 1, 1919, Admiral Benson issued a secret order abolishing the navy's Aviation Division. Somehow, Mitchell got a copy of that order and told the Senate Military Affairs Committee on September 12, 1919, that the navy did not have a separate bureau of aviation. Unaware of the order, Assistant Secretary of the Navy Franklin D. Roosevelt came to the defense of the navy. Mitchell's comments, said Roosevelt, showed that he "knew absolutely nothing about the organization of the Navy Department." Mitchell then embarrassed Roosevelt by reading the order to the committee.[8]

Mitchell was the best known, but he was not the only army flier to attack publicly the navy and General Staff. Benjamin D. Foulois—who had been Chief of the Air Service, American Expeditionary Force, during World War I—also launched public attacks on the opponents of air power. While advocating a separate air arm before the Senate Military Affairs Committee on October 16, Foulois accused the General Staff of being reactionary and lacking interest in aerial research and development. Turning his ire toward the navy, he complained that the navy had upset the army's wartime logistics by taking away priorities for engine and aircraft procurement. He then disclosed, for the first time in public, how the navy had negotiated independently with the Italians to buy a large number of Caproni bombers already purchased by the army. In closing, Foulois denounced Roosevelt's earlier claim that "not only the Navy Department officially, but the entire naval service, is absolutely opposed to the creation of another branch of national defense." He challenged Roosevelt's testimony and criticized him personally by stating that "our naval authorities at home" had hampered the growth of the Army Air Service in France.[9]

While both Mitchell and Foulois attacked Franklin D. Roosevelt, they were not conspiring. Mitchell had been Foulois's subordinate during the war, and their relationship had been strained. In 1919, Foulois had been made subordinate to Mitchell, and the situation became worse. The antagonism between the two became so great that, in spite of having adjacent offices, they never spoke. Besides the importance of air power, anti-navy feelings were about the only thing that Mitchell and Foulois could agree upon. They lumped together anyone connected with the navy into a monolithic enemy, and their narrow views blinded them to the fact that Roosevelt felt differently about the role of aviation than did most of the admirals. James Wadsworth, Jr., chair of the Senate Military Affairs Committee, asked Roosevelt if aviation could become the principal factor in the army or navy. Exhibiting greater foresight than Admiral Benson, Roosevelt answered: "It might conceivably, in the Navy, become the principal factor. I don't know whether the Chief of Naval Operations will agree with me, but I might say that later on, in the future, aviation might make surface ships practically impossible to be used as an Arm."[10] Twenty-two years later, on the eve of America's entry into World War II, President Roosevelt believed that bombers had made that possibility come true.

Franklin Roosevelt did not believe that aviation should be separated from the navy. In the fall of 1918, Roosevelt had inspected U.S. Navy facilities in France, and he found naval aviation to have the greatest problems. While praising the efforts of navy personnel at naval air stations, he complained to Secretary of the Navy Josephus Daniels about what he called the scandalous condition of American-built seaplanes shipped to France. The problems, he told Daniels, resulted from the poor system of procurement by which different bureaus of the Navy Department supplied various aircraft components. Roosevelt recommended strengthening the authority of the Office of Naval Aviation. Otherwise, although he opposed the creation of an air ministry, Roosevelt said that "the present situation will strengthen the hands of those who would take Naval Aviation away from the Navy Department."

In June of 1919, Roosevelt publicly denounced the idea of taking aviation away from the navy. He viewed the role of naval aviation as one of "co-operation with the fleet . . . : bombing enemy's men-of-war and bases; protection of its own fleet from hostile craft; scouting, reporting movements of enemy over smoke screens in low visibility, and over the horizon; detecting mine fields, torpedoes, and submarines; spot-shooting, and escort and convoy work."[11] Franklin Roosevelt had formulated definite ideas about the offensive and defensive employment of naval aviation by 1919.

Mitchell's efforts in 1919 to separate the air service from the army through congressional legislation failed. The National Defense Act of 1920 left the General Staff in control of the air service. Furthermore, the General Staff retained control over promotions, which was a tight rein over the airmen. Even though the National Defense Act recognized the air service as a combat arm of the army, put fliers in command of tactical units, and authorized flight pay at 50 percent of base pay, the hopes of those wanting a separate air force were crushed. Bitter over the turn of events, Mitchell and his followers refused to accept an inferior status for army aviation quietly.[12]

In magazine articles, books, and lectures, Mitchell made sensational claims that airplanes could do anything. Specifically, Mitchell pressed his claim that airplanes could sink battleships. The navy replied by saying that Mitchell's claims were unproven, but they refused to let Mitchell test his theories on the surrendered German battleships. Two summers after Mitchell had spoken to Arnold in El Paso, the navy, under pressure from Congress, gave the air service permission to conduct bombing tests.

Attracting wide press coverage, the tests took on a circus atmosphere as both sides made wild claims. Former Secretary of the Navy Josephus Daniels bragged that he would be safe standing bareheaded on the bridge of any battleship while it was being bombed. Daniels regretted that the planes could not attack under real combat conditions to find out how quickly they would be shot down. When the army fliers heard Daniels's boast, they begged Mitchell to have the navy shoot back. Fortunately, cooler heads prevailed, and nobody was on board the *Ostfriesland* when the air service sank it on July 20,

1921. However, the airplane-versus-battleship question remained unsettled. The Joint Army and Navy Board report on the bombing tests stated that airplanes were valuable auxiliaries, but it concluded that the battleship was "still the backbone of the fleet and the bulwark of the nation's sea defense." The air service sank three more obsolete American battleships over the next two years, but the official results remained the same.[13]

The refusal of the Joint Army and Navy Board to accept the results of the battleship tests as proof of the airplane's superiority over the battleship frustrated the Army Air Service, but the failure of the joint board to support sufficient funding for equipment left the air service in a very poor condition. The situation became so bad that in his annual report for 1922, Chief of the Air Service Mason M. Patrick, who opposed the creation of a separate air force, pointed out the shortage of personnel and the unsafe equipment. In response, the General Staff created the Lassiter Board in March, 1923, to investigate the situation. The Lassiter Board recommended a ten-year expansion program and agreed with Patrick's suggestion to mass most of the air service's offensive aircraft into a strike force under one general headquarters, rather than individual ground commanders. The secretary of war approved the Lassiter Board's report, but the navy's opposition to spending such a large amount on the army prevented the report from being sent to Congress for action. After four years of hard work, Mitchell had little to show. He became very depressed. "Air power," he told Arnold, "doesn't seem to be getting anywhere at all." He had interested the American public, but the leaders in Washington with the power to do something would not listen to him.[14]

In an unsuccessful effort to calm him, the army sent Mitchell to the Orient after the battleship tests in September of 1923. Alarmed by what he saw on his tour of Hawaii, Guam, the Philippines, Japan, China, India, Java, and Singapore, Mitchell returned in July, 1924, more vituperative than ever. He filed a 323-page report in October, which noted Japan's interest in air power. Judging the Japanese to have the second most powerful air force in the world, he warned of the virtual absence of American air power in the Orient. The army and navy officers he had spoken to had been ignorant of and indifferent to the disparity between Japanese and American air power. Believing that the United States and Japan would eventually go to war over control of the Pacific, he made his famous prediction that Japan would start that war with an air attack on Pearl Harbor. When the War Department ignored his report, Mitchell took his message elsewhere.[15]

Secretary of War John Weeks had tried to muzzle Mitchell in 1923, he ordered the vocal aviator to submit all of his articles to the War

Department for clearance before publication, but Mitchell soon found a way to get around Weeks's order. At the ceremonies for the army fliers, who had just completed the first flight around the world, Mitchell saw that President Coolidge seemed interested in aviation. Therefore, he went over Weeks's head and asked Coolidge for permission to write a new series of articles. Unaware of the articles' contents, Coolidge granted Mitchell permission but stipulated that his superiors had to approve the articles before they were published. Mitchell interpreted Coolidge's stipulation to mean only his direct superior, the chief of the air service; he submitted his articles for publication without showing them to the General Staff. Later, the chief of the air service denied having given Mitchell his permission, but it was too late. The *Saturday Evening Post* ran the articles from December, 1924, through the following March.[16]

As always, Mitchell continued to blast the navy in the articles. The second article, carrying the headline "How Should We Organize Our National Air Power," included six photographs of the *Ostfriesland* being sunk. In the same issue as Mitchell's third article, the *Post* ran a cartoon showing Uncle Sam as an ostrich with his head stuck in the sand. "I don't see anything in the air," Uncle Sam said as airplanes flew overhead. Although the cartoon was not part of Mitchell's article, it fit. With a circulation of more than two and a half million, the *Saturday Evening Post* gave Mitchell's articles a large audience. However, the *Post* allowed Secretary of the Navy Curtis D. Wilbur to state the navy's case. In an article titled "A Balanced Navy," Wilbur warned against placing too much emphasis on one type of weapon. He stated that the fundamental naval policy of the United States was to maintain a navy strong enough to support the nation's policies, commerce, and overseas possessions. "Only a Navy—a well balanced Navy —with its surface and subsurface vessels and its aircraft and aircraft carriers, can accomplish this," he wrote. The effect of Mitchell's articles was tempered, but he was not.[17]

When Mitchell again carried his campaign to congressional hearings that spring, he expanded his attacks to the War Department, including the navy and General Staff. Mitchell charged them with opposing improvements in the air force, not listening to suggestions by air officers, and using veiled threats to try to control the public testimony of air officers. This time, the War Department did more to silence Mitchell. When his tour as assistant chief of the air service ended in March, 1925, Secretary Weeks (with the approval of Coolidge) refused to reappoint him to the position. Mitchell reverted to his permanent rank of colonel and was sent to Texas as the Aviation Officer for the Eighth Corps Area.[18]

Undeterred, Mitchell continued to press the cause of air power through public attacks on the navy, General Staff, and War Department, but in September he finally went too far. After the navy's dirigible *Shenandoah* crashed during a thunderstorm, Mitchell released a nine-page statement to the press on September 5, 1925. Remembering how public pressure had forced the British government to create the RAF, he tried to form the same type of pressure by blaming the crash on "the incompetency, criminal negligence, and almost treasonable administration of the National Defense by the Navy and War Departments." The army responded by court-martialing Mitchell. Coolidge himself drew up the charges. Aware of the seriousness of Mitchell's charges, the secretaries of war and the navy asked President Coolidge on September 10 to form a committee to study national defense.[19]

A year earlier, Coolidge had escaped being tarnished in the Teapot Dome scandal by appointing a special counsel to prosecute the accused. Similarly, he took much of the political threat out of the Mitchell court-martial by quickly naming Dwight W. Morrow to head a committee to study military aviation in the United States. Together, Coolidge and Morrow chose committee members who had the confidence of the American people and Congress. Coolidge knew that the existence of the Morrow Board would counter any claims that the government was unconcerned about American military aviation. The president then took another step to lessen the impact of the court-martial by directing the Morrow Board to produce its report by the end of November, which was about the time Mitchell's court-martial would be over.[20]

The Morrow Board allowed Mitchell to testify, but he squandered the opportunity. Rather than presenting a spirited defense, he just read his recently published book, *Winged Defense,* to the board. He continued to read his book until board member Sen. Hiram Bingham, a former air officer and a supporter of air power, reminded Mitchell that each member had a copy of the book. Mitchell snapped back, "I'm trying to make a point!" That remark lost Mitchell his chance to influence the board. The Morrow Board released its report on December 3, 1925. Opposing the creation of a separate air arm, the board said that air power had not "demonstrated its value for independent operations," and it recommended only superficial changes. At his court-martial, Mitchell staged a better show. He often put the prosecution on the defensive. Airmen from across the United States came to Mitchell's defense. Hap Arnold, Carl Spaatz, Herbert Dargue, Robert Olds, and other army airmen who supported Mitchell sat through the trial. In a show of support, they directly quoted Mitchell when they were on the stand. However, the court found Mitchell guilty on December 17 and issued a harsh sentence. It suspended him from duty for five years, which forced his early resignation from the army.[21]

Angered by the trial, Arnold and Dargue tried to keep up the fight by contacting friends on Capitol Hill and writing letters, but the War Department frowned upon their actions. Both were called in to answer for their "irregular" correspondence concerning changes in the status of the air service. Dargue received a reprimand, and Arnold found himself "exiled" to Fort Riley, Kansas. The army had taken care of its internal critics.[22]

Mitchell's court-martial aroused a great deal of public interest and spawned a host of bills in Congress to create a separate air force. But public interest and support for the legislation in Congress withered away when Congress passed the Air Corps Act on July 2, 1926. The law changed the name of the air service to the Air Corps, created the position of assistant secretary of war for air, and authorized a five-year program to expand the Air Corps to 20,000 officers and men and 1,800 serviceable aircraft. In reality, however, the Air Corps Act changed little more than the name of the air service. The new organization remained inferior to the infantry, and the effectiveness of the assistant secretary of war for air was limited by the secretary of war. Its authorization of men and planes meant little because funds were not made available to carry out the expansion. The Coolidge and Hoover administrations emphasized economy, small government, small military establishments, and disarmament. Coolidge succinctly explained his unwillingness to spend tax money on the military by asking, "Who's gonna fight us?" Congress agreed with both administrations — or at least followed the wishes of its constituents — and never appropriated enough funds to fulfill the Air Corps Act. Still, the passage of the Army Air Corps Act did not end all agitation. From 1926 to 1933, twenty-nine bills were introduced into Congress to give aviation a greater freedom, but none of the proposed legislation reached the floor. More importantly, nobody in the Air Corps stepped forward to take Billy Mitchell's place as the champion of air power.[23]

The depression increased the Hoover administration's unwillingness to spend money on the Army Air Corps. Hoping to stabilize his budget for the next few years, in the fall of 1930 Secretary of War Patrick J. Hurley cut the department's estimates for the fiscal year 1932 by $20 million, with the bulk coming out of the Air Corps's budget. However, Hoover's Bureau of the Budget refused to accept the scaled-down estimates and instructed Hurley to make even further cuts from the Air Corps. In an effort to come up with the additional budget cuts, Hurley looked for ways to cut back on the cost of airplanes.

3. Equipped with obsolescent aircraft, such as this Keystone B-6A bomber, the leaders of the Army Air Corps were limited initially in their efforts to prove their theories of air power. *Courtesy U.S.A.F.*

Mass production would lower the price, but building military airplanes by mass production techniques is very difficult. To take full advantage of the cost savings of mass production, the article being produced must be standardized, but unlike an automobile assembly line, an airplane production line requires a great deal of flexibility. If a new improvement is presented to an automobile manufacturer, it can be added to the next year's model, and the advertisements for that model can emphasize the improvement. But when an aircraft manufacturer is presented with an improvement, he wants to incorporate it immediately. Even a slight improvement that adds one or two miles per hour to an airplane's speed could save a military pilot's life. Obviously, military aviators want the most up-to-date aircraft possible, but once an airplane has gone into production, any change increases the final cost of production. Increased production costs mean that fewer planes can be purchased, especially when budgets are fixed.

As a result, clashes are bound to occur between fliers wanting the most up-to-date aircraft and budget officers wanting to buy the most planes their fixed budget allows.

Secretary Hurley found himself in quite a dilemma. He had to cut the Air Corps budget just when its five-year expansion program was supposed to be finished. Congress had failed to provide enough funds to complete the expansion, but the War Department officials, fearing they would be blamed for the failure, opted to purchase the most planes instead of improved planes. Chief of the Air Corps Maj. Gen. James F. Fechet objected loudly. He told the House Subcommittee on Military Appropriations that the attempt to stabilize the costs of the Air Corps with lower priced, standardized aircraft left it with inferior aircraft. He tried to explain that aircraft improved so much every year that by the time production of a standard model started it was obsolescent, but his complaints were ignored. As a result, the Air Corps received planes that were new but lacking the recent improvements available on commercial airplanes.[24]

The study of air power doctrines in the United States progressed as slowly as aircraft procurement and development. The Air Corps Tactical School at Maxwell Field, Alabama, served as the Air Corps's center for doctrinal development, but without the guidance of a strategic bombing advocate, the study of strategic bombing languished. Dominated by the General Staff, the Tactical School worked only on air defense and ground support. The influence of the General Staff was demonstrated in a 1928 Tactical School paper titled "The Doctrine of the Air Force," which stated that, regardless of how decisive the air force's operations were or how indirect the support, the air force "always supports the ground forces." General Fechet rejected the paper because it suggested that the air force was an auxiliary of the ground forces. Worried about the Tactical School's submissiveness, Fechet reminded them air power had removed the necessity "of ground forces ever coming in contact."[25]

Feeling that he could best promote the cause of aviation as a civilian, Fechet retired from the service on December 19, 1931, ten years before he reached the age limit. As his farewell act, Fechet told the *New York Times* that America's great wealth made it the most hated nation in the world, and he said that its wealth was virtually unprotected. Fechet warned that unless the nation prepared to meet the impending trouble, "our fool's paradise" would soon be lost. Upon leaving the service, Fechet started a campaign to shape public opinion with denunciations and scare tactics. Speaking to the L'Enfant Chapter of the Daughters of the American Revolution on January 20, 1932, Fechet warned that the United States had fallen too far behind other

4. Brig. Gen. Benjamin D. Foulois, on left, speaking with Eddie Rickenbacker and Maj. Gen. James E. Fechet at the 1931 Army Air Corps Maneuvers at Wright Field, Ohio. *Courtesy U.S.A.F.*

nations in air defense. To scare his audience, he claimed that the major cities of the United States could be leveled in twenty-four hours by air attacks.[26]

Brig. Gen. Benjamin D. Foulois replaced Fechet as chief of the Army Air Corps, and he readily entered a struggle between the House Subcommittee on Military Appropriations and the General Staff over budget cuts. The General Staff proposed keeping personnel while cutting back on materiel, but Rep. Ross Collins, believing that the decisive element in a future war would be weapons and machines rather than men, opposed their plans. Foulois sided with Collins and told the subcommittee that "it would be a splendid thing if additional expense would be put in materiel, meaning heavy bombers, rather than into personnel." Through the strenuous efforts of Chief of Staff Gen. Douglas MacArthur, the General Staff succeeded in keeping its personnel-oriented army, but Foulois had demonstrated that he would follow in his predecessor's footsteps and continue to antagonize the General Staff.[27]

Foulois used his new position to attack publicly any opponent of air power. In late January, 1932, Rep. Charles Martin of Washington, a former assistant chief of staff, told reporters that the Air Corps personnel were the most extravagant and unruly group of men in the world. He criticized the fliers for going up several times in an airplane, then calling the planes flaming coffins in an effort to get more money for airplanes. "If we had followed Mitchell's program," Martin said, "we would bankrupt the government. Those fellows have no sense of economy." Foulois went before the House Committee on Expenditures in the Executive Departments on February 4 to give testimony for creating a Department of Defense, and he used the opportunity to attack publicly Representative Martin, who sat on the committee. Foulois enlivened the session by saying that Martin's remarks showed a pitiful lack of knowledge regarding the administration and operation of the Army Air Corps" and were an "unwarranted public criticism of a body of men who . . . are not exceeded in efficiency today by any other branch of the United States army."

During the ensuing questioning, Representative Schafer mentioned a magazine article in which Fechet had claimed that Congress was killing national defense units by inadequate appropriations. "I am going to insist that we call General Fechet," stated Schafer, "and see who is paying him to carry on this propaganda—the airplane builders or who." Foulois came to Fechet's defense and, in a statement that could have easily been attributed to Billy Mitchell, told the committee that it was the duty of any soldier to point out defects in the national defense system. Though enemies, Foulois and Mitchell used the same method to press the cause of air power: public confrontation.[28]

Despite being the chief of the Air Corps, Foulois had little direct control over the air arm. For organizational purposes, the army had divided the United States into areas, and operational control over the tactical units belonged to the corps area commanders. Still, his control over aircraft procurement, equipment dispersal, personnel assignments, writing of regulations for aircraft operation and training, and expenditure of Air Corps funds gave him a great deal of power to supervise each tactical unit. However, Foulois left the actual running of the Air Corps to his staff. He concerned himself with getting the General Staff and the navy to recognize the Air Corps as the agency primarily responsible for coastal defense. The agency charged with coastal defense would be assured of funding, and Foulois's concentration on securing that duty was a matter of practicality.

5. Maj. Gen. Oscar Westover. *Courtesy U.S.A.F.*

Control over air force doctrine fell to Assistant Chief of the Air Corps Brig. Gen. Oscar Westover. Under his direction, the Air Corps Tactical School began formulating a specifically American view on the employment of strategic bombing. Since 1919, Westover had opposed the separation of the air force from the army and believed that officers who advocated independence were insubordinate. But he strongly advocated the development of air power. At his insistence,

Capt. George C. Kenney and a civilian at the Air Corps Tactical School translated an article by Giulio Douhet into English. Arguing that air power would be the decisive factor in any future war, Douhet reduced the role of the army and navy to preventing a surface invasion while the air force destroyed the enemy's industrial capability and morale. Douhet felt that the nation whose air force finished its work first would win. Foulois approved the translation and had it distributed widely through the Air Corps. He also gave copies to the House Committee on Military Affairs.

Billy Mitchell continued writing to Air Corps officers after he left the army in 1926, and he tried to press his arguments on them. By this time he had started to echo Douhet. He too preached that the bombing of an enemy's industrial and population centers would bring about a quick victory. However, his efforts had little impact on the formulation of air power doctrines at the Tactical School. Neither did the translated writings of Douhet.

Independently of Douhet and Mitchell, the Air Corps Tactical School had developed its own doctrine of strategic bombing. Its textbook on bombardment for the 1933–34 class stated that bombardment can "shatter a nation's will to resist; it can destroy the economical and industrial structures which make possible the very existence of modern civilization." It also noted the defensive role of bombardment in preventing the establishment of enemy airfields close enough to strike American industry. Unlike Douhet and Mitchell, the Air Corps Tactical School did not advocate the bombing of population centers.[29] By the early 1930s, the influence of Billy Mitchell on the Air Corps had started to decline.

Within the Air Corps, the emphasis turned increasingly toward long-range bombers. The Air Corps Tactical School allowed the study of attack (or ground support) aviation to languish. Also, pursuit aviation, which had been the dominant branch of the air arm during the 1920s, lost its position during the first five years of the 1930s. Claire Chennault, an instructor of pursuit tactics at the ACTS, continued to champion pursuit aviation, but he had little influence. The trend toward long-range bombardment was reversed only by the need for ground support aircraft in North Africa and long-range fighter escorts over Europe.[30]

The Air Corps and the General Staff held differing views on the decisiveness of strategic bombing and the importance of ground support, but they agreed on the importance of army control over coastal defense. For over a century the army had been charged with coastal defense, and the navy had been recognized as the nation's first line of defense. The dividing line between their areas of responsibility had been determined by the range of the army's coastal artillery, but the advent of airplanes forced a reconsideration of where the dividing line rested. The army wanted its jurisdiction extended to the range of the army's planes, but the navy refused to surrender its traditional domain. The dispute dragged on from the sinking of the *Ostfriesland* until President Hoover took interest. He wanted to avoid the expense of two services duplicating a single function; he encouraged Chief of Staff Douglas MacArthur to settle the matter. In January, 1931, MacArthur and Chief of Naval Operations Adm. William V. Pratt signed an agreement recognizing the army as primarily responsible for coastal defense. The navy would have absolute freedom of action without having to worry about coastal defense. But naval officers were never happy with the arrangement and wanted to control all aviation over the water. Soon after Pratt retired, the navy renounced the MacArthur-Pratt agreement, and the dispute started up again. Despite the personal attention Foulois gave to the problem, the dispute continued until the Japanese attacked Pearl Harbor.[31]

Within a few months of the MacArthur-Pratt Agreement, however, the Air Corps embarrassed itself in the public eye. Given an old freighter, the *Mount Shasta*, the Air Corps intended to use the ship for routine target practice and made no effort to publicize it. Unfortunately for the Air Corps, the press found out about the *Mount Shasta* and played up the bombing practice until it appeared to be as important as the *Ostfriesland* sinking. Not expecting so much publicity, the Air Corps failed to plan the bombing exercises carefully. On August 11, 1931, Air Corps bombers, led by Maj. Herbert Dargue, failed to find the ship anchored only fifty-five miles out. Three days later, Dargue found the freighter, but he used bombs that were too small. The Air Corps bombers set the ship on fire, but it was sunk by a Coast Guard cutter. Hanson Baldwin, an Annapolis graduate who was a military affairs correspondent for the *New York Times*, wrote that the test showed the "inefficiency of land-based pilots over water." He pointed out that flying over water was something that naval fliers did regularly.

The poor showing inspired little confidence in the Air Corps's ability to defend the coastline. On August 26, Hap Arnold told Carl Spaatz that he could not "help but feel that it will have a very detrimental effect on this newly assigned Coast Defense project." He also showed other officers cartoons that ridiculed the Air Corps. Yet, the *Mount Shasta* farce made Air Corps officers realize that many of the problems faced by the Air Corps resulted from their own mistakes. Lt. Col. Frank M. Andrews, executive officer of the Office of the Chief of the Air Corps (OCAC) in Washington, D.C., told Hap Arnold that his office had issued instructions that no publicity was to be given to the bombing, "but it was reversed higher up." Obviously vexed, he admitted that what was originally simply a target more interesting than a circle on the ground had let the navy "have a good laugh at us." But what bothered the OCAC most, Andrews explained, was "the possibility that something is wrong with our training and our ability to attack targets at sea."

Andrews realized that the Air Corps had to do more than just make claims. It had to substantiate its claims to win support. "What we have got to do," he told Arnold ten days later, "is to get down a proper system of training in navigation and bombardment, improve our equipment, and keep out of the limelight for a while until we know exactly what we can do." Unfortunately, Andrews was not in a position to put his suggestions into effect. The Air Corps opened an over-water navigation school in April, 1932, but it provided no formal training in over-water navigation for the tactical units. As a result, most Air Corps pilots had little navigation training. More importantly, however, the Air Corps failed to stay out of the limelight and soon found itself in a situation more embarrassing than the *Mount Shasta* fiasco.[32]

Thus, before Franklin D. Roosevelt was elected president of the United States, a few officers in the Air Corps realized that the method of public confrontation used by Billy Mitchell, James Fechet, and Benjamin Foulois was inappropriate for winning support from the public, government, and military. They knew that the Air Corps had to prove itself deserving of support by fulfilling its claims. Within a year of Roosevelt's inauguration, these officers rose to positions from where they could carry out their ideas.

II. The Army Air Corps and the New Deal

The Democratic party held its 1932 convention at Chicago and chose Franklin D. Roosevelt as its presidential candidate. Customarily, the candidate waited for official notification before accepting the nomination; Roosevelt, however, physically flew in the face of tradition. Without waiting, he boarded a trimotor airplane on July 2 and flew into strong head winds to the convention to make his acceptance speech. Roosevelt told the convention that his flight from Albany to Chicago symbolized a breaking of traditions, and he promised the American people a new deal. His bumpy flight also foreshadowed the rough and bumpy growth of the Army Air Corps during his presidency.[1]

During his presidential campaign, however, Roosevelt's experiences with aircraft manufacturers varied. In Seattle, Roosevelt ran into open political partisanship at the Boeing Aircraft Company. They refused to let him enter the factory to address their employees, but Boeing allowed Republicans inside. Back on the East Coast, however, Roosevelt found himself courted by R. H. Fleet, president of Consolidated Aircraft Corporation; T. P. Wright, vice president of Curtiss Aeroplane and Motor Corporation; and L. D. Bell, president of the Aero Club of Buffalo. They cabled Roosevelt from Buffalo, New York, on October 15 to remind him that thousands of skilled aircraft workmen were unemployed. Arguing that seventy-five cents out of every dollar spent on airplanes went to skilled labor, they suggested that Roosevelt come out for spending money on aircraft because it would be "more effective in relieving distress than other forms of public building [and a] great factor toward guaranteeing peace and national security." The three men told Roosevelt that his flight to the Chicago convention had been a "hit with airminded people." They promised that Roosevelt would win thousands of votes in Buffalo and across the nation if he would announce his support of aviation.[2]

Fleet tried to cover his bets by sending President Hoover a letter similar to his telegram to Roosevelt. He sent General Foulois copies of his messages to Roosevelt and Hoover. Fleet confided to General Foulois his plan to get Roosevelt's commitment to support the aeronautical industry, "and then perhaps Hoover would fall in line." Foulois noted with interest the efforts of the aircraft manufacturers in Buffalo, but he wisely declined any comment on Fleet's plans. The chief of the Air Corps explained to Fleet that he could not comment because it was a matter "outside of [his] official province."[3] Foulois fully understood that military men should stay out of politics, and he also knew that whatever he said could be used against him later.

Roosevelt's election on November 8, 1932, ended the partisan political struggle for the presidency but started an internal political struggle for control of air power policy. Freely approaching their commander in chief, the army and navy involved Roosevelt in their rivalry from the very start. Impressed by Roosevelt's flight to Chicago, both services told the press on election day that they expected Roosevelt to make full use of their airplanes. The navy bragged about having several large-cabin planes that the president and his council could use. The army replied that its "land" planes were superior to navy planes. Trying to outdo the navy, army flyers emphasized that they would have a trimotored, metal transport plane ready for the president when he took office on March 4, 1933. A naval official said "he ought to use the navy one time and the army the next." An army man replied that Roosevelt "should use army equipment all the time unless he flies out over the ocean." A civilian further clouded the issue by suggesting that Roosevelt use the Ford trimotor, belonging to the Department of Commerce, and "avoid any fights."[4] Amid the depression and bank holidays, the incoming president had more important considerations than how he would travel, and Roosevelt solved the tit-for-tat squabble in a way that neither side expected. He traveled by car or train.

The Air Corps could not be blamed for overestimating President Roosevelt's commitment to aviation. In February of 1933, the press was still reporting that the new administration would be more airminded than the old because both Franklin and Eleanor Roosevelt preferred flying to any other form of transportation. However, people returning from visits with Roosevelt at Warm Springs warned against expecting too much. They reported that neither Roosevelt or James Farley, the incoming postmaster general, seemed impressed by claims that the air transportation industry needed air mail lines where there was no mail to survive. Nor were Roosevelt and Farley convinced by the claims of Edward P. Warner, editor of *Aviation* magazine, that survival of the aviation industry depended on military purchases. Fiscally conservative and wanting cuts in military expenditures, the *New York Times* stated that increased military spending was unnecessary because "the naval arm is strong and capable, and army aviation lags a bit, but is efficient with new squadrons authorized."[5] Roosevelt soon showed that he agreed with the *Times*. In his campaign speeches, Roosevelt had promised to cut federal spending by 25 percent. At Pittsburgh in October of 1932, Roosevelt said, "I regard reduction in Federal spending as one of the most important issues of this campaign." To the surprise of the Air Corps, Roosevelt carried out his pledge by cutting back on military expenditures.[6]

During the celebrated "Hundred Days" from March 9 to June 16, Roosevelt asked for and Congress passed the Agricultural Adjustment Act, Civilian Conservation Corps, Federal Emergency Relief Act, Tennessee Valley Authority, Home Owners Refinancing Act, Farm Credit Act, and the National Industrial Recovery Act with $3.3 billion for the Public Works Administration. Roosevelt realized that his New Deal programs would be expensive; he warned Congress on March 10 that the federal government would have a deficit of more than a billion dollars unless immediate action was taken. "Too often in recent history," Roosevelt said, "liberal governments have been wrecked on rocks of loose fiscal policy." To contain the projected deficit, he asked Congress for the power to make economies within the government, and Congress gave it to him.[7] President Roosevelt knew that spending tax dollars on defense would provide relief, and the cable from the East Coast aircraft manufacturers told him that laborers would receive most of the benefits from increased aircraft purchases. Nevertheless, Roosevelt refused to support a military increase that might wreck his liberal programs.

Congress passed the War Department appropriations bill for the 1934 fiscal year on March 4, 1933, and most of the army took cuts. Through hard work, the Air Corps had managed to get almost all the funds it requested, but those efforts went for naught. In April, Roosevelt carried out his campaign pledge and ordered the War Department to cut $144 million from its 1934 budget. He also mentioned furloughing 3,000 to 4,000 army officers and cutting flight pay.

Roosevelt's plans for economy caused great concern in both the army and navy flying services. Since he had not specified which officers would be released, the fliers feared that reductions in personnel would come from their ranks. Acting without the approval of the General Staff, General Foulois and his staff argued before Congress that funding for the Air Corps should be increased rather than decreased. Their actions upset the General Staff, because extra funds for the Air Corps meant reduced funds for the rest of the army.[8]

The General Staff also tried to prevent the cuts, and at a White House meeting Chief of Staff MacArthur angered the president with his arguments. MacArthur said that when the United States lost the next war, "and an American boy, lying in the mud with an enemy bayonet through his belly and an enemy foot on his dying throat spat out his last curse, [he] wanted the name not to be MacArthur but Roosevelt." The president replied lividly, "You must not talk that way to the President!" MacArthur apologized and offered his resignation, but Roosevelt, showing remarkable self-control, refused to accept it. "Don't be foolish," Roosevelt told him, "you and the budget get together on this." As they left the White House, Secretary of War George B. Dern told MacArthur that he had saved the army, but MacArthur replied by vomiting on the White House steps.[9]

MacArthur quickly got over his illness, and he continued to protest loudly about the proposed cuts. Again, he threatened to resign if the cuts were not put back. The administration compromised and restored nearly half the cuts, but appropriations for the Air Corps were reduced from $26 million to $12 million.[10]

Despite the budget cuts, the supporters of air power had hopes for improvement under Roosevelt because of his connections with Billy Mitchell. In July, 1931, Mitchell met Roosevelt and became convinced that Roosevelt recognized the increased importance of aviation. Mitchell supported Roosevelt for the Democratic nomination and helped in the presidential campaign. Mitchell and his supporters assumed that Roosevelt would name Mitchell the assistant secretary of war for air. However, when Roosevelt delayed in filling the post, rumors circulated that he would never fill it. The hopes of Mitchell and his supporters fell when the New York Times reported on April 9, 1933, that Roosevelt would cut the assistant secretaries for air in the army and navy.[11]

Since the assistant secretary for air gave the troublesome army fliers direct contact with Congress, the War Department wanted to abolish the post. The War Department got its chance when the director of the Bureau of the Budget asked Secretary of War George B. Dern on May 23 for recommendations for money-saving changes in the War Department. Dern turned the matter over to General MacArthur, and the General Staff recommended only that the office of the assistant secretary of war for air be abolished. The administration accepted MacArthur's recommendation and announced the abolition of the assistant secretaryship in June.[12]

The army fliers recognized what had happened. By cutting the Air Corps's budget and abolishing the assistant secretary of war for air, the General Staff significantly increased its control over the Air Corps. Maj. Carl Spaatz expressed the dismay felt throughout the Air Corps. "As was anticipated," he complained to Hap Arnold, "the War Department is hot on the trail of the Air Corps since the buffer [assistant secretary for air] has been removed."[13]

The rest of the army also felt dismay over the budget cuts. It must have appeared that Roosevelt was cutting the military budget in a blind disregard for national defense. That was not the case. His cuts in military spending were matched by his effort to reach an international arms reduction at the Conference for the Reduction and Limitation of Armaments. Better known as the Geneva Disarmament Conference, the conference sponsored by the League of Nations had opened in February of 1932, with hopes of reaching a worldwide arms agreement. Although neither were members of the League of Nations, both the United States and the Soviet Union had sent representatives to the conference.

Representatives attending the conference made great efforts to place limitations on military aircraft. In November, 1932, Stanley Baldwin expressed the conference's concern with aircraft before the British House of Commons. He said that a failure to abolish bombing planes would mean the end of European civilization. The fear Baldwin and others expressed over bombers during the interwar years reflected their perception of the horrors an air attack would bring. They envisioned the first wave of bombers dropping explosives on cities to drive civilians into underground shelters. The second wave of airplanes would sweep overhead spraying poison gas. The gas, heavier than air, would seep into the basements and shelters and find the people hiding there. Very small children would be helpless, because there were no gas masks their size. The image of thousands, perhaps millions, of people hideously choking to death in shelters—as well as buildings, toppled by high explosive and incendiary bombs, crushing and burning to death those people on the surface—approached that of the modern fear of nuclear war, with its instantaneous incineration and subsequent nuclear winter. Yet, their fear of not having bombers outweighed their fear of air raids.

France proposed placing all bombing planes under the control of the League of Nations for use as an international police force; but, as if the ghost of the Versailles Treaty had arisen, the United States refused to allow its military forces to be used in any European squabble and rejected the French proposal. Operating under the popular assumption that civilian planes could be converted into bombers overnight by simply adding machine guns and bomb racks, the French then suggested placing all civilian aviation under League supervision. This proposal was also rejected. Great Britain proposed outlawing all bombing planes except those used for police actions. Because the Royal Air Force had been used successfully in Iraq as a police force, the British were unwilling to give up the right to use bombers in policing their empire. They apparently felt differently about bombs falling on their homes than those falling in their territories. President Hoover suggested doing away with entire categories of arms. He proposed ending all military aviation except naval observation planes, but his proposal was rejected as well. In spite of all their fears and efforts, no agreement had been reached by the time Adolf Hitler and Roosevelt came to power.[14] Hitler cared little for disarmament and demanded parity in armaments. Roosevelt, however, worked hard at trying to achieve a reduction in offensive armaments through the Geneva Disarmament Conference. As the president-elect, Roosevelt asked Under Secretary of State William Phillips on April 27 for the Soviet delegate's definition of "an aggressor nation." Phillips reported that on February 6, 1933, Maxim Litvinov had defined an aggressor nation as one that declared war; invaded without a declaration of war; used bombardment by land, sea, or air; crossed frontiers without permission or infringed on that permission when granted; or conducted a naval blockade.[15]

Once he had been inaugurated, Roosevelt became involved personally with the disarmament efforts. Meeting with Dr. Hjalmar Schacht, president of the Reichbank, on May 6, 1933, Roosevelt expressed his ideas on reducing offensive armaments. Explaining that the United States regarded Germany as the only possible obstacle to a disarmament treaty, Roosevelt insisted on the status quo in land armaments for Germany. But he promised that the United States would support any effort to bring the offensive armaments of all other nations down to Germany's level. Roosevelt reiterated his idea of limiting offensive weapons during a White House press conference four days later. "If you remove the weapons of offense and thereby strengthen the weapons of defense," he said off the record, "you give security to every nation." He named gas, airplanes, and tanks as the offensive weapons that render defensive weapons ineffective.[16]

On May 16, President Roosevelt made public his ideas about limiting offensive weapons in a message to the leaders of all nations represented at the Disarmament Conference and the World Monetary and Economic Conference, better known as the London Economic Conference. He blamed the need for armaments on two causes: either governments desired to enlarge their territories at the expense of another nation, or they feared being invaded. Believing that "only a small minority of Governments or of peoples" wanted expansion, Roosevelt said that the "overwhelming majority of peoples" kept excessive armaments out of fear of aggression. Their fear, he continued, came about because fixed fortifications were vulnerable to attack by airplanes, heavy mobile artillery, tanks, and gas. "If all nations will agree wholly to eliminate from possession and use the weapons which make possible a successful attack," he reasoned, "defenses automatically will become impregnable, and the frontiers and independence of every nation will become secure." Roosevelt proposed that the ultimate objective of the Disarmament Conference should be the complete elimination of all offensive weapons.[17]

The War Plans Division of the General Staff opposed the president's plans for abolishing bombers. While not favoring an independent air force, the WPD recognized the potential value of aerial bombardment. On May 3, Brig. Gen. Charles Kilbourne, chief of the WPD, prepared a memorandum for the American Delegation at Geneva stating that the abolition of bombing planes would be a real sacrifice for the United States. Explaining that the army's bombers "were primarily valuable in defense of our overseas possessions and coasts," Kilbourne said he could see "very little possibility" of the United States fighting an offensive war. MacArthur approved the memorandum on May 6 and sent it to the State Department. Clearly at odds with his military advisors, President Roosevelt ignored their wishes. When the British proposed in late May to limit the United States to only 500 military and naval aircraft as part of a disarmament plan, Roosevelt approved it without consulting the army or navy. On May 28, a member of the American Delegation told the Geneva Conference that the United States government wanted an absolute abolition of bombing. The only way to make it effective, he said, would be to capitalize on "the growing conviction that bombing from the air is a crime."[18]

Even as he attempted to reach a disarmament agreement in Geneva, Roosevelt received warnings about Germany and Japan. Samuel Fuller, the president of the American Bemberg Corporation, often sent Roosevelt reports about his visits to Germany. On May 27, Fuller warned Roosevelt that Hitler would cause a war someday. Roosevelt sent Fuller's warning to the State Department, which replied with a memorandum from Ambassador Joseph C. Grew warning that the United States was inferior to Japan in land forces, about equal in naval forces, but "probably potentially superior in the air."[19]

Concerned by these warnings, President Roosevelt decided to strengthen America's naval forces. Knowing that the navy had fallen well below the limitations placed on it by the Washington Treaty of

1921 and the London Treaty of 1930, Roosevelt authorized in June the expenditure of $238 million in PWA funds for thirty-two new ships. Hailing it as a measure to aid the economy, Roosevelt said that his ship-building program would employ people all across the nation.[20]

Already suspicious about Japanese intentions, the United States rejected in June a proposal from the Japanese Delegation at Geneva to abolish aircraft carriers while allowing an increase in Japan's naval strength. On June 29, Secretary of the Navy Swanson announced that the United States would "maintain the navy in sufficient strength to guard the continental and overseas possessions of the United States, . . . create, maintain and operate a navy second to none and in conformity with treaty provisions, . . . provide great radius of action in all classes of fighting ships, . . . [and] develop national aviation primarily for operations with the fleet." Swanson's declaration was directed at Japan, and they understood it immediately. *New York Times* correspondent Hugh Byas reported from Tokyo that Swanson's statement directly confronted the Japanese. His reference to guarding overseas possessions meant the Philippines, and Japan presented the only threat to the islands. Also, a navy second to none with a great radius of action would be needed in a war with Japan. Byas added that if "national aviation is developed primarily to give wings to the shells of that fleet, the inflammable wooden cities along the coast in which Japan's industry is concentrated may be menaced with risks greater than those of earthquakes." The Japanese would not be indifferent to any improvement of American naval aircraft, he warned.[21] The only American planes capable of reaching Japan's cities were those launched from aircraft carriers; Japan's willingness to abolish that threat made sense. More important, the public mention of threatening to burn Japanese cities appeared seven years before the attack on Pearl Harbor evoked American hatred of the Japanese. Eventually, that threat became part of America's foreign policy.

In addition to upsetting the Japanese, Roosevelt's naval expansion program drew protests at home. When Rev. Malcolm E. Peabody protested to him about the naval expansion, Roosevelt explained how Great Britain, the United States, and Japan had agreed to a naval ratio of 10:10:7. Although the British and Japanese had built up to the treaty limits, the United States had not built enough ships to keep up with the Japanese's smaller ratio. He assured Peabody that the new building program would just keep the United States even with the Japanese and not come close to the British. He confided, "I am not concerned about the latter, but I am about the first."[22]

Convinced that the army would receive PWA funds too, the General Staff instructed the Air Corps to draw up estimates for completing the five-year expansion program. To the army's surprise, Roosevelt gave the Air Corps only $7.5 million in PWA funds, the same amount given to the Naval Air Service. After much effort, Secretary of War Dern convinced the president to release another $3 million from impounded Air Corps funds. This total of $10.5 million provided the Air Corps with just enough money to replace the planes it lost to normal attrition and left it short of the 1,800 planes authorized in the Air Corps Act.[23] Since army and navy aviation received only one-tenth as much in PWA funds as the surface fleet, most people thought Roosevelt was prejudiced in favor of battleships. They were wrong. He opposed offensive weapons. From his days as the assistant secretary of the navy, Roosevelt viewed the navy as America's first line of defense. And as he told Peabody, building up the navy was a defensive measure against the only naval threat facing the United States: Japan.

Budget cuts and President Roosevelt's determination to reduce offensive weapons put the Air Corps in a precarious position. Lacking a specific purpose for existing, the Air Corps was susceptible to additional budget cuts. Therefore, General Foulois's efforts at getting the General Staff to recognize the Air Corps as the agency primarily responsible for coastal defense became increasingly important. The MacArthur-Pratt agreement of 1931 had given the Air Corps responsibility for coastal air defense, but the General Staff failed to give it directions on how it should carry out that mission. Foulois pressured the General Staff to formulate a policy, and in January, 1933, General MacArthur finally issued a directive detailing the Air Corps's duties. Titled "Employment of Army Aviation in Coast Defense," this directive divided the Air Corps's mission into three phases. First, the Air Corps would operate "to the limit of the radius of action of the airplanes" to find and destroy approaching enemy vessels and forces. Second, when the enemy came within range of the ground defenses, the Air Corps would assist them with continued observation and offensive operations. Third, if the enemy made a successful landing on American shores, the Air Corps would provide ground support. Foulois got his policy, but he also made a powerful enemy on the General Staff. General Kilbourne supported the Air Corps and appreciated the military value of airplanes, but he was a stickler for team spirit. By endlessly demanding that the General Staff formulate a policy, Foulois convinced Kilbourne that he lacked team spirit.[24] General Foulois was as unconcerned about making enemies in high places when FDR was elected as he had been in 1919.

With a definite policy as a guideline, Foulois planned extensive maneuvers for May, 1933, under the command of Oscar Westover. By quickly concentrating the Air Corps's airplanes on the West Coast, he hoped Westover would demonstrate that the Air Corps could defend either coast. Foulois believed, furthermore, that the maneuvers would prove the need for long-range aircraft to carry out the first phase of the Air Corps's mission and conduct operations against enemy fleets far from American shores. The maneuvers had just started when they had to be cancelled, because the Air Corps officers were needed to administer the Civilian Conservation Corps.[25]

Despite the early end of the maneuvers, the combined fighter and bomber operations that were conducted influenced Westover. The newly arrived Martin B-10 bombers, monoplanes with a top speed of more than two hundred miles per hour, outran the Air Corps's P-12 biplane fighters. Westover realized that any interceptor would need to be faster than the bomber, but he believed that fighters could not operate efficiently or safely at such high speeds. He concluded, therefore, that fighters could not stop formations of bombers from reaching their target. If the bombers flew in close formation, they could reach their target without fighter escort. Since Foulois had left the formulation of doctrine to Westover, who believed the bomber could get through fighter defenses, the Tactical School moved unhindered by the Office of the Chief of the Air Corps toward the policy of daylight strategic bombing that the Army Air Forces practiced in World War II.

Foulois wanted to prove the need for long-range bombers for defensive purposes, but he still believed in using airplanes for offensive duties. He recognized the strong antiwar feelings in America and realized that efforts to secure an offensive role for the Air Corps would be a waste of time. When his air staff complained that the General Staff would not give the Air Corps the bombers it requested, Foulois advised them to stop asking the General Staff for bombers to conduct offensive operations. He told them to ask for bombers to carry out defensive operations and especially bombers to reinforce the Hawaiian Islands. Unconcerned about the language used in papers sent to the General Staff, Foulois only wanted bombers with longer range and greater bomb loads. Eventually, Foulois's impertinence toward superiors, use of expedient methods, and willingness to employ deceptive language caused him trouble with the General Staff and Congress.

In July, 1933, the Air Corps Materiel Division reported that an airplane capable of carrying a one-ton bomb load 5,000 miles at a speed of 200 miles per hour was feasible. On the basis of that report, the Air Corps asked the General Staff in December for a plane with those specifications. Taking his advice, Foulois's air staff justified the request by pointing out that the bomber could reinforce Hawaii and

Panama. Their argument worked. On May 16, 1934, the General Staff authorized the Air Corps to negotiate contracts for an experimental aircraft, named Project A. The General Staff required the experimental plane to be able to destroy "distant land or naval targets" and "reinforce Hawaii, Panama, and Alaska without the use of intermediate servicing facilities." Boeing won the contract, and the airplane it produced was designated the XB-15. Completed in 1937, the XB-15 proved to be too underpowered for use in combat, but Boeing gained valuable experience that it used to create the highly successful B-17.[26]

While the Air Corps was working out the proposal for Project A, the Geneva Disarmament Conference collapsed without reaching an agreement on arms reduction. In October of 1933, Germany withdrew from the conference and the League of Nations. The other delegates continued meeting in Geneva until the spring of 1934, but the conference was effectively over. Efforts at international arms reduction had failed. France announced a return to its traditional methods of security: armaments and alliances.[27]

In the fall of 1933, President Roosevelt became convinced that the leaders of Germany and Japan were preventing arms reductions. From Germany, Ambassador William E. Dodd reported that more than half of Germany was liberal at heart and opposed arbitrary and minority government, but they "dared not speak out." Walter Lippmann told the president during the first week of November that "about 8 per cent of the population of the entire world, i.e., Germany and Japan, is able, because of imperialistic attitude, to prevent peaceful guarantees and armament reductions on the part of the other 92 per cent of the world."[28] The influence of these two men on the president became apparent when he spoke at the Woodrow Wilson Foundation Dinner on December 28, 1933. Roosevelt enunciated his belief that the "blame for the danger to world peace lies not in the world population but in the political leaders of that population." Echoing Lippmann, he estimated that at least 90 percent of the world's population would be willing to reduce armaments if all nations would do so. Without mentioning Germany or Japan, Roosevelt said that the 90 percent would not disarm because they feared the 10 percent would follow their leaders in seeking territorial expansion. "If," he continued, "that 10% of the world population can be persuaded by the other 90% to do their own thinking and not be so finely led, we will have practical peace, permanent peace, real peace throughout the world." Again, he called on the world to eliminate every offensive weapon and have international inspections to assure that no new offensive weapons would be built.[29]

After ten months in office, Roosevelt had little to show for his efforts to disarm the world. His attempt to lead the way by reducing America's offensive armaments had failed, but he believed that his budget cutting had not seriously hampered army or navy aviation. On January 11, 1934, six navy seaplanes flew from San Francisco to Pearl Harbor, breaking the record for a mass flight. The commander of the flight told reporters that it demonstrated the possibility of sending any number of squadrons to Hawaii in a time of national emergency. Assistant Secretary of the Navy Col. Henry L. Roosevelt claimed that the flight was "in no sense a stunt." He said they "did an extraordinary thing in a routine way" with unaltered service planes. The navy proved it could reinforce Hawaii while the army was still secretly considering the long-range, Project A bomber. The flight demonstrated the soundness of naval aviation, and President Roosevelt offered his congratulations to the navy fliers.[30]

This flight signified the increasing importance of air power in the Pacific Ocean, and it did not go unnoticed. A *Washington Post* editorial stated that when "six Navy planes make the trip [to Hawaii] in formation without accident or undue difficulty the range of the airplane as an instrument of destruction in war time is graphically illustrated. Even more graphic, to the thoughtful observer; is the object lesson—the necessity of insuring peace in the Pacific." An accompanying editorial cartoon showed six seaplanes flying from San Francisco toward the palm trees of Hawaii, and the caption read: "A Routine Performance."[31] A Chicago *Daily Tribune* editorial called the flight "an important demonstration of the possibilities of defending our Pacific bases against a surprise attack." Looking to the future the *Daily Tribune* offered that if "our planes can now make Hawaii in a single day without much difficulty, it may not be long before they can reach Manila in a single hop from the American mainland." Although the editorial quickly disavowed the notion of an airplane being able to sink a battleship, it argued that airplanes could hold off an invasion fleet until the battle fleet arrived.[32] The Japanese also grasped the meaning of the flight. A spokesman for the Japanese navy office said the flight showed the increased powers placed in the hands of men. "It remains to be seen," he said, "whether these powers will be used beneficently or destructively."[33]

The annual report of the National Advisory Committee for Aeronautics, the forerunner of the National Air and Space Administration, made Roosevelt feel confident about America's civilian aviation. The NACA report boasted that aeronautical development in the United States equaled or surpassed that of any other country. Roosevelt concurred with the NACA report. When he submitted the report to Congress, Roosevelt said that fundamental research in aeronautics was "essential to the national defense" and "to the future of air transportation."[34]

President Roosevelt had every reason to feel confident about the condition of the Army Air Corps. He soon discovered, however, that the Air Corps was poorly equipped and inadequately trained. He was presented evidence on February 9 that President Hoover's postmaster general had misused his authority to make air mail contracts. By altering the competitive bidding procedures and preventing smaller airlines from receiving contracts, the Republican postmaster general had allowed three large holding companies to create a monopoly on the profitable air mail carrying business. On the basis of this information, Roosevelt prepared to cancel the contracts. He instructed the assistant postmaster, Harllee Branch, to ask General Foulois if the Air Corps could carry the air mail. Unaware that Roosevelt meant to take immediate action, Foulois said that the Air Corps could be ready in "about a week or ten days." Informed of Foulois's statement, President Roosevelt cancelled the air mail contracts that day, and he ordered the Air Corps to start carrying the mail as of February 19.[35]

When he spoke to Branch, Foulois knew that the Air Corps was unprepared to fly the mail. The air mail had to be flown at night, and the commercial carriers had cargo planes designed for the work. Equally important, the commercial pilots were trained to fly on instruments in darkness or bad weather. The Air Corps possessed few cargo planes, and the army pilots had not been trained to fly on instruments. Nevertheless, Foulois believed that the Air Corps's bombers and observation planes could carry the mail, and he thought that the Air Corps could use this opportunity as a training exercise. He also felt obligated to say yes to a request from his commander in chief. Furthermore, Foulois saw an opportunity to win support for the Air Corps through public pressure. Later, he remembered thinking that any problems encountered "would focus national attention on the Air Corps and maybe we would then get the funds we needed for expansion. . . ."[36] Like Billy Mitchell after the *Shenandoah* crash, Foulois felt that the way to get changes would be to use a bludgeon.

In ordering the Army Air Corps to carry the mail, FDR wanted to use the Air Corps to further his domestic policies. Having already used the army to administer the CCC, he had no hesitation about using the Air Corps to implement another policy. The Air Corps would become a trust buster to ensure fair competition among the air carriers, just as the Tennessee Valley Authority did with the utilities holding companies. A few years later, Roosevelt would use the army air arm to further his foreign policies.

The air carriers, as well as Will Rogers, Capt. Eddie Rickenbacker, and Charles Lindbergh, denounced the president's decision, but Roosevelt refused to rescind the order. Before the airlines relinquished air mail operations to the army, they insulted the Roosevelt administration with a publicity stunt. Flying a special Douglas DC-2 transport plane, Rickenbacker, who worked for one of the airlines, and two other airline pilots carried a partial load of mail from California to Newark, New Jersey. Leaving on the evening of February 18, Rickenbacker set a new, cross-country speed record. Adding to the insult, a storm that had chased Rickenbacker across the country forced the Air Corps to cancel its East Coast mail flights on the first day of operations.[37]

Given command of the air mail operations, Westover set up his headquarters in Salt Lake City and divided the air mail routes into three zones. Designed for combat rather than carrying cargo, the army's planes were poorly suited for their new assignment. The War Department's earlier decision to standardize its aircraft meant that the army planes lacked the night-flying instruments and the radio navigation equipment found on the more modern commercial planes. In addition to the Air Corps's difficulties, the winter of 1934 was one of the worst in American history. Aware of these deficiencies and knowing that the younger pilots would fly under suicidal conditions in their eagerness to carry the mail, Foulois gave orders to sacrifice delivery rather than pilots. But a number of pilots died in crashes anyway. Rickenbacker called the deaths "legalized murder," and Republicans in Congress used the deaths to attack the Roosevelt administration.[38]

In the field, the Air Corps commanders willingly accepted their new assignment but complained about the way it had been given to them. Maj. C. L. Tinker, commander of the Seventeenth Pursuit Group, explained to reporters that army and commercial pilots had different training for their different tasks, and he complained that the Air Corps had not had enough time to retrain its pilots. In Salt Lake City, Westover blamed the deaths on a lack of equipment and unfamiliarity with the routes rather than a lack of experience. "When you consider how the job was dumped in our laps, how little warning we had, how little time for preparation, the men have done exceptionally well, particularly with our present equipment." Air Corps pilots in the New York area resented statements that sending them on air mail flights amounted to legalized murder. Eager to carry out their assignment, they promised to "drag those mail sacks" once they got organized. Air Corps spokesmen in Washington, understandably, made no mention of how little time the Air Corps had to prepare for carrying the mail, since the chief of the Air Corps had been responsible for the mere ten days of preparation.[39] Actually, Foulois's telling the press that the army pilots had been warned to be careful made it sound like the Air Corps had fallen into such poor condition that nothing more could be done.[40]

Like Billy Mitchell, General Foulois concluded that the best way to win increased support for the Air Corps was to rally public opinion. Foulois hoped the air mail problems would force the government to make changes in the Air Corps. To publicize the changes he desired, Foulois contacted Russell Owen, a sympathetic aviation writer for the *New York Times*. After conferring with Foulois, Owen reported in his paper on March 2 that proponents of a separate air force saw the air mail operations as an opportunity to attain their objective. Rather than divulging that Foulois was his source, Owen referred to him as unnamed "Air Corps officers" in Washington. Owen said the unnamed officers exhibited suppressed jubilation over getting their first "man's size job." However, their excitement was mixed with a desire to show the poor condition of the Air Corps's equipment. Claiming that the United States needed airplanes capable of intercepting enemy bombers, aircraft carriers, or battleships far out to sea, they complained that not enough had been done to produce those planes. The officers hoped that the air mail problems would prove the need to place the aviation industry under government supervision and stimulate the design of faster aircraft with longer range. If they were given these planes, they promised to form an almost impenetrable barrier around the United States. Admitting an inability to find their objectives in difficult weather, such as low fog or clouds, he assured Owen that carrying the mail was training the Air Corps to carry out their mission. "Given training in flying the air mail," Owen wrote, "over mountains and through all sorts of weather, by means of instruments, these pilots would be able successfully to ride through any conditions and meet the enemy." Nine days later, Owen revealed in a second article that Foulois was his source. Reusing several direct quotations attributed to "Air Corps officers" in his first article, Owen attributed the comments to Foulois. Whether or not Foulois wanted to be identified, his plan for playing up the bad aspects of the air mail duties to get better planes for the Air Corps became public knowledge.[41] In his comments to Owen, Foulois extended his efforts to win the coastal defense mission for the Air Corps to the press. Denied the opportunity to prove that the Air Corps needed long-range bombers with the West Coast maneuvers, General Foulois hoped the air mail duties would serve the same purpose. By complaining that not enough had been done to produce the necessary planes, he took a slap at the War Department and the General Staff. Billy Mitchell could not have done better.

Despite Foulois's efforts to reduce the risks involved in flying the mail, more army fliers died in crashes. As a result, public pressure forced President Roosevelt to act. He ordered the post office to draw up new commercial air mail contracts, and he took the Air Corps off air mail duty. On March 10, after giving Foulois the worst tongue-lashing of his career, Roosevelt asked Congress for an additional $10 million to buy more army airplanes and to improve facilities.[42]

Obviously, Foulois had forced President Roosevelt to spend more money on the Air Corps by arousing public pressure. Only ten months before, Roosevelt had proposed the abolition of military airplanes because they were offensive weapons, had approved a British plan to limit the United States to only five hundred army and navy planes, and had grudgingly approved the spending of PWA funds on the Air Corps. But political necessity was not the only factor motivating President Roosevelt. German rearmament, Japanese aggression in Manchuria, and the collapse of the Geneva Disarmament Conference had convinced Roosevelt before the air mail fiasco that his policy of disarmament by example had failed. With the New Deal moving toward increased government spending as a way out of the depression, he had little reason to continue reducing expenditures on aircraft for the army and navy. Furthermore, Roosevelt had demonstrated a willingness to increase spending on aircraft before he cancelled the air mail contracts. In January, he had given his full support to the Vinson-Trammell bill, which proposed the construction of one hundred new ships and more than one thousand new airplanes for the navy over a five-year period. These additional ships and planes would have increased the navy only to the limits set for it by the Washington Treaty of 1922 and the London Naval Treaty of 1930. However, adverse public reaction and threats from isolationists in Congress to hamper his domestic programs forced Roosevelt to abandon naval expansion. Congress approved the Vinson Naval Parity Act in March, but without presidential support for the measure, Congress appropriated only enough funds to replace overaged ships.[43]

A more important change occurred among the junior officers of the Air Corps as a result of the air mail episode; they learned the right and wrong way to press their case. While on air mail duty, Capt. Ira Eaker saw that the mail had been delivered with little trouble or delay in California, and he wondered why the higher authorities had not publicized what the Air Corps had been doing well. Keeping a scrapbook with newspaper clippings about the Air Corps, Eaker noticed that the Air Corps had managed to keep everything derogatory out of the newspapers in California. Only the Los Angeles *Times,* whose owner held stock in an airline that had its mail contract canceled, attacked the Air Corps. Eaker concluded that the favorable press was the result of personal contact with aviation editors, and he suggested that the Office of the Chief of the Air Corps use the public relations techniques employed by the airlines.[44]

A meeting with an editor further impressed upon Eaker the need to make personal contacts with newspapermen. When Eaker offered him an Air Corps press release, the editor refused to take it. He said that he had no confidence in the army's ability to carry the mail and that he refused to print propaganda. Eaker explained that his mail route carried more mail than the commercial companies had carried before the army took over. The information changed the editor's mind about using the press release, and he asked Eaker why the Air Corps had not "let somebody know this." Eaker realized the importance of having spoken to the editor personally. If the press release had been sent through the mail, the editor would have thrown it away without reading it. But by meeting with him, Eaker had been able to correct the editor's misconceptions and win his support.

Eaker told Hap Arnold about the meeting, and Arnold said that he could not tell whether the truth about the Air Corps was being kept out of the newspapers by politics or by propaganda. Although the Air Corps had flown over 138,000 pounds of mail through Salt Lake City, Arnold doubted that anyone outside of his staff knew it. "I have talked the matter over with the Chief of Air Corps," Arnold informed Eaker, "expecting that something would be done there but to date they have not used or not been able to get published the data which they and they alone have available."[45]

Foulois could have gotten Arnold's information printed in the *New York Times* through his connection with Russell Owen. Yet, rather than proclaiming the Air Corps's achievements, Foulois denounced the poor condition of its equipment. Foulois had praised the abilities of the Air Corps before the air mail operations, and he was taking an opportunity to defend himself against hostile attacks in the press. However, Foulois used his connection with Owen in an effort to force Roosevelt to give the Air Corps more funds. Of course Foulois did not intend or expect the death of his pilots. He, unlike Eaker and Arnold, simply did not understand the proper method for advertizing the Air Corps's needs. Like Billy Mitchell, Foulois used this opportunity to present the negative side of the Air Corps to the press in order to show what was needed. As he had stated in his memoirs, Foulois thought that problems encountered "would focus national attention on the Air Corps and maybe we would then get the funds we needed for expansion. . . ."[46] Eaker, on the other hand, understood that the Air Corps had to use its personal contacts to present a positive picture to advance the cause of air power. Eaker wanted to project a positive attitude that expressed, "see what we can do" and "just think what we will be able to do with more support," while Foulois took the negative approach of "we cannot do anything unless we have better equipment." It was a subtle difference, but it would have a profound effect in future perceptions of the Air Corps.

The navy already used the approach advocated by Eaker. Meeting with the press on the last day of March, Chief of Naval Operations Adm. William H. Standley discussed the tactical maneuvers conducted by the fleet in January. He praised the Naval Air Service for making more than 1,000 flights in two days without a single casualty. Then, taking a dig at the army, Standley said that an "excellent idea of the flying efficiency of the navy can be derived from the fact that approximately 80 per cent of the total aircraft operating strength of the fleet was engaged in the exercises and without a single actual casualty." He felt that the official reports were gratifying to all interested in the national defense of the United States.[47]

After years of practice, the Office of the Chief of the Air Corps knew how to handle attacks from the navy, and it released a photograph of the U.S.S. *Lexington* taken by an Air Corps photographer. Published in the *New York Times*, the photograph showed the U.S.S. *Lexington* shortly after being caught and "sunk" by army bombers. The caption read: "THEORETICALLY SUNK IN THE CANAL WAR GAME: THE AIRCRAFT CARRIER LEXINGTON."[48]

While the Office of the Chief of the Air Corps continued its traditional policy of embarrassing the navy, Hap Arnold started presenting the Air Corps along the lines suggested by Eaker. On the same day that the *Times* ran the Air Corps's photograph of the *Lexington*, Arnold admitted to the press that the Air Corps had lacked enough planes equipped with blind-flying instruments and radios to meet the mail requirements, but he said that the problems experienced by the Air Corps had brought attention to the deficiency. He also stated that funds had been provided for the necessary equipment. While not advocating the continuation of army air mail operations, he declared that the experience had improved the equipment and the capabilities of the Air Corps. He claimed that the Air Corps had learned more while flying the mail than it had on any single project since the World War. Budget cuts had forced the Air Corps to limit flying time, and the detailing of officers to the Civilian Conservation Corps had kept army pilots from flying at all. Explaining that pilots cannot be taught to fly on the ground, Arnold admitted that the army's pilots had become inefficient. But in flying the mail, the army pilots had become efficient flyers by logging thousands of hours in good and bad weather. He bragged, furthermore, that the Air Corps had "shown a remarkable economy of operation" while flying the mail.[49]

Unlike Foulois, Arnold used his access to the press to promote the achievements of the Air Corps. Although he mentioned the deficiencies of the Air Corps, as had Foulois, Arnold pointed out what the Air Corps could do with proper funding. Army pilots then backed up Arnold's words with actions. Still fuming over Rickenbacker's flying the last commercial transcontinental air mail in record time, several pilots wanted to show the world what the Air Corps could do with their new B-10 bombers. On May 7, Lt. Elwood Quesada flew a B-10 from Oakland to Newark only forty-nine minutes short of Rickenbacker's record. However, the Air Corps pilots let it be known that Rickenbacker had made three fewer stops and had flown 279 fewer miles on his flight.[50]

The negative approach used by Foulois and his predecessors had its greatest effect on the General Staff. In 1934, Brigadier General Kilbourne complained that for "many years the General Staff of the Army has suffered a feeling of disgust amounting at times to nausea over statements publicly made by General William Mitchell and those who followed his lead." He believed that Mitchell and his followers made unsubstantiated claims about the effectiveness of air power to get preferential treatment over the other arms. Officers in the War Plans Division concluded that zealots in the Air Corps "adopted the tactics of attacking and belittling all other elements of our national defense forces, sea and land. This course of action led many officers to instinctively close their minds to perfectly legitimate and honest claims" made by the Air Corps.[51]

Hap Arnold recognized the problems caused by the tactics that Mitchell and his followers used. In his memoirs, Arnold said that the War Department did not profit from the Mitchell period. Members of the War Department, he wrote, "seemed to set their mouths tighter, draw more into their shell, and if anything, take even a narrower point of view of aviation as an offensive power in warfare. Our Navy, on the contrary, made a study of the entire affair and of all the incidents relating thereto, and became air-minded in a big way. They even went out of their way to find new means of using aircraft in naval operations."[52]

Although the War Department as a whole failed to profit, many of his supporters profited from the Mitchell period. These supporters took Mitchell's teachings to heart, but a few took away much more. These few learned the lesson of how not to press their cause. For them, Billy Mitchell became a dual symbol of the right message but the wrong presentation. Hap Arnold was one who learned the lesson well. When finally recalled from "exile," he put that lesson to practice.

III. A New Army Air Arm

General Foulois soon discovered that the air mail fiasco had marked only the beginning of his troubles in 1934. When people saw the poor condition of the Air Corps's equipment, they wanted to know what had happened to their tax dollars. In February, the House Military Affairs Committee began investigating aircraft purchases and found hints of improprieties.

As written, the Air Corps Act of 1926 embodied the congressional desire for competitive bidding. The purchase procedure called for the Air Corps to test aircraft submitted by manufacturers and then purchase the best design. The manufacturer submitting the lowest bid would receive the contract to build the plane. Often, the contract was not given to the company that designed the plane. Looking askance at airplanes built by the lowest bidder, the Air Corps believed that negotiated contracts provided better aircraft. Using loopholes, the Air Corps ignored the intent of the law and purchased aircraft through negotiation.[1] In 1929, the army judge advocate general reversed an earlier ruling and declared illegal the method used to skirt the law, but the judge advocate general and the secretary of war continued to approve all purchases of aircraft through negotiated contracts. Despite the new ruling and warnings from his staff in 1932, Foulois continued to purchase airplanes through established but questionable procedures. Foulois's main concern was the purchase of the best planes for his pilots, but trouble came in December of 1933, when Foulois prepared to purchase aircraft with the $7.5 million in PWA funds released by President Roosevelt. Hoping to spend the PWA money to create jobs quickly, Foulois purchased more planes of the types already on order.

Rather than going through the lengthy competitive bidding process, he negotiated contracts with Northrop, Glenn L. Martin, and Boeing to increase their existing aircraft orders. As expected, the other aircraft manufacturers felt cheated and complained to Assistant Secretary of War Harry H. Woodring. A staunch believer in competitive bidding, Woodring rejected the negotiated contracts and told Foulois to write up a new proposal based on competitive bidding.

Woodring did not order a change in the aircraft specifications. However, to allow at least two companies to make bids, the Air Corps significantly lowered the speed, range, and load specifications in its new proposal. Woodring approved the new plan, and the Air Corps declared the original three winners of the negotiated contracts to be the winners of the competitive bids. Woodring did not approve the new contracts. He had become the target of a federal grand jury looking into army purchases of motor vehicles and disposal of surplus materiel. The grand jury found him innocent of wrongdoing, but the investigation caught the attention of Congress. Cautiously, Woodring decided to defer approval of the new contracts. William E. Boeing, chair of the board of United Aircraft and Transport, made matters worse when he testified before a Senate committee investigating air mail contracts. Boeing bragged that his companies had profited greatly from airplane and engine sales to the army and navy. In February, the House Military Affairs Committee, chaired by Rep. John J. McSwain, began an investigation into previous Air Corps purchases. Another believer in competitive bidding, McSwain was shocked to discover that the Air Corps had evaded the law. Upon learning that the Air Corps had lowered its original specifications, the committee suspected that the specifications had been changed to grant special favors. Already skeptical of the assistant secretary, they questioned the ease with which the aircraft manufacturers had convinced Woodring to reject the Air Corps's original proposal.

The Military Affairs Committee had no reason to suspect Foulois when they called him to testify on February 14. Relations between Foulois and the committee had always been cordial, and the chief of the Air Corps went to Capitol Hill with no misgivings. However, relations between Foulois and the committee soon deteriorated. Asked who was responsible for the changes in the specifications, Foulois left the impression that Woodring had specifically ordered the changes. Foulois compounded the problem by promising to provide all documents pertinent to the proposal.[2] He told the committee, "We will give you all the documents that were set up or prepared in connection with our procurement or expected procurement of the types which we had recommended, and also all documents with reference

to the present which are available."³ Misunderstanding, the committee thought that he possessed papers proving that Woodring had ordered the changes.

Responding to the deaths of Air Corps pilots flying the mail, the
Military Affairs Committee created a subcommittee, chaired by William N. Rogers, to conduct a deeper investigation of the Air Corps's
methods of procuring aircraft. Woodring told the subcommittee that
he had intended to ensure competitive bidding and denied ordering
the changes in aircraft specifications. Foulois tried to correct the problem by saying that Woodring had not changed the specifications.⁴ After
further investigation, the subcommittee found no sign of collusion,
and on March 17 it announced that Secretary Woodring was "above
reproach in handling airplane bids."⁵ But the committee showed hos-
tility toward Foulois. On March 1, Foulois promised the Rogers Subcommittee that the Air Corps could fly the mail, and he blamed the
deaths on the weather. Accepting Foulois's assurances, Rogers and
other committee members defended the Air Corps on the House floor.
To their great embarrassment, more army pilots died. Convinced that
Foulois had tried to dupe them, the Rogers Subcommittee unanimously charged him with violating the Air Corps Act.⁶

When the War Department failed to act upon its charges, the
Rogers Subcommittee put direct pressure on Secretary of War Dern.
In June, the subcommittee unanimously recommended that Dern immediately replace Foulois as chief of the Air Corps. While praising
the Air Corps fliers, the subcommittee accused Foulois of dishonesty,
gross misconduct, inefficiency, inaccuracy, unreliability, incompetency, and mismanagement. These charges, especially the charge of
dishonesty, brought forth expressions of indignation from Foulois's
many associates. Everyone acquainted with Foulois admired his hon-
esty. It was well known that Foulois refused small gifts from busi-
nessmen or politicians in order to protect his integrity. To his credit,
Secretary Dern refused to act too hastily, and the White House refused
to act without his recommendation.⁷ Roosevelt had every reason to
dump Foulois, who had publicly embarrassed him years before. Also,
he could have used Foulois as the scapegoat for the air mail trouble.
The Rogers Subcommittee's recommendation had given Roosevelt an
opportunity to get even with Foulois while appearing to follow the
wishes of Congress. That he did not use the opportunity indicates
Roosevelt's self-restraint.

Undeterred, the Rogers Subcommittee continued pushing for the
general's removal, and Dern ordered the inspector general to conduct
an investigation. In June, 1935, the inspector general reported that he
had found nothing wrong in Foulois's claim that the Air Corps could

fly the mail. Nor did he find any improprieties in aircraft purchases. However, the inspector general reprimanded Foulois for making unfair and misleading statements about the General Staff before the Military Affairs Committee. Foulois wanted to drop the matter, but Rogers complained on the House floor that the reprimand was little more than a "slap on the wrist." Rogers's persistence convinced Foulois that the Air Corps would suffer. Rather than see the Air Corps hurt, Foulois chose to leave the Air Corps. In September, he went on terminal leave and retired at the end of the year.[8]

Like Billy Mitchell, Foulois had been forced to retire from the army. Foulois had done nothing to justify forced retirement, but with his departure, officers with different ideas on how to promote the Air Corps moved into positions of authority. These new officers also received the organization and the airplane with which they carried out their ideas.

After the passage of the Air Corps Act, the supporters of a separate air force continued their efforts. They introduced into Congress a number of bills to create a separate air force over the following years, but none made it out of committee. Thus, by 1933, many Air Corps officers had concluded that independence was impossible to achieve. Turning to a more realistic goal, they sought to deny local ground commanders control over offensive aviation. By gathering all the Air Corps's offensive tactical units under a single commander, the organization would be the unified striking force the airmen envisioned. Concurrently, the General Staff decided that the fulfillment of the MacArthur-Pratt agreement required a unified air arm for coastal defense. To choose a workable plan for unifying the offensive units, the General Staff created a review board, headed by Maj. Gen. Hugh A. Drum. The Drum Board recommended the creation of a General Headquarters Air Force with 1,800 airplanes under one commander, and MacArthur approved the recommendations on October 12. Keeping the recommendations secret, the General Staff did nothing to implement the recommendations until the following January.[9]

Unaware of the General Staff's plans, advocates of an independent air force continued attacking the General Staff. Retired General Fechet wrote a series of virulent articles for the *Washington Herald* that elicited a strong response from General Kilbourne. In a memorandum for the deputy chief of staff, Kilbourne said that Fechet had renewed "the effort to get results through frightening people" by referring to "devastatingly disastrous" bombing attacks on the United States. He bitterly denounced this type of article for causing a "false indoctrination of members of our Air Corps" and misleading "the uninstructed civilian." Also, he explained that Fechet's attack on the cost of the navy was "the type of public statement that has embittered the Navy to a degree threatening cooperation between the services."[10]

In the end, Fechet only stirred up bad feelings. On January 31, 1934, the army sent a bill to the House Military Affairs Committee creating the GHQ Air Force, but not because of Fechet's articles. Rather, Chairman McSwain's announcement that his committee would once again consider creating an independent air arm forced the General Staff into action. McSwain introduced the army's bill on February 1 and called Foulois to testify. Still on good terms with Congress, Foulois attacked the General Staff for being the "main obstacle" to the growth of the air force. Although willing to accept the GHQ Air Force if necessary, Foulois said that the ultimate solution for national defense was a separate air force. Much to the General Staff's surprise, McSwain introduced a bill calling for independence the next day. When asked by the General Staff, Foulois pleaded ignorance about the bill, but a few months later, the General Staff discovered that Foulois had lied. The Office of the Chief of the Air Corps had drafted the McSwain bill. The General Staff opposed McSwain's bill, and Foulois's claim that the General Staff had hindered the growth of the air arm angered General Kilbourne as much as Fechet's articles had. In a twelve-page memorandum to the chief of staff, Kilbourne admitted that there had been conflicts. Nevertheless, he protested that the WPD had supported the Air Corps "whenever such support could logically be extended." The Air Corps, he concluded, had little reason to complain, because it had been "accorded a greater latitude than has any other arm or service."[11]

McSwain's bill and Foulois's testimony also upset Secretary of War Dern. In a letter to McSwain, Dern rejected the idea of independence for the Air Corps. Denying the ability of airplanes alone to defeat an enemy or protect the coasts of the United States, Dern stated that a fleet "can operate at night, in fog, and in weather when airplanes are helpless, if not indeed chained to the ground." Unconvinced and resentful, McSwain continued his efforts to separate the Air Corps from the General Staff, but the air mail fiasco sidetracked him.

Public uproar over the air mail episode forced both the War Department and the White House into action. In March, 1934, Secretary Dern named Newton D. Baker to chair a board studying the Air Corps. As Wilson's secretary of war, Baker had opposed a separate air force.[12] Nonetheless, the General Staff feared the influence of Foulois and McSwain upon the board and packed it with opponents of independence. Ignoring pleas from Air Corps pilots, the Baker Board rejected independence or increased autonomy for the Air Corps. Too many of Foulois's enemies sat on the board for him to have any influence. Furthermore, his trouble with the Rogers Subcommittee forced him to support the General Staff's proposal for the GHQ Air Force.[13]

The General Staff voiced legitimate complaints about the Air Corps to the Baker Board. While testifying on May 22, General Kilbourne cited an air defense plan presented the day before as evidence of the problems caused by the Air Corps. Kilbourne complained that the plan was unrealistically expensive and tactically faulty. More importantly, it failed to provide "a defense dependable in all kinds of weather." Despite personal requests and warnings, he said, the Office of the Chief of the Air Corps submitted "over and over again" this type of unworkable plan. As a result, his small staff in the WPD was prevented from doing constructive work. He attributed the problems between the General Staff and the Air Corps to the influence of men like Foulois and Fechet. The attitude of the Air Corps and its advocates, "who write articles for the press indicating the Navy to be obsolescent," made it difficult for the General Staff to discuss controversial matters with the navy. Furthermore, they indoctrinated the "rank and file of the Air Corps . . . with this idea of unfair treatment and soaked them with the idea of standing together *against* the Army instead of *for* the Army, as the Navy aviators stand together for the Navy."[14] Kilbourne's testimony demonstrated how the continuous attacks launched by the advocates of air power had embittered the General Staff. As a result, they refused to listen to any proposals coming from the Office of the Chief of the Air Corps. In turn, the fliers attacked the General Staff for not listening, further angering the General Staff. To break the cycle, Kilbourne wanted to foster an esprit de corps throughout the army, but that sense of teamwork could grow only when men of a like mind took command of the Air Corps.

The final report of the Baker Board read like something written by the General Staff. Rejecting a separate air force, the report approved the General Staff's proposal for a GHQ Air Force. Armed with this report, the General Staff announced the creation of the GHQ Air Force on July 27. The fact that the Baker Board supported the General Staff did not make its report worthless. Explaining why the board rejected a separate air force, the report presented a realistic appraisal of the limitations and inherent weaknesses of air power: airplanes could not capture or hold territory; their bases needed protection from land, air, and sea attacks; and airplanes depended "on at least fairly good weather" to conduct operations. Moreover, the warnings of air attacks on America were unjustified, because current airplanes lacked the range to cross the ocean, successfully attack America's "vital areas," and return home. Most significantly, the report stated that "aviation is so expensive a weapon that no nation can afford to base its organization and supply thereof on visionary approaches but rather on proven facts and possibilities."[15]

In explaining its reasons for rejecting a separate air force, the Baker Board clearly stated the prerequisites for independence. Fortunately, some Air Corps officers understood that using negative publicity campaigns would not provide the "proven facts and possibilities" required by the Baker Board. They saw, as Frank Andrews did after the *Mount Shasta* fiasco, that the Air Corps had to demonstrate what it could do before people would accept the possibilities.

Public opinion also forced Roosevelt to start his own investigation of American aviation. In June he appointed Clark Howell, editor of the *Atlanta Constitution* and a strong supporter of aviation, chair of the Federal Aviation Commission. To prepare for the investigation, Howell crossed the Atlantic to study the administration of aviation in Europe, and the other four members of the commission gathered information in the United States and the Caribbean.[16] While the commission made its preliminary investigation, Foulois put the time to good use. He selected Hap Arnold to organize and command a flight of bombers from Washington, D.C., to Alaska and back. Officially, Foulois said the flight would demonstrate how rapidly the Air Corps could move its units to remote areas. But in reality, he wanted to redeem his and the Air Corps's reputation with a spectacular flight.

At Wright Field in Dayton, Ohio, Arnold received ten new Martin B-10 bombers for the 8,290-mile round trip. Maj. Hugh Knerr, normally in charge of developing bombardment, was assigned as his executive officer for the flight. With new planes and an experienced aide, Arnold began a month of careful preparation before leading the ten bombers from Wright Field to Washington, D.C., on July 17. During that month, Air Corps officers courted congressional interest by boasting to investigating committees that the new bombers were faster than pursuit planes. Also, the Air Corps arranged for Arnold to address a national radio audience and for live radio reports to cover the departure from Washington. When a flight of navy patrol planes started a "routine" flight from San Diego to Alaska and back on the same day that Arnold left Dayton, the Air Corps heightened public interest by making the two flights seem like an off-field continuation of the Army-Navy football game.[17]

Arnold's bombers put on a colorful show for the residents of Washington, D.C. Instead of the olive drab fuselage and yellow wings of the Air Corps's tactical aircraft, his planes sported light blue fuselages with yellow wings.[18] Suitably impressed, the *New York Times* reported that the planes arrived in Washington with "their bodies and wings glistening in the sunshine . . . exactly on schedule. The flight had been

6. Lt. Col. Henry H. "Hap" Arnold, commander of the 1934 Alaskan Flight, and Maj. Ralph Royce with maps showing the route of the flight. *Courtesy U.S.A.F.*

made with the precision of a railroad train."[19] After the air mail fiasco, this praise meant a great deal.

Soon, a flight of ten bombers to Alaska became so common that it received no notice outside air force reports; but, in 1934 that was not the case. Special enough to warrant nationwide radio hookups, the flight to Alaska offered a golden opportunity for the Air Corps to redeem itself or dig a deeper grave if it failed. Fortunately, the flight was a great success. Only one mishap occurred during the entire trip. When one of his two engines failed, a pilot ditched his B-10 in Cook's Bay, Anchorage. But Air Corps mechanics recovered the plane from forty feet of water, repaired it, and put it back into service in time to join the return flight to Washington, D.C. All ten of the B-10s re-

7. All ten of the B-10s making the Alaskan Flight returned to Bolling Field on August 20, 1934, on schedule. Here, the Alaskan fliers are posing for photographs with Assistant Secretary of War Harry H. Woodring. To his left is Hap Arnold and Maj. Gen. Benjamin D. Foulois. Note the newsreel camera in the lower left and the Alaskan Flight emblem painted on the nose of the B-10s. *Courtesy U.S.A.F.*

turned to Bolling Field on August 20 on schedule again. Climbing out of their planes, the fourteen officers and nineteen enlisted men were greeted by a large crowd. Secretary Dern congratulated Arnold for demonstrating "the skill and daring of our army and its fliers and the thoroughness of their training."[20]

The Alaska flight recouped some of the Air Corps's lost prestige, but it did nothing to ease Foulois's predicament. Having purchased the B-10s through negotiated contracts, he had hoped the flight would vindicate his actions. Unfortunately, the Rogers Subcommittee wanted to oust him. Nothing changed their minds.[21] For the Air Corps, however, the flight provided a guide to follow. In the years to come, army fliers conducted a number of meticulously planned flights, proving the Air Corps's abilities and efficiency.

Meeting in late September, the Howell Commission took little notice of the Alaska flight. As with the Baker Board, the General Staff acted to ensure the Howell Commission's support for the GHQ Air Force. The General Staff gave the commission a written statement strongly supporting the new organization, and it tried to control the testimony of the Air Corps officers by making them submit their statements for examination. Foulois's statement, actually written by his subordinates, proclaimed the decisiveness of air power and called for an autonomous air force. After the General Staff objected, he watered it down. Assistant Chief of the Air Corps Westover also watered down his prepared statement. Yet he denounced the claim of the Drum and Baker boards that the United States was invulnerable to air attack. Other officers refused to submit; they continued to press the claims for air power. Officers from the Air Corps Tactical School, especially Maj. Donald Wilson and Capt. Harold L. George, adamantly professed the ability of airplanes to crush an enemy's will to resist before the land armies came into contact. For the air force to be properly prepared for war, said Captain George, it had to be separated from the ground forces.[22]

Free from any restrictions, the civilians testifying before the Howell Commission made Wilson and George sound tame. Billy Mitchell again called for an independent air force and told the commission that he wanted the United States to acquire fifty airships to make possible the "annihilation of Japan." Igor Sikorsky claimed that warlike Japanese fliers would cheerfully make a one-way flight to get the chance to drop bombs on New York City, or more probably poison gas.[23]

The remarks by Mitchell and Sikorsky angered the Japanese press and threatened the future of the Washington and London Treaties. The London Treaty would expire in December, 1936, unless Great Britain, Japan, and the United States agreed to extend its provisions in 1935. The Washington Treaty would expire in 1936, if one of the three signatories repudiated it by the end of December, 1934. Irreconcilable differences between the three signatories put the future of both treaties in doubt. Feeling slighted by the 5:5:3 tonnage ratio, Japan demanded parity. Great Britain wanted to keep the same ratio but cut back on battleships and heavy cruisers while increasing the allowed tonnage for light cruisers. American interests in the Pacific required the long-range capabilities of heavy cruisers, and the United States feared that giving the Japanese parity would spark a new arms race.[24]

As the December deadline for the Washington Treaty approached, the United States, Great Britain, and Japan sent negotiators to London to discuss the extension of the naval treaties. On October 5, Roosevelt told Norman H. Davis, the American negotiator, to extend the treaties and obtain further naval limitations if possible. The president emphasized that he would not approve a treaty allowing larger navies. Later that day, Roosevelt told reporters that the United States hoped to carry on the progressive reduction in naval armaments started in the Washington and London Treaties. Mitchell's talk of annihilating Japan had upset Roosevelt. He knew that Mitchell's volatile remarks would enable the Japanese to justify abandoning the treaty ratios, effectively ending any hope of arms reduction. "Of course," he complained to the reporters, "things are not in the least bit helped— this is off the record entirely—by the kind of statement that was made by our old friend Billy Mitchell the other day. . . . Billy Mitchell would be a much more useful person to this country if he would not talk that way."[25]

But Roosevelt soon discovered that the Japanese had already decided to end the treaties. Secretary of the Navy Claude A. Swanson informed him on November 28, 1934, that the Japanese cabinet had recommended increased appropriations for national defense. Realizing that any chance for reduction in naval armaments was gone, Roosevelt prepared for an arms race. In a memorandum on December 17, Roosevelt instructed Swanson to look confidentially into producing new long-range ships should the Washington and London treaties be discarded. "At the same time," Roosevelt wrote, "I should like to have a study made of the possibility of establishing one or two very large air bases in the Philippines, with a smaller base in Guam, and still smaller bases in the Midway-Hawaiian chain and in the Aleutian chain of Islands."[26] Roosevelt wanted the capacity to extend American naval and air power across the Pacific Ocean.

While Roosevelt looked into transoceanic defenses, supporters of air power sought the construction of new airfields to guard America's borders. In November of 1934, General Fechet and Florida Congressman James M. Wilcox created the National Air Frontier Defense Association to lobby for those air bases. On January 17, 1935, Wilcox introduced a bill for ten new air bases. The War Department, fearing that Wilcox's bill would reduce appropriations for the rest of the army, proposed a less ambitious construction program of six air bases. Both Wilcox and the War Department agreed, however, that one air base had to be placed in Alaska. Wilcox told the House Military Affairs Committee that an "Oriental country" could seize mineral-rich Alaska, and he warned the committee that "Alaska is closer to Japan than it is to the United States."[27]

Billy Mitchell thought more along the lines of President Roosevelt. On February 11, he told the Committee on Patents that the Manufacturers Aircraft Association had impeded progress in civil and military aviation through a monopoly over patents. Then, he took the opportunity to warn America once again about Japan. "If Japan seizes Alaska," he told the committee, "she can bomb New York in twenty hours. We know they have ships designed for that purpose. We have got to have planes that can fly to the Midway Islands, to Japan and back."[28]

The army and civilian supporters of the air base proposals thought of aircraft as merely an extension of coastal artillery. Besides embodying the current isolationist view of remaining behind coastal defenses, their plans to build a number of air bases around the frontiers of the continental United States differed from nineteenth-century harbor fortifications only in the range of the weapons. Basically, they saw the airplane as a long-range cannon. Unknowingly, they were attempting to make a new weapon fit old concepts, instead of formulating new concepts to fully utilize the potential of the new weapon.

As Roosevelt's memorandum to Secretary Swanson and Mitchell's testimony before the Committee on Patents showed, both thought of air power as more than a weapon for static defense. They wanted to project American air power into the Pacific through Midway Island, even as others only sought to defend the United States with a ring of airfields. Realizing the mobile and destructive nature of modern warfare, Roosevelt saw the importance of taking the war to the enemy and not letting the enemy bring the war to the United States. Since Japan was the most likely enemy in a Pacific war, Roosevelt wanted the two weapons best suited for carrying a war to Japanese shores: long-range ships and airplanes.

Japan denounced the Washington Treaty in December, and rumors quickly spread that President Roosevelt had decided to ask Congress for increased national defense funds. He first tried to convince the world of America's peaceful intentions in his annual message to Congress on January 4, 1935. Roosevelt said there was "no ground for apprehension that our relations with any nation will be otherwise than peaceful."[29] Three days later, the president asked Congress to increase the army's budget for military spending by more than $48 million, with almost half to go to the Air Corps. He also wanted the navy to receive more than $16 million for aircraft.[30]

The Japanese objected to plans for placing an American air base in the Pacific. On February 8, the House Military Affairs Committee considered the construction of another air base in Hawaii. Afterward, Chairman McSwain told the press that it was only a defensive measure, but the Japanese protested that a Hawaiian air base would be a direct threat to Japan.[31] President Roosevelt knew that the Japanese would object strenuously if the United States put large air bases in the Philippines, as he had suggested to Secretary Swanson.

The Japanese had good reason to worry about American air power in the Pacific. It threatened their sea communications. In 1930, Billy Mitchell had stated in his book, *Skyways,* that Great Britain and Japan depended upon overseas commerce. Any breakdown in their trade routes would be their downfall. "Air power," he wrote, "is entirely capable of breaking down these lines of communications by sinking the ships and causing the evacuation of the ports. . . ."[32] On February 3, 1935, Edwin L. James refined Mitchell's argument. Writing about the post–Washington Treaty strengths of the British, Japanese, and American fleets for the *New York Times,* James pointed out that strategic parity did not necessarily mean parity in tonnage or guns. For Japan, parity depended on fuel rather than ships. In peacetime, the Japanese home islands produced only half the oil consumed by the navy. Wartime usage of oil would multiply, making the Japanese even more dependent upon imported oil. He suggested that Great Britain, the Dutch East Indies, and the United States—the three countries most affected by Japanese expansion—could stop the Japanese by cutting off their foreign oil supply and waiting only six months for the Japanese navy to run out of fuel. "It is this factor," wrote James, "which constitutes the weakest point in the naval strategy of the Japanese."[33] Understandably, the proximity of American aircraft worried Japan. In early 1935, American planes stationed in the Philippines, Guam, Midway, Hawaii, and the Aleutians could have threatened Japan's sea communications.

From Europe, Roosevelt received more distressing news. Hitler had made Anschluss with Austria his primary foreign policy, but Mussolini, fearing a powerful nation on his northern border, opposed the German unification. In January, 1935, he and the French signed a consultative pact, promising to discuss joint action if Hitler threatened the independence of Austria.[34] Hitler continued to push the issue, and on February 2, Mussolini told Ambassador Breckinridge Long that war with Germany appeared imminent. Reporting the conversation to President Roosevelt, Long made a suggestion: "you might consider

giving instructions to somebody that a good equipment for your diplomatic and consular officers in Europe would be gas masks, because
when it comes it will come over night and come from the air. There
will be no long drawn out mobilization. I am serious about the gas
masks."[35] Like the Europeans, Long feared aerial gas attacks. Since the
Germans were not supposed to have an air force, only American dip-
lomats in Germany should have needed masks. However, the Germans secretly had kept a small air force disguised as flying clubs, and
Long's warning suggests that he knew about the German air force.

Adolf Hitler became chancellor of Germany on January 30, 1933,
and three days later he put Hermann Goering in charge of all civil
aviation and air raid protection. Goering, commander of the Richt-
hofen Squadron at the end of the First World War, placed all flying
club members into uniform, and the German air force became an open
secret. In March, 1935, the Nazis officially announced the existence
of an air force, the Luftwaffe. Goering, its commander, publicly denounced the Versailles Treaty on March 16 and boasted that he would
build the Luftwaffe into the world's strongest air force.[36]

Germany's announcement of the Luftwaffe coincided with the establishment of the GHQ Air Force. When the Howell Commission
submitted its final report to President Roosevelt, it too supported the
General Staff's plan for a GHQ Air Force. Armed with favorable reports from a military and a civilian investigation, the General Staff
hammered out the details for the GHQ Air Force. Although people
continued referring to all army aviation as the Air Corps, the General
Staff essentially split the Air Corps into two organizations: the Air
Corps and the GHQ Air Force. Foulois, as chief of the Air Corps, controlled supply, procurement, and training at the Air Corps schools.
Lt. Col. Frank M. Andrews, as commander of the GHQ Air Force, controlled the tactical units with the temporary rank of general. To maintain its control over the GHQ Air Force, the General Staff made Andrews report directly to the chief of staff rather than the chief of the
Air Corps.[37] Emphasizing the separation, the General Staff physically
separated the two branches. Andrews set up his administrative headquarters at Langley Field, Virginia. The tactical units, divided into three
wings, established headquarters at Langley Field, Barksdale Field
(Bossier City, La.), and March Field (Riverside, Calif.). Looking on the
GHQ Air Force as an experiment, the General Staff gave it a trial period of one year.[38]

Becoming operational on March 1, 1935, this new organizational
scheme had a number of inherent flaws. The local ground commander
retained control over the airfields. To get anything done at the airfield,
the Air Corps needed the approval of the ground commander. Also,

the split command fostered internal dissension within the Army Air Corps as each branch tried to impose its will upon the other.[39] Nevertheless, after more than fifteen years of acrimonious debate, advocates of a separate air arm and advocates of ground-support aviation had compromised. Advocates of strategic air power finally had a strike force capable of carrying out strategic missions. At the same time, however, that strike force remained under the General Staff's control. Despite giving neither group all that it wanted, the GHQ Air Force satisfied both enough to stop their vicious fighting. The airmen demonstrated their pleasure with the new organization when Representative McSwain introduced another bill to create a Department of Aeronautics in April of 1935. Telling Congress that they opposed McSwain's bill, Westover, Arnold, and Lt. Col. Follett Bradley expressed satisfaction with the new arrangement.[40]

To mark the operational debut of the GHQ Air Force, the Office of the Chief of the Air Corps planned a spectacular, long-distance flight. On February 25, the Air Corps announced that ten bombers would demonstrate the mobility of army planes and show the need for air defenses in the Pacific. The plans called for the planes to fly from March Field to Washington, D.C., and on to Miami. After refueling, the planes would then fly over 900 miles of water to Panama. All previous mass flights to Panama had taken the time-consuming route along the Gulf of Mexico. A spokesman said that the 2,129-mile flight from Washington to Panama would take only eleven hours of flying time.[41] The Air Corps had high hopes for the flight. "I believe it very essential," Maj. Carl Spaatz told Hap Arnold, "that a flight of this nature take place in order to bolster up the Air Corps."[42]

On March 1, the officers at Langley Field confidently told reporters that the GHQ Air Force would prove that coastal air defenses should be entrusted to the Army Air Corps. They also promised that the Panama flight would prove the ability of land planes to fly over water with the same precision as the navy flying boats.[43] General Andrews, however, decided to cancel the flight. After wresting control of the flight from Foulois, Andrews discovered that the pilots and planes were not prepared for such a flight. Until both were ready, he told Arnold, "the political effects of anything unfavorable happening now—not on our personal fortunes but on the future role of the GHQ Air Force in National Defense—are such that no chances must be taken on its happening."[44]

Finally, the Army Air Corps had an officer in a position of authority who realized that public and political support would not come from demonstrating the poor condition of the Air Corps. Andrews's cancellation of the Panama flight revealed his knowledge of how to conduct a successful political and publicity campaign to win increased support for the air force. Andrews understood that support from the government, the War Department, and the American people would come by proving that trust, and thereby funds, could be placed in the Army Air Corps. Furthermore, Andrews's careful check of the preparations and efforts to get control of the flight indicated that he did not trust Foulois's planning ability. After the air mail fiasco, Andrews had every reason to be wary.

Andrews recognized that the antagonistic attitude of his men toward the General Staff had hurt the Air Corps. To remedy the problem, he started an education campaign within the GHQ Air Force. Telling his officers and men to submerge their personal feelings for the "good of the Air Corps," Andrews said that the War Department genuinely wanted the GHQ Air Force to succeed because it wanted to keep coastal air defense under army control. Addressing the problem of niggardly congressional funding, Andrews said that Congress had wanted to do something for air defense, but it had lacked confidence in the previous Air Corps set up. Now, he assured his men, Congress planned to appropriate money to see what the GHQ Air Force could do. Finally, Andrews emphasized the need for unified action and thoroughly prepared maneuvers to get favorable publicity. He insisted that the public must not be confused with differing pronouncements. To achieve this unified action, Andrews ordered the various units to share all information with each other.[45]

Andrews's education campaign worked. By submerging animosities and showing that the Army Air Corps could deliver what it promised, Andrews helped win the trust and support of the War Department, the president, the Congress, and the American people. During the last six months before the Japanese attack on Pearl Harbor, the confidence in the abilities of the Army Air Corps to deliver what it promised greatly influenced America's military and civilian leaders.

By cancelling the Panama flight, General Andrews deprived the GHQ Air Force of the opportunity to celebrate its creation with a publicity stunt. But Andrews planned on following his advice to Hap Arnold after the *Mount Shasta* farce. As commander of the GHQ Air Force, Andrews improved navigation and bombardment skills, procured better equipment, and kept the GHQ Air Force "out of the limelight" until he knew its limitations. When Andrews demonstrated his strike force, he left nothing to chance.[46]

Although rumors had been circulating for several months, Pan American Air Lines formally announced in March, 1935, its plans to establish a transpacific airline from San Francisco to Manila with stops at Honolulu, Midway, Wake, and Guam. These plans to extend American commercial aviation across the Pacific dovetailed with the directions Roosevelt had given Secretary of the Navy Swanson three months earlier. Pan American had aided American foreign policy since its formation in 1922,[47] and the Roosevelt administration supported the transpacific air route. Postmaster General Farley predicted that Congress would provide funds for companies making transoceanic flights. The United States Navy granted Pan American permission to use Wake Island for a landing field, and the Federal Communications Commission considered Pan American's request for radio stations along the Pacific air route.[48]

Even when the Pan American route was only conjecture, some Americans viewed the projection of American commercial air power across the Pacific as a means to thwart Japan's economic domination of China. "The door into China," wrote Harris Hull in the *Washington Post*, "which Japan has been eager to slam in the face of Western nations who dared peep in, may soon be pushed completely open with a wedge that will stay—an airplane propeller."[49] The Japanese clearly saw the threat. In November, 1934, the Japanese government provided subsidies in the 1935–36 budget to extend air routes to the mandated islands. The route from Japan to Saipan intersected the American line from California to the Philippines, but the Japanese gave no indication that they would allow foreign airlines to use their facilities.

The Roosevelt administration recognized the importance of the American air route to the Philippines. In March of 1935, Governor General of the Philippines Frank Murphy returned to the United States and conferred with Roosevelt. Afterward, Murphy told reporters that foreign nations were trying to get landing rights in Hawaii, Guam, Wake Island, and the Philippines. Thus, it was clear by early 1935 that aviation would play an important role in the military and economic affairs in the Pacific Ocean.

To justify giving Pan American access to landing facilities at Wake Island, the navy stressed the commercial aspects of the transpacific air route. Secretary Swanson promised that Pan American had not received a monopoly on the landing facilities.[50] However, the commercial aspects failed to disguise the military potential. The Washington Treaty prohibited the United States from building fortifications or naval bases at Midway, Wake, or Guam, but navy officials claimed that they were commercial landing fields. Not fooled, the Japanese navy complained that the air bases could easily be transformed into naval air bases. As such, they threatened Japan's mandated islands. Adm. Nobsmasa Suetsugu, the former commander of the Japanese Fleet, explained that the mandated islands formed Japan's first line of marine defense. "Should they be occupied by an enemy," he stated, "they would at once endanger our defense. The islands are natural air-craft 'carriers,' affording enemy squadrons ideal places from which to operate."[51] Japanese naval officials told the press that the planned route indicated military preparation in the guise of civilian enterprise, and Japanese headlines carried such comments as, "American air force shakes finger under Japan's nose," and "American concealed power in the Pacific."[52]

The Japanese knew that air bases on these islands threatened sea communications with their mandated islands, but they harbored a deeper fear. "Most of All Japan Fears an Air Attack" proclaimed the title of an article published by the *New York Times Magazine* in August of 1935. The author, Hugh Byas, recounted how fires had burned most of Tokyo and had killed over 71,000 people during the earthquake of 1923. Their homes constructed of wood and paper, the Japanese worried constantly about fire. They responded to shouts of "fire" more quickly than any other cry for help. Modern brick build-ings and fire departments had reduced the threat from normal fires, Byas explained, but air attacks offered new threats. If, he wrote, "Japan is ever engaged in war with a power of any military standing the enemy will find in those cities a target such as no other country in the world offers." The Japanese realized that Soviet bombers from Vladivostok could reach Tokyo with ease. Gen. Vassily Bluecher, the Soviet com-mander in the Far East, stated that "three tons of bombs can destroy Tokyo as completely as the earthquake did." American aircraft car-riers presented an equal threat. A Japanese naval writer claimed that only 10 percent of the U.S.S. *Saratoga*'s bombers could do as much damage to Tokyo as did the great earthquake.[53]

Six years before the Pearl Harbor attack created overwhelming hatred for the Japanese in the United States, the firebombing of Tokyo was openly discussed in the American press. The idea gained further exposure from foreign soldiers and military writers who described the firebombing of Japanese cities. Russians, Japanese, and Americans de-scribed the Japanese cities as military targets, although all three groups grossly underestimated the number of aircraft needed to burn Tokyo. During the Second World War, racial hatred shaped American mili-tary policy toward Japan, but the idea of burning down Tokyo, a city like none in Europe, had entrenched itself firmly in popular thought before the Pearl Harbor attack created a desire for revenge.

Secretary of State Cordell Hull and President Roosevelt knew of Japan's fears, and they worried about the effect of the Pan American route on relations with Japan. On April 16, Hull suggested that Juan T. Trippe, the president of Pan American, invite the Japanese to join the venture with their own air route from Japan to Guam. Hoping that the Japanese would reconsider their denunciation of the Washington Treaty, Roosevelt told Hull that "this is a good suggestion," and he approved it the next day. Roosevelt's willingness to accommodate the Japanese influenced his policy toward the Philippines. On April 22, Secretary Swanson suggested designating naval reservations in the Philippines before they became independent in 1946. Roosevelt rejected the suggestion. The president believed that Japan would interpret such a move as contrary to America's stated desire to extend the Washington Treaty. Roosevelt also rejected the proposal for military reasons. He considered a military-naval base in the Manila–Subic Bay area a liability. "It is well known," he told Swanson, "that this area could not be defended over a long period of time against an army attacking it from the land side."[54]

Nevertheless, President Roosevelt remained interested in establishing airfields across the Pacific. On April 2, 1935, a small party of soldiers and civilians secretly occupied Baker, Howland, and Jarvis islands in the central Pacific to gather information and prepare landing fields. As protection, the Roosevelt administration prepared a cover story. If the press discovered the expeditions, the Post Office Department would claim that they were part of an effort to expand air mail service across the Pacific. The Commerce Department informed Roosevelt of the operation and the cover story on April 8, and Secretary Swanson gave him copies of the landing parties' log books on May 28. Two days later, Roosevelt told Swanson that he was "greatly interested" in the expeditions and instructed Swanson to keep him informed of the "progress of the men landed on these Islands." The president wanted to colonize those islands for at least a year, even if the personnel had to be replaced every three months.[55]

While Roosevelt quietly projected American aviation into the Pacific, the army became involved in an international incident. Through his involvement, the president demonstrated his support for General Andrews. At a secret session of the House Military Affairs Committee about the army's air base bill, General Andrews warned that an enemy could use Newfoundland, Saint Pierre, Niquelon, Bermuda, the Bahamas, Jamaica, Trinidad, British Honduras, or the Lesser Antilles to launch air attacks on the United States. As a precaution, Andrews recommended keeping these potential bases under surveillance. Should a base be discovered, Andrews recommended either bombing or occupying it. Whether he understood it or not, Andrews had advocated preemptive strikes on the territories of other nations. Much to the general's surprise, the committee published his secret testimony. He quickly stated that he had spoken only of an "abstract military study with no concrete political thought or reference." Coming to An-

8. Formation of six Curtiss YA-8 attack airplanes over the seawall at Galveston, Texas. *Courtesy U.S.A.F.*

drews's aid, President Roosevelt warned Chairman McSwain that any further publication of secret testimony would force him to allow future testimony "only after approval by me." McSwain listened to the president. Calling it a mistake, McSwain took full responsibility for the publication. In a public apology, he praised Andrews as an efficient, patriotic, and honorable officer.[56]

Saved from further embarrassment by Roosevelt's intervention, General Andrews proceeded with his plans to prove the capabilities of the GHQ Air Force. The GHQ Air Force's obsolescent aircraft, however, limited Andrews's efforts. When asked to send bombers and attack planes to an army demonstration, Andrews had to send old B-6s and A-8s. The slow B-6s worried him. Andrews said sarcastically to Westover, "People are getting so they laugh nowadays when a ship goes thundering by at 90 miles per hour."[57] Yet even as Andrews proceeded with obsolete airplanes, the first B-17 neared completion at the Boeing plant in Seattle. With this plane, Andrews ended the laughter.

Despite tight security, the press learned that Boeing had built a new bomber. Newspapers carried reports of a giant "mystery" bomber and called it "the deadliest air weapon in the world." Pressed by reporters, War Department officials confirmed that Boeing had constructed an "aerial battle cruiser." They expected Boeing to enter the plane, designated the Boeing 299, in the Air Corps's open competition in August. Excited about the new bomber, officials hailed it as the most formidable aerial defense weapon ever offered to the United States.

Boeing mechanics rolled the highly polished airplane out of its hanger for public view on July 17. Upon seeing the five gun turrets on the bomber, Dick Williams of the *Seattle Times* nicknamed it a Flying Fortress. Boeing copyrighted the name, and it stuck with the bomber throughout the Second World War. However, the Air Corps soon adapted the nickname to lessen opposition to the purchase of long-range bombers. The Air Corps referred to the plane as a mobile fort, capable of roaming the skies in defense of America's coasts.[58]

At the bomber competition, the four-engine Boeing bomber made its two competitors, twin-engine bombers entered by the Martin and Douglas companies, appear archaic. The Boeing enhanced this appearance by flying from Seattle to Wright Field with an average ground speed of 233 miles per hour, a remarkable achievement for the time. After winning every phase of the competition, Boeing's luck ran out on October 30. The bomber crashed on takeoff and burned, killing two test pilots. Although clearly superior to its two competitors, the Air Corps judges disqualified the Boeing bomber for not completing the competition. On that technicality, Douglas won the competition and an order for 133 Douglas B-18s. Development costs for the Boeing 299 came out of company pockets, and Boeing expected to recover its expenses with an army contract. The loss of the plane almost ruined Boeing, but a small order from the Army Air Corps saved the company. Determined to purchase the bomber, the Air Corps ordered 13 for test models. Boeing contracted to deliver the 13 planes, redesignated the YB-17, within ten months. Although small, the order kept Boeing in the bomber business.[59]

Prospects for the Army Air Corps appeared bright in the summer of 1935. In addition to the Flying Fortress, Congress and the president seemed ready to provide more funds. The House Military Affairs Committee and the General Staff asked Congress for an additional $40 million to purchase 600 to 800 new planes. Representative Rogers, who spoke to the president on July 24, announced that Roosevelt supported the increased purchases. Congress also passed Wilcox's air base bill, but FDR warned that few funds from the PWA would be provided to implement the bill.[60]

General Andrews boosted morale in the Army Air Corps on August 24. Using a B-12 with its wheels exchanged for pontoons, he broke three world seaplane records and almost broke a fourth. The Army Air Corps did not fly seaplanes, and the press wondered why Andrews wanted to break seaplane records. Because coastal air defense duties required flying considerable distances out to sea, explained a GHQ Air Force spokesman, Andrews's flight prepared army fliers for that duty. The press saw through that weak excuse and reported that Andrews wanted to improve morale by setting an unusual aviation record.[61]

Since he had cancelled the Panama flight, Andrews felt obligated to do something spectacular, but he realized the need for success. He showed brilliance in choosing to set a seaplane record. First, Andrews knew that Charles Lindbergh owned the previous record, increasing the importance of a successful attempt. Second, he knew that his B-12 could fly more than forty miles per hour faster than Lindbergh's plane. Therefore, even with pontoons slowing him down, he had plenty of speed. Third, by flying the plane himself, Andrews drew attention to himself. He was not seeking glory, however; rather, Andrews realized that critics would blame him, not the GHQ Air Force, for failure.

As he awaited the arrival of his new B-18s and YB-17s, Andrews used the planes on hand to impress the War Department and American public. At a demonstration for the Command and General Staff School at Fort Leavenworth, he watched three B-6 bombers accurately hit a target from eight thousand feet. The demonstration impressed the ground officers. Andrews overheard one say, "You can't tell me that the Corps can't hit anything from bombers."[62] Andrews knew that hitting an undefended target from eight thousand feet was not difficult, but the ground officers seemed unconcerned by the altitude from which the bombs fell. The accuracy impressed the spectators. Andrews noted the importance of showing people accurate bombing, and he employed it whenever possible.

On November 7, Andrews's men impressed a much larger audience. Fourteen army planes from Mitchel Field on Long Island flew down the Hudson River toward lower Manhattan. Continuing around the tip of Manhattan and up the East River, the planes filled the sky with a smoke screen. High winds quickly dissipated the smoke, but a GHQ Air Force spokesman claimed that the exercise had proved the feasibility of concealing other planes from the guns of ground

9. Army aircraft laid a smoke screen around New York City, theoretically to conceal other aircraft from antiaircraft guns on the ground. High winds quickly dissipated the smoke, but the event was captured by newsreel photographers carried aloft by Army Air Corps aircraft. Movie theaters across the United States showed the newsreels. *Courtesy U.S.A.F.*

forces. The exercise also served as a publicity stunt. To guarantee wide exposure, army planes carried newsreel photographers to record the event. The newsreels played in movie theaters across the nation.[63]

On October 2, 1935, a major change occurred in the General Staff with important implications for the Army Air Corps. Malin Craig replaced MacArthur as the chief of staff. Believing that the General Staff had been too concerned with theory, Craig tried to make the army a combat-ready force. With his limited funds, Chief of Staff Craig emphasized the need to replace the army's World War vintage weapons. Research and development lost priority. He wanted to arm his troops with new, if not the most modern, weapons. Craig's outlook put him at odds with the GHQ Air Force over aircraft procurement. As Chief of Staff, he wanted the most airplanes for the dollar, but the Air Corps sought the best airplanes for the dollar. Hence, Craig opposed the purchase of one four-engined B-17 when two B-18s could be bought for the same price. To reach the authorized goal of 2,320 airplanes, Craig pressured the GHQ Air Force to accept more B-18s. Andrews opposed the purchase of anything but the best planes, and he believed the B-17 was the best airplane available. In defiance of the Chief of Staff and the War Department, Andrews campaigned for more B-17s.[64]

Although General Craig opposed the creation of a separate air force, he supported the Army Air Corps. In a memorandum for Oscar Westover, Craig spelled out his policy toward the Army Air Corps.

> The Air Corps plays an important part of the Army team in national defense. Its role as a combat arm is increasing very rapidly, and its use as a strategic weapon is influencing national defense policies and international political policies throughout the world. The extent of such influence can only be registered by the march of time and the results of history.

Craig promised to provide enough aircraft to bring the Army Air Corps up to its authorized level. To fulfill his promise, however, Craig demanded of Westover the "loyal support and hearty cooperation," not only of "those in direct authority in the Air Corps and in the G.H.Q. Air Force," but the entire air arm. Since Westover would replace Foulois as the chief of the Air Corps in December, Craig made Westover responsible for the "leadership and direction of the Air Corps." Craig wanted to see "constructive action," and he ordered Westover to proceed before Foulois retired.[65]

Himself a team player, Westover rejected the methods used by Mitchell and Foulois. Westover wanted his subordinates to stop attacking the opponents of air power. He also hoped to create a unified front that could successfully win the support of the General Staff, War Department, and Congress. Armed with Craig's order to take command, Westover implemented his ideas on winning increased support for the Army Air Corps. In a directive, which he ordered disseminated throughout the Air Corps, Westover denounced the methods of confrontation and intrigue practiced by Mitchell and Foulois. Without mentioning Mitchell and Foulois by name, he said that most of the Air Corps's problems stemmed "from the aggressive and enthusiastic efforts of some of its personnel in seeking remedial measures" outside proper channels. He ordered the Air Corps to heed the wishes of the president and Congress and support the recommendations of the Drum and Baker boards. Hopes for an independent air force would be forgotten. To ensure that the Army Air Corps received the eight hundred airplanes a year authorized by Congress, Westover called for "effective teamwork" and "support and hearty cooperation" from the entire Air Corps. By cooperation, he meant some very specific things:

sending criticisms and recommendations through proper channels; not going to the press or Congress with complaints; presenting to Congress only properly prepared plans having the support of the War Department; and not expressing public opposition to measures recommended by the General Staff. These practices had angered the War Department and General Staff, making them unreceptive to Air Corps proposals, and he wanted them stopped. Furthermore, he carried his ideas to the public. Westover ordered his officers, "particularly the senior grades," to participate in public speaking programs "to enlighten the public as to the part which the Air Corps and the G.H.Q. Air Force play in the Army team of national defense." Westover told them to inform the public about "the civic cooperation, if any, needed to assist the War Department in carrying out its Army program."[66]

Andrews took advantage of his freedom to report directly to the chief of staff. In a memorandum to Craig, Andrews warned that Chief of Naval Operations Admiral Standley had ignored the MacArthur-Pratt agreement and had organized a strike force of a thousand shore-based aircraft. The navy was "planning to usurp some of the functions now charged to the Army." Opposed to teaching over-water navigation to army pilots, the navy had offered to guide army planes to their target and back. "Navigation over water," explained Andrews, "is an essential part of our training in order to carry out our function of off shore reconnaissance and for off shore operations." The army had to guard against navy encroachments at all times. The only defense against navy encroachment would be "an adequate Air Force actually in being, properly equipped, thoroughly trained and with sufficient bases to operate in any possible theater."[67]

This memorandum appeared to be just another attack on the navy. In reality it was skillful propaganda. By telling Craig that the navy wanted a thousand airplanes, Andrews quietly presented proof of the need for more airplanes. After all, if the navy needed that many planes, then the army also needed that many. By relating King's remarks, Andrews tried to win support for more over-water navigation training. Although nothing came of his memorandum, Andrews definitely projected an image that the GHQ Air Force was made up of team players.

During the interwar years, air races attracted public attention, and the air services sent planes to capitalize on the free publicity. Andrews scheduled maneuvers in Florida for December, 1935, to take advantage of the media coverage of the Miami air races. From across the nation, GHQ Air Force planes rushed to Florida, demonstrating the ability of the GHQ Air Force to meet an assault on either coast. Once his planes had gathered in Florida, Andrews exploited the press. The *New York Times* always devoted special coverage to the major air races. Sending to Miami one of its most respected aviation writers, Reginal M. Cleveland, the *Times* printed daily reports about the maneuvers and races. Fed stories by the army fliers, Cleveland reported what the GHQ Air Force wanted known. Many of the Air Corps's problems during the air mail fiasco had resulted from the lack of radios and navigation skills. The Army Air Corps had rectified the problems, and through Cleveland and the *New York Times,* the GHQ Air Force publicized the changes.[68]

By December, 1935, the GHQ Air Force, which had satisfied the army fliers, threatened the cohesiveness of the Army Air Corps. A serious split arose between the Air Corps and the GHQ Air Force. Westover wanted the GHQ Air Force to report to the chief of the Air Corps rather than the chief of staff, but those in the GHQ Air Force preferred reporting directly to the chief of staff. Thinking he had found a solution, Westover decided to take an officer from the GHQ Air Force and make him the assistant chief of the Air Corps. With Westover's approval, General Craig named Hap Arnold to the post in December.

After almost a decade of "exile," Arnold returned to Washington in January 1936. To his embarrassment, Arnold found himself "ranged with the Air Corps Headquarters, across the fence from the G.H.Q. Air Force, whose side of the intramural arguments had been my own enthusiastic side in California." Nevertheless, personal involvement in the affairs of the Army Air Corps gave Arnold "a new kind of sympathy" for the previous chiefs and assistant chiefs of the Air Corps, and he developed an ability to perceive the air force as a whole. "The ramifications of the job," he later wrote, "spread far beyond any jurisdictional rivalry with the G.H.Q. Air Force."[69]

During his years away from Washington, Hap Arnold grew considerably in his political capabilities. Less than ten years after the War Department had exiled Arnold for supporting Billy Mitchell and attacking the General Staff, people recognized his ability to "sell" the air force to the General Staff. Col. G. C. Brant, Commander of the Third Wing, GHQ Air Force, congratulated General Andrews for not being made the chief of the Air Corps. Brant recognized the importance of the chief of the Air Corps in securing legislation and appropriations, but he also knew that the success of army aviation depended upon the efficiency with which the tactical units were commanded. "If they fail to function," he told Andrews, "appropriations and legislation mean nothing." Brant saw Andrews as the best tactical commander. He believed the team of Westover and Arnold made a fine contribution to the Army Air Corps. "Westover can do all the detail work," Brant explained to Andrews, "and Arnold can sell our ideas to General Staff, Bureau of the Budget and Congress."[70]

10. On March 1, 1937, the first Boeing YB-17 "Flying Fortress" arrived at Langley Field, Virginia. Here, Maj. Gen. Frank M. Andrews greets the pilot, Maj. Barney M. Giles. Hap Arnold later called this first Flying Fortress "Air Power that you could put your hand on." *Courtesy U.S.A.F.*

As Brant realized, the three men best suited to lead the Army Air Corps took command in 1935. By rejecting the negative publicity campaigns employed by their predecessors, Andrews, Westover, and Arnold successfully promoted the cause of air power. They understood that success won support. Just as they came to power, the tool they used to promote air power arrived. Arnold later recalled that "almost at the same moment I arrived in Washington, the first real American Air Power appeared. Not just brilliant prophecies, good coastal defense airplanes, or promising techniques; but, for the first time in history, Air Power that you could put your hand on."[71] He referred to the arrival of the Army Air Corps's first two Boeing B-17 bombers at Langley Field.

IV. Early Attempts to Shape Public Opinion

Events in Europe influenced President Roosevelt's thinking about warfare. The military policies he followed after the Munich Crisis in 1938—such as increasing production of aircraft and using air power as a deterrent—had their roots in 1935.

In December, 1935, the War Department announced plans to accelerate its purchase of aircraft. An Army Air Corps officer told reporters that it would give, "with the possible exception of Germany," the United States the most modern air fleet in the world.[1] His statement showed a high regard for the Luftwaffe. But in reality, the Luftwaffe was more powerful as a propaganda weapon than as a military weapon. When Hitler came to power in 1933, the German air force consisted of only four pursuit, three bomber, and eight reconnaissance squadrons. Hitler gave the Luftwaffe a high priority, but it grew slowly. Yet, by the end of 1935, the Germans had convinced the world that they possessed a large and modern air force.[2]

Soon after he unveiled the Luftwaffe, Hitler announced plans to form a 550,000-man army. In response, President Roosevelt devised a plan to force the Germans to disarm. He suggested to Secretary Morgenthau that England, France, Italy, Belgium, Holland, Poland, and perhaps Russia sign an agreement doing away with all armaments, except those carried by a soldier on his back or in his hand. Then, the Germans could be shown the agreement. Should Germany refuse to join, said Roosevelt, the signing nations could force German acquiescence with a total blockade. After receiving unenthusiastic replies from the State Department, Roosevelt dropped the plan.[3] Roosevelt remembered his plan and returned to it during the Munich Crisis in 1938.

Italian aggression caused President Roosevelt more immediate problems. Mussolini dreamed of rebuilding the Roman Empire through the military conquest of Ethiopia, but his ambitions clashed with British interests. A strong Italian presence in Ethiopia threatened Great Britain's route from India to the Suez Canal, and a war between the two nations seemed likely. Fearing American involvement in another European war, isolationists in Congress passed the Neutrality Law of 1935. It placed a mandatory embargo upon all "instruments of war" to belligerents once the president declared that a state of war existed, it prohibited American ships from transporting munitions to the belligerents, and it empowered the president to withhold protection from Americans traveling on ships of belligerent nations. President Roosevelt tried to keep control of arms exports in the hands of the executive, but he failed.[4]

The possibility of a major war in Europe increased President Roosevelt's interest in American aircraft production. Unlike Germany, Italy possessed a large number of combat aircraft in 1935. After the World War, the Italian air force had been allowed to disintegrate, but Mussolini rebuilt the air force. Naming himself air minister, Mussolini created a separate air force, the Regia Aeronautica. Reflecting Italy's inability to fight another war of attrition, the Regia Aeronautica adopted Douhet's theories about bombing civilian populations to win a quick victory.[5] Aware of the Regia Aeronautica, Roosevelt asked Secretary of War Dern for information on the production capabilities of the American aircraft industry. Dern reported that the industry lacked the capacity to meet wartime needs. But once the industry mobilized and expanded, Dern promised, "the capacity to produce aircraft will be enormous."[6] Italy and England avoided war in 1935, and FDR took no steps to increase aircraft production. Three years later, during the Munich Crisis, he responded differently to the threat of the Luftwaffe by increasing production.

The Regia Aeronautica influenced Britain's decision to avoid war. From Italy, Ambassador Breckinridge Long informed Roosevelt that Italian air power could cause Britain an "enormous amount of trouble" in the Eastern Mediterranean. From Poland, Ambassador John Cudahy reported that the British recognized the vulnerability of the British Isles to air attacks and to an effective blockade. Having dispatched their entire home fleet and a quarter of the Royal Air Force to the Mediterranean, the British had left their home islands inadequately defended.[7] When Italian troops attacked Ethiopia on October 11, 1935, President Roosevelt invoked the Neutrality Law. Choosing to avoid war, the British convinced the League of Nations to impose economic sanctions against Italy. However, the sanctions meant little because coal, steel, and oil—the major implements of modern warfare—were left off the sanction list. Also, the British allowed the Italians to continue using the Suez Canal.[8] The *Washington Post* reported that British Conservatives believed the government should not put virtually the entire Royal Navy "at the mercy of an Italian air attack." More concerned about Germany and Japan, the British feared the Regia Aeronautica would cripple their fleet and backed off.[9]

The Regia Aeronautica provided President Roosevelt with a concrete example of the importance of air power. The Royal Navy was superior to the Italian Navy, but just the threat of Italian planes causing widespread damage to their fleet had forced the British to back away from war. There were other influences behind the British decision, such as a lack of cooperation with the French, but the vulnerability of ships to air attack caught Roosevelt's attention. Over the next few years, he became interested in using air power to deter aggression.

Oscar Westover's first opportunity to shape public opinion came on January 1, 1936. Annually, the *New York Times* published articles written by the heads of federal agencies. These synopses of achievements gave the authors an opportunity to brag about their work. In his article, Westover broke away from the traditional argument that the lack of funds prevented the Army Air Corps from doing anything. After listing what the Army Air Corps had done on limited funding, the chief of the Air Corps promised to do much more with enough money. "If sufficient funds are provided for procurement of additional new aircraft and for the establishment of operating bases at strategic locations as provided in the Wilcox bill of the last congressional session an adequate program of national defense will be well underway."[10]

Adhering to Westover's directive to participate in speaking programs, Lt. Col. Russell L. Maxwell, ordnance officer for the GHQ Air Force, spoke to the Engineer's Club of Philadelphia in January. With a degree of realism heretofore missing in statements by army airmen, he explained that only airplanes launched from aircraft carriers or nearby air bases could reach the United States. But the GHQ Air Force lacked the men and weapons to destroy these "nests." To enable the GHQ Air Force to carry out its mission, he asked the engineers to support increased funding for weapons.[11]

Soon after speaking in Philadelphia, Colonel Maxwell received a more important assignment. He became the public relations officer for the GHQ Air Force's cold-weather maneuvers scheduled from January 27 to February 15 in the New England–New York area. Given few instructions and no staff, Maxwell initiated his own plan to ensure that the press heard what the GHQ Air Force wanted it to hear. Maxwell wanted to guard against conflicting statements about the maneuvers, so before they started he forwarded a series of press releases to Boston, New York, and Washington for release on simultaneous dates. He won the cooperation of the leading press, radio, and newsreel services by giving them a general outline of the maneuvers, thus simplifying the job of reporting them. Once the maneuvers began, Maxwell offered the reporters official Air Corps photographs, but the newsmen rejected them, saying that they lacked the degree of professionalism required by editors of the day. Maxwell encouraged the news photographers to take their own pictures, and many of their photographs were published in daily and Sunday newspapers across the country. All the major newsreel companies sent film crews to cover the events, and movie theaters around the nation carried their films for several weeks afterward. To provide correct information, Maxwell arranged for press conferences to be held at several locations.

Maxwell failed to get extensive radio coverage of the maneuvers because of the high cost of relaying the programs from Mitchel Field to the New York City radio stations. But Maxwell did convince NBC to air a live broadcast of pursuits intercepting a flight of bombers over New York City with the commentator on board one of the participating airplanes. Maxwell arranged for GHQ Air Force personnel to give radio interviews in Boston and New York City, and his persistence paid off. With the cooperation of the Gulf Refining Company and Maj. Al Williams, CBS broadcast Williams's fifteen-minute interview of Brig. Gen. H. C. Pratt and Maxwell. This program was so successful that Williams offered Maxwell the use of his regular Thursday night program and promised to publicize the maneuvers in his syndicated newspaper column, which had a circulation of about eight million.

After the maneuvers, Maxwell reflected upon his experience as the public relations officer, and he concluded that the GHQ Air Force's preparations had been too haphazard. In his report to the General Staff, Maxwell recommended the creation of a permanent Public Relations Section at GHQ Air Force. At least one specially selected officer needed to gain the confidence of the press to ensure that the press's "interpretation of events" would be what the army wanted. Complying with Westover's demand for teamwork, Maxwell told the General Staff that the objective of GHQ Air Force publicity should be "the maintenance of friendly relations with all arms and services of the Army, the aviation industry, and the public." Colonel Maxwell also presented his ideas to other Army Air Corps officers and asked for comments.[12]

The colorful aerial maneuvers over New England and New York won the GHQ Air Force a lot of publicity,[13] but they had little impact on Congress. On Valentine's Day, the House passed an army appropriations bill without additional authorizations for aircraft. Hitler's reoccupation of the Rhineland in March had a greater impact on Congress. It responded to his action by authorizing an increase of the Army Air Corps to a maximum strength of 2,230 airplanes, and Roosevelt signed the bill on June 25. However, Congress refused to provide the necessary funds.[14]

In January, 1936, Japan withdrew from talks on extending the London Naval Treaty, and the decade-old naval-limitations system died. Great Britain responded by stepping up its building program, and Roosevelt asked Congress for the largest peacetime naval appropriation in American history.[15] When American pacifists denounced the large naval expenditures, Roosevelt attempted to educate them about the need to extend America's defenses beyond the coastline. In the process, the president revealed his views about America's military needs. He told Rev. G. Ashton Oldham, Bishop of Albany, that William Jennings Bryan's belief that "a million men would spring to arms overnight" in case of an attack was too simplistic. A successful attack on Hawaii, Roosevelt pointed out, would leave the entire West Coast and the Panama Canal open to attack. For this reason, the United States needed its expensive naval and land defenses in Hawaii.[16] Using an anecdote about a reassuring but useless harbor defense as an illustration, President Roosevelt told the representatives from the People's Mandate to End War Committee that coastal defenses provided an illusory defense. By early 1936 Franklin Roosevelt had concluded that the threat of air attacks frightened Adolf Hitler. During his meeting with the People's Mandate to End War Committee, Roosevelt said that Hitler was giving tax breaks to Germans who built bomb shelters in their basements. Furthermore, Roosevelt recognized the weak condition of the Army Air Corps. "We are way behind. The army has only eight hundred planes, England has twenty-five hundred, France four thousand, Germany is working up to five thousand and Russia has six thousand."[17] Despite his efforts, pacifists continued to oppose increased military spending.

The Royal Navy noted the importance of aircraft also. On March 22, 1936, "Augur," the *New York Times* special correspondent in London, reported that the Regia Aeronautica had forced the Royal Navy to replace the Mediterranean with the Indian Ocean as the British empire's vital link. The western approaches to the Indian Ocean were secure since no nation had bases on the African continent to threaten them. But Augur concluded that Singapore alone could not protect the Indian Ocean from the east. Singapore needed an advanced base, but Japanese aircraft and submarines had rendered Hong Kong ineffective. After surveying the area, Augur chose Camranh Bay, Indochina, as the best forward base.[18]

There is no way of knowing whether Augur's article influenced Roosevelt, or even whether he read it. Nevertheless, the president had become interested in the effectiveness of modern bombers against ships, and he asked General Westover for information about tactics and the accuracy of air attacks on ships. Westover sent the request to the GHQ Air Force. Knowing that it had been requested by the president, General Andrews presented the information in a way that would convince Roosevelt of the need for more B-17s. Listing the ranges and bomb loads of the bombers flown by the GHQ Air Force, General Andrews emphasized that the greater range and bomb load of a B-17 allowed it to do the work of two B-18s. After describing the number of hits on a target from different heights and with various sizes of bombs, Andrews claimed that a ship could not move fast enough to avoid all the bombs. He also boasted that hitting targets accurately from as high as eighteen thousand feet would be "merely a matter of training."[19]

Alerted to the president's interest, Andrews realized that the GHQ Air Force might be called upon to demonstrate its ability to bomb ships from high altitudes. As a precaution, he ordered his bomber units to intensify their training in high-altitude bombing and search-and-location techniques. Andrews made the right decision. Unaware that Andrews had begun preparations, Westover warned him of rumors that the president wanted a test of the GHQ Air Force's efficiency in attacking naval vessels. Mindful of the air mail fiasco, Westover suggested he make a preliminary study to select the needed personnel, increase training in ship recognition, and gain familiarity with the characteristics of navy smoke screens. "The main thing," explained Westover, "is that we must not fail in the test for reasons well known to both of us."[20] Not only would their personal futures ride on this test, but the future of the Army Air Corps was at risk. If Andrews's men failed to demonstrate their efficiency at bombing naval targets, the Army Air Corps could lose its coastal defense mission.

The possibility of the GHQ Air Force proving its ability to repel a naval assault worried the navy. Before the House Subcommittee on Naval Appropriations, Assistant Chief of Naval Operations Rear Adm. J. K. Taussig complained about army plans to patrol the Panama-Hawaii-Alaska triangle. He said it was "none of their business," because the Joint Army and Navy Board had assigned that duty to the navy. "If you let those army air fellows go," Taussig added, "they will take up the whole business, of course." Instead of answering the navy's attack in kind, General Andrews told the Associated Press only that no plans for the GHQ Air Force to patrol that area had been "perfected." If an enemy did enter that triangle, Andrews explained, "it might be necessary for the army to make sure that there would be no attack on land defenses under army control."[21] In his answer, Andrews did two things. First, he justified having Army Air Corps planes in the area by presenting them as a backup should an enemy get by the navy. Second, he furthered the idea of teamwork within the army by stating that the army, not just the Army Air Corps, might need to protect the land defenses.

Rather than publicly attack the navy, Andrews preferred to show what the GHQ Air Force could do by making a non-stop flight from San Juan, Puerto Rico, to Langley Field.[22] Boake Carter of station WCAU in Philadelphia described the flight on his radio broadcast, and Andrews sent him a thank-you note. Emphasizing that the GHQ Air Force had done something spectacular, while making it appear routine, Andrews told Carter that this flight was "the forerunner of flights which will become more or less routine when we get our new long-range equipment in the GHQ Air Force." By implying that the flight was made with inadequate equipment, Andrews suggested that the GHQ Air Force would do really spectacular things once its new, long-range airplanes arrived. Andrews praised the skill of his navigators on the flight to point out that the men of the GHQ Air Force were trained well and awaited the new airplanes.[23]

By now, the army fliers had learned to lodge complaints about the navy with their superiors instead of the press. Maj. Robert Olds, the GHQ Air Force Inspector, heard numerous complaints about the navy's practicing unfair methods to build up naval aviation. Although the complaints were unsubstantiated, Olds heard so many that he decided the matter required investigation. The most frequent complaints dealt with the navy's use of higher pay and privileges to lure pilots and mechanics away from the Army Air Corps. He also heard complaints about a navy campaign to convince the American people that the GHQ Air Force, by conducting over-water flights, was usurping the navy's responsibilities for national defense. Instead of going public with the complaints, Olds passed them on to Andrews with the observation that there were too many complaints to not have some validity. Unless the War Department took remedial action, he warned, the morale of the Army Air Corps would be undermined. Andrews relayed the information to Westover in memorandum, but he advised moderation in reacting to the problem. Referring to an article Westover had recently published in *National Aeronautic Magazine,* Andrews praised Westover for "very properly" not pointing to the navy as one of the main reasons for the decline in students at the Air Corps Training Center. Unlike Billy Mitchell, who would have gone to the press, Andrews suggested seeking redress through proper channels. To handle the problem of unfair practices, Andrews recommended the securing of "legislation or regulations to permit us to compete on an equal footing with the Navy." Like Westover, Andrews also wanted to get the support of the War Department for corrective legislation.[24]

Although many GHQ Air Force officers had become team players of the kind that Westover and Chief of Staff Craig wanted, they still stated publicly that air power would play the decisive role in warfare. But they were careful not to antagonize the ground officers. In his critique of war games held around Camp Custer, Michigan, Lt. Col. Follett Bradley, acting chief of staff of the GHQ Air Force, explained that the bomber units had only hinted at their capabilities during the maneuvers because of time and space limitations. After making the standard disclaimer that the GHQ Air Force did not want war and that the policy of the United States was one of defense only, Bradley claimed that bombers could destroy nearly anything built by man. "It can destroy ships easily," he said, "and an enemy must come to us in ships." In closing, however, Bradley assured the ground officers that the Army Air Corps no longer sought independence from the army. "We of the Air Corps often speak of independent air operations and are occasionally misunderstood in our use of the term. We refer to the unquestioned *tactical* independence of Bombardment Aviation from ground troops. Strategically, there is the greatest of interdependence under one commander, the Chief of Staff in peace and the commander of the field forces in war. We are proud to be a member of the Army team, and we expect, should war come to this country, to acquit ourselves well of the responsibility which will inevitably be reposed in us."[25]

When not around ground officers, the GHQ Air Force officers made less reserved comments. At the Air Corps Tactical School, General Andrews told the class of 1936–37 that it was the only school where an officer learned how to use an arm "which is more and more dominating warfare in all its phases both land and sea." Pointing to Ethiopia, Andrews said that the preponderance of Italian air power in the Mediterranean "made it much easier" for Britain to decide against going to war with Italy. "Russian bombers at Vladivostok capable of bombing Japanese cities," he added, "are certainly contributing toward Japanese expansion in China rather than in the eastern provinces of Siberia." Noting the expansion of air forces around the world, Andrews prophesied that the Army Air Corps and its defense responsibilities would be expanded.[26] Despite making bold claims for the future of air power, Andrews did so out of any ground officer's earshot. His methods differed from those of his predecessors, but his ideas did not.

As the summer of 1936 passed away, the navy made plans for the GHQ Air Force to simulate an air attack on destroyers. Knowing that his B-10s and their bomb sights were inadequate, General Andrews faced a dilemma. If the bombers failed the test, President Roosevelt might conclude that the army's air arm could not defend the coasts. But he feared the unfavorable reaction if he refused to go through with the tests. Believing the latter situation to be the less damaging, Andrews postponed the tests. He explained to General Craig that he preferred to wait until the new B-18s and B-17s arrived. Andrews added that a new bomb sight undergoing testing promised better results. The commander of the GHQ Air Force also refused to participate in tests with destroyers because battleships, not destroyers, would attack America's coasts. He told Craig that the loss of a destroyer would not stop an attack, but the destruction of one battleship would affect the outcome of the battle. Furthermore, he knew that a destroyer offered a poor target from any height because it was more maneuverable than a battleship and had only one-seventh the vulnerable area of a battleship. "When we do agree to attack," he said, "the naval target should be a battleship."[27]

Frank Andrews envisioned an Army Air Corps armed with long-range bombers and capable of delivering bombs far from American shores. Like General Foulois, Andrews emphasized the defensive role of bombers in order to receive the support of the General Staff. However, Andrews realized that winning control over coastal air defenses would not be enough. An arbitrary boundary could be placed on the Army Air Corps's jurisdiction, and the General Staff might limit the purchase of aircraft to those capable of reaching the boundary. The possibility of an arbitrary boundary materialized during the Joint Coastal Defense Air Exercise Number 1, which was held off the East Coast in mid-October of 1936. The B-10s used by the GHQ Air Force during the exercise had radii of only 336 miles, and Andrews feared that the Joint Army and Navy Board would adopt it as the line separating army and navy jurisdiction. General Andrews used his critique of the exercise to discredit arbitrary boundaries. Pointing out that the B-18 and the B-17 possessed greater ranges than the B-10, he said that "no one can now predict the radii of land based bombers of the future." He proposed assigning jurisdiction by the type of target. The navy would have responsibility for enemy naval forces intending to raid shipping, and the army would bear responsibility for enemy forces threatening to invade the United States. In the spirit of team play, Andrews said that either service should feel free to request the assistance of the other. General Andrews realized that the General Staff, unhindered by limits on range, would be compelled to purchase even longer-ranged airplanes.

Joint Coastal Defense Air Exercise Number 1 did not provide the bombing test President Roosevelt wanted, but he was interested in it. When the last two days of the exercise were cancelled, some newspapers reported that the weather had been too bad for the army's planes to operate. To prevent "incorrect conclusions from being drawn by higher authorities," Andrews stated in his critique that the army planes had been ready to fly in any weather. Only inadequate facilities at the Norfolk Naval Base and the navy's decision to cancel the exercises scheduled for the last day had kept the army planes on the ground.[28] Remembering the air mail fiasco, Andrews made certain that President Roosevelt knew of the Army Air Corps's ability to fly through bad weather.

While Andrews believed that nobody could predict the radius of land-based bombers of the future, he wanted to arm the GHQ Air Force with as many B-17s as possible. The Flying Fortress was the best long-range bomber available, and Andrews wanted the best plane for his crews. To win the General Staff's approval, Andrews tried to elicit the support of Maj. Gen. Hugh A. Drum. Made the commander of the Hawaiian Department of the United States Army after chairing the Drum Board, General Drum believed that Hawaii would become the center of commercial air traffic in the Pacific, and he thought the islands had inadequate air defenses. Hoping to get a recommendation for a specific number of B-17s, Andrews requested Drum's views on the GHQ Air Force's requirements in the Western Pacific. Instead of giving Andrews a number, Drum objected to plans for flying bombers to the Hawaiian Islands in time of emergency. He wanted bombers stationed there permanently.[29] Since the Army Air Corps had justified the need for the B-17 with the argument that it could reinforce Hawaii, Andrews sought other ways to prove the need for more B-17s.

The reports about air power that Roosevelt saw in 1936 came from civilians. William C. Bullitt warned him that everybody in Europe, including the British ambassador to France, expected a war by the spring or summer of 1938. The French government had considered providing gas masks for the entire population of Paris until they discovered the prohibitive cost. "It was decided to let the population take its chances." Bullitt told Roosevelt that the "airplane has made Europe an absurdity." The speed of airplanes meant that the "dinky little European states can not live in an airplane civilization." Either Europeans had to submerge their national pride and unify the continent, or destroy themselves and hand Europe "over to the Bolsheviks."[30] Agreeing with Bullitt about the importance of airplanes, Acting Secretary of State R. Walton Moore said that every month of delay by "leaders who have the warlike inclination" afforded "Great Britain the opportunity to build up her Air Force and strengthen her Navy."[31] President Roosevelt already understood what air power meant to modern warfare. At Buenos Aires, he told the Inter-American Conference for the Maintenance of Peace that modern warfare entailed more than the clash of armies. It meant poverty, the destruction of cities and farms, and the threat of broken societies and constitutional governments.[32] When Franklin D. Roosevelt supported the expansion of the Army Air Forces in World War II, he did so with a full knowledge of the horrors that total war brought with it. The claims that air power would bring a quick victory did not blind him to the devastation that would accompany aerial bombardment. As demonstrated by his address to the Inter-American Conference, Roosevelt foresaw the horror. This explains why he vacillated about measures that could have brought war between the United States and Germany and Japan.

Although preoccupied with Europe, the Roosevelt administration remained interested in the Far East. Throughout 1936, the United States further expanded and improved its air links with the Philippines. On November 14, Maj. Gen. Edward M. Markham, chief of the army engineers, asked Congress for improvements in the seaplane facilities at Midway and Wake Islands to ensure regular schedules for Pan American Airways's transpacific service. Afterward, rumors circulated around Washington that Guam would be fortified. R. Walton Moore denied the rumors, saying that the improvements were intended to aid commercial planes. But Japanese naval authorities complained that the bases would increase the striking power of the United States in Asian waters. Pointing out that Midway was only two thousand miles from their mainland, the Japanese said that the United States threatened them from the Philippines, the Aleutians, and Midway Island.

The Japanese had reason to worry about a seaplane base at Midway Island. Consolidated Aircraft had started producing flying boats with a flying radius of 1,500 miles and a large load capacity. The navy called them scout planes, but some navy officials regarded them as a strike force. Since the future seemed to promise airplanes of even greater range, the 2,000 miles between Midway and Japan did not seem insurmountable. Speaking to the National Aeronautical Association on November 30, General Westover announced that the day of the 3,000-mile bomber had arrived. On December 2, Boeing conducted a successful test flight of its second B-17. The *New York Times* ran the story on page one with the headline: "Army Bomber, Called World's Largest, Soars Over Seattle in Test; Can Cruise 3,000 Miles."[33] Because of pronouncements like these, Japan seemed to be more accessible to American bombers with each passing year.

Thoughts of striking Japan from the air had been mentioned by the American press. From Shanghai, Mark J. Ginsbourg reported in the *Washington Post* that the skepticism about Pan American's flying boats crossing the Pacific Ocean had given way to consternation. It had forced the Japanese into a program of aerial expansion. "Japan more than any other nation is concerned over the transpacific flights of American aircraft." Long the major power in the Far East, Japan had been free to "draw the map of the Orient as she pleased," but the Soviet Union had shocked Japan when it sent "an air armada to her Siberian frontiers" to contest Japanese moves in Manchuria. Another shock came when United States Navy planes flew over the Aleutian Islands, "only 24 hours away from the Nipponese shores." However, Ginsbourg explained that the Pan American flights "brought Japan face to face with a realization that she was being brought within striking distance of the United States."[34] In 1936, the Japanese still viewed the greatest threat as coming from the Soviets, and posters illustrating the threat were displayed in Japan.[35]

Despite the interest of the press, the War Department refused to purchase more B-17s. Westover and Arnold asked the General Staff in May of 1936 for fifty more B-17s and eleven more Project "A" long-range bombers. The General Staff concluded that the international situation did not indicate a need for more long-range bombers. Explaining that the B-18 met the army's military and cost requirements, the General Staff rejected the request. Secretary of War Harry Woodring, who replaced Dern after his death, instructed Westover to order no more B-17s until the thirteen on order had been delivered and tested. Like General Craig, Woodring wanted to purchase the maximum number of bombers. Boeing delivered the thirteen YB-17s over the first eight months of 1937.[36] With these thirteen YB-17s, the Army Air Corps conducted a publicity campaign to win appropriations for more Flying Fortresses. In the process, Andrews, Westover, and Arnold won converts to the cause of strategic bombing.

V. Arrival of the Flying Fortress

In July of 1936, Generals Andrews, Westover, and Arnold told a congressional committee about their opposition to separating the Army Air Corps from the army. They understood that a separate air force needed its own medical, police, quartermaster, signal, and even food service personnel; the Army Air Corps lacked all of these. Until the vast expansion of the Army Air Forces during World War II, the army provided all these personnel and everything else needed.[1] Outside of the military establishment, however, efforts to separate the air arm from the General Staff continued. On January 18, 1937, Representative Wilcox introduced another bill in Congress calling for a separate air force.[2]

Frustrated at not being given more B-17s, General Andrews started looking toward a separate air force once again. He and Hugh Knerr had secretly written the Wilcox bill. When General Craig sent him a copy of the bill, Andrews wrote a critique supporting it. He later told Craig that he had not read the bill. Andrews lied to the chief of staff to avoid antagonizing him.[3]

With their criticism of the General Staff, the civilian supporters of air power often antagonized the General Staff more than the airmen did. Since Andrews, Westover, and Arnold wanted to promote good relations with the General Staff, they had to muzzle the more outspoken critics. The trick was to quiet the criticism without alienating their civilian supporters. Arnold often used a third party to approach the critic. When Swanee Taylor, the vice president of *Popular Aviation* magazine, made slanderous remarks about army and navy procurement officers, Arnold asked John Jouett of Fairchild Aviation to intercede, which he did. "There are times," Arnold told Jouett, "when we of the Military Service are at a distinct disadvantage and the Swanee Taylor case at hand is one of them."[4]

Although the Army Air Corps officers hoped to avoid public controversy, there were times when it could not be helped. But even then, they tried to separate themselves from the controversy. For example, when the *Saturday Evening Post* ran an article entitled "Airplanes Can't Sink Battleships," the Army Air Corps could not let such pronouncements go unchallenged. Instead of answering the article himself, Ira Eaker decided to write a rebuttal and ask General Fechet to sign it. Having second thoughts about acting on his own, Eaker asked Arnold if he thought the article was a good idea. "The reason I thought of General Fechet for the article," Eaker explained, "was that I thought it impolitic for you to sign it at this time. The proper answer would undoubtedly be slightly controversial." Arnold gave Eaker his permission.[5]

Pressure groups, such as the Air Defense League, also threatened relations between the General Staff and the Army Air Corps. The General Staff could interpret criticisms from the ADL as originating from the Army Air Corps. Harvey L. Williams, chair of the northeastern branch of the ADL, increased the danger by claiming that the league cooperated with "the best informed air officers" in the army and navy. Again, a third party acted for Arnold. Stating that "a very hearty spirit of co-operation now exists between the General Staff and the Army Air Corps," Reed G. Landis asked a member of the ADL to avoid jeopardizing that spirit by pursuing a separate air force. Landis's efforts failed, and the ADL proceeded with its plans to support the Wilcox bill. Concerned, Landis asked Arnold for instructions. In his reply, Arnold offered no specific directions. Instead, he related a story about an injured mule with the "blind staggers" he had seen in the Philippines. No matter what, the mule always walked in a straight line, even if the "mess tent or the cook's fire" were in the way. "That in short," Arnold explained, "is my opinion of the Defense League — I think they have blind staggers!"[6]

Arnold gave Landis no instructions, because the General Staff had already become quite distressed about the Wilcox bill. Chief of Staff Craig told Secretary Woodring that the supporters of the Wilcox bill were confined to Wilcox and a "small group of dissatisfied Air Corps officers who were adherents of former Brigadier General William Mitchell." Craig informed Woodring that these dissatisfied officers planned to use the congressional hearings on the Wilcox bill "as a forum for the airing of opinions and charges in the sensational manner of those that occurred under the leadership of General Mitchell."[7]

With the damage done, Arnold did not want to anger the ADL too.

While Arnold tried to maintain friendly relations with the General Staff, General Andrews demonstrated that his fliers had sharpened their navigation skills. By 1937, Andrews felt secure enough with their skills to allow the first mass flight of land planes across the Caribbean. On February 6, nine B-10s flew eleven hundred miles non-stop from Miami to Albrook Field, Panama Canal Zone. Two days later, they completed the return trip. The flight impressed General Craig. Congratulating Andrews, Craig said the flight "was well planned and has demonstrated that our Army navigators are thoroughly capable of navigating our airplanes over extensive stretches of water." The army fliers continued to make spectacular flights over water, and with each success, the General Staff became increasingly certain that the fliers could fulfill all their promises.

The Panama flight marked the last time that Andrews had to depend on the old B-10s for demonstrations. On March 4, the 2d Bombardment Group received the first YB-17. After flying by in review twice, the big bomber landed on a snow-covered Langley Field. Showing the importance of the event, the officers and men of the 2d Bombardment Group lined up in parade formation to greet that lone airplane. The group's second airplane arrived a week later, along with four navigators fresh from the new course taught at the Navigation Unit at Langley Field. However, Andrews did not wait for the second plane to advertize the delivery. The 2d Bombardment Group flew its first YB-17 to Bolling Field on March 9. Over the next four days, crowds and journalists from Washington viewed the plane. On April 4, the 2d Bombardment Group showed off its new planes to the whole nation. The National Broadcasting Company aired a live, six-minute broadcast from one of the new YB-17s flying over Washington, D.C. After interviewing Gen. Gerald C. Brant, commander of the 2d Bombardment Group, the announcer gave an account of the crew going through its combat drills.[8]

Enthusiastic about the YB-17s, General Andrews adamantly opposed the purchase of more B-18s. On June 16, Andrews spent half an hour complaining to Arnold about the army's mistake in purchasing B-18s instead of B-17s. Having learned the supply officer's problems, Arnold explained that the Air Corps needed a balanced program that did not lean too much on four-engine bombers. Arnold had a responsibility to consider the evaluation of two-engine bombers for possible tactical needs. He also reminded Andrews that the "General Staff, Secretary of War and possibly The President" had opposed the purchase of more B-17s. But Arnold was wasting his time; Andrews refused to listen.[9]

Andrews and Col. Hugh Knerr, chief of staff of the GHQ Air Force, became impatient with anyone who gave less than total support to purchasing more B-17s. Knerr credited Arnold's measured support for more B-17s to personal ambitions. When Arnold refused to speak up for more Flying Fortresses, Knerr thought that Arnold remained silent because he "didn't want to get in the wrong" with the General Staff. However, Arnold was only adhering to what he had told Reed Landis: "When things are rolling along toward your goal, a little encouragement does more good than criticism and a fight." Also, Hap Arnold hesitated to put too much faith in one type of airplane. In 1923, Billy Mitchell had purchased an experimental, long-range bomber named the Barling. Since the Barling had cost the Army Air Service $500,000, an astounding figure at the time, it had aroused public interest. But it proved to be a dismal failure and was placed in storage at the air depot at Fairfield, Ohio. The Barling sat as a reminder of Mitchell's failure. Arnold, stationed at the air depot five years later, found the old Barling in dilapidated condition, but the army refused to destroy the worthless plane. The great expense of the plane had made it a matter of continued interest in Congress. Thereafter, every time a request for permission to destroy the plane had been sent to Washington, the answer was no. To get around that problem, Arnold requested permission to dispose of an experimental plane, without mentioning the Barling by name. As soon as he received approval, Arnold had the plane burned. Like the Barling, the Flying Fortress was expensive, which drew the attention of critical Congressmen and generals. Arnold worried that the B-17s might use up too much of the Air Corps's meager funds. As he later recalled, Arnold feared that entrusting the future of the Army Air Corps to the B-17 might put "too many eggs in one basket."[10]

Arnold was looking beyond the B-17. Like everybody in the Army Air Corps, he knew that Boeing was about to complete the XB-15. Back in 1935, Arnold had expressed his enthusiasm about the plane.[11] On April 17, 1937, the New York Times carried a front-page story on the new plane based on information released by Army Air Corps officers in Washington, D.C. Refusing to give specific details about the plane, the officers said that the new plane would "startle the world" with its capabilities.[12] Two weeks later, the Air Corps News Letter repeated verbatim parts of the Times story, and both articles referred to the new bomber as the "natural successor" to the "compromise type" B-17. Moreover, the News Letter called the plane "an indication of the constant desire of the Army Air Corps to explore every potentiality of the airplane in National Defense." Arnold had influenced the author of the News Letter article, as shown by the author's description of

11. Maj. Hugh J. Knerr, wearing the 1934 Alaskan Flight emblem on his flight jacket. *Courtesy U.S.A.F.*

the provision for a five-lens aerial camera on the XB-15. The author noted that the potential for aerial photography had been demonstrated by the army flight to Alaska in 1934. He neglected to mention that Arnold had led that flight, but few army airmen would have forgotten. Since the projected range of the XB-15 was 5,000 miles, Arnold did not want the Army Air Corps saddled with too many B-17s if the new bomber proved better.[13]

Andrews, on the other hand, did not have the luxury of time. It could have been several years before the XB-15 reached production, and as the commander of tactical units, General Andrews needed the best, currently available planes.[14] Believing that an aggressive publicity campaign would overcome resistance to increased congressional appropriations, on March 9 he proposed sending three of his new B-17s on an around-the-world flight. Brig. Gen. W. Kruger, Assistant Chief of Staff WPD, rejected the flight because it would not be a pioneering flight. Also, Kruger preferred special long-distance flights

12. The XB-15, shown here making its initial flight on October 15, 1937, proved to be too underpowered for use in combat, but Boeing gained valuable experience that it used to create the highly successful B-17. *Courtesy U.S.A.F.*

within the Western Hemisphere or to and from American overseas possessions.[15]

Andrews soon discovered that the GHQ Air Force had a more important task than an around-the-world flight. On May 17, Roosevelt's Naval Aid requested a report on bombing exercises from the secretary of the navy.[16] The service given control over costal defenses had to be able to hit its targets. Upon learning about the request, Andrews began searching for a radio-controlled boat to give his men practice in hitting a moving target. When he failed to locate one, Andrews desperately looked for anything, even a radio-controlled automobile, for use on Muroc Lake. In the end, his men had to practice on outlines of capital ships drawn on the desert, but the chief of the Air Corps Materiel Division told him about a new bomb sight being used by the navy. General Andrews looked at the Norden bomb sight and decided that he wanted it for his planes. "We cannot afford," he told Westover, "to have our bombing records unfavorably compared with those of the Navy."[17]

Made suspicious of the airmen by the Wilcox bill, Chief of Staff Craig refused to let the adherents of Billy Mitchell turn Coastal Frontier Defense Joint Air Exercise No. 4, as the tests were designated, into another *Ostfriesland* show. Craig personally ordered Andrews to avoid publicity about the bombing tests. Explaining that "the President stated the exercise was for the information of himself and the Secretary of War and the Secretary of the Navy only," Craig instructed Andrews to say only that it would be a routine training exercise in conjunction with the navy.[18]

Starting at noon on August 13 and ending at noon the following day, Joint Air Exercise No. 4 simulated an attack on the West Coast by a "Black" aggressor force of two battleships, one aircraft carrier, and nine destroyers. Three squadrons of B-10s, with nine to twelve planes per squadron, and eight YB-17s gathered in California to defend the coast. The exercise took on an unrealistic atmosphere from the start because the entire Black force was represented by one ship, the overaged battleship *Utah*. Efforts at army-navy cooperation soon fell apart. The navy provided the practice bombs, which were a type unfamiliar to the army fliers, and navy spotters gave the army incorrect information about the location of the *Utah*. The GHQ Air Force fliers countered by unexpectedly using civilian airfields and taking off before the navy expected.

Despite the navy's efforts to mislead them, the army fliers found the *Utah* in heavy fog on the second day. Only the YB-17s reached the ship in time, but the fliers successfully "bombed" it. The navy observers complained afterward that the bad weather had prevented sailors on the *Utah* from seeing the YB-17s in time to take evasive action. So, the army fliers offered to attack the ship in clear weather. On the third day of the exercise, the fliers attacked the *Utah* with all their bombers. They systematically bombed the battleship from different altitudes ranging from eight to eighteen thousand feet. The army fliers registered hits with 11.9 percent of their bombs, a higher percentage than the navy had scored in tests made from a lower altitude, pleasing the entire army.[19] After reading the final report on Joint Air Exercise No. 4, General Craig expressed "high satisfaction and gratification" about "the efficiency and dependability of the G.H.Q. Air Force."[20] Winning the approval of the chief of staff was very important to the future of the GHQ Air Force, but the approval of the president was critical.

Unfortunately, the jubilation felt by Craig was never expressed to the president. In their joint report, Secretaries Woodring and Swanson left out a number of important facts. Neglecting to mention that the navy had reported the wrong location, they said that the army fliers had failed to find their target on the first day. The report also downplayed what happened when the fliers found the *Utah* by stating that they scored only three hits out of ninety-eight bombs dropped. Even a near miss would have damaged a battleship in combat, but the secretaries made no mention of how close the other ninety-five bombs had come. Clear weather on the third day of the exercise had allowed photographs to be taken of the bombs crashing all around the ship, and those photographs were included with the report. Still, the secretaries waffled, claiming that the "artificialities" involved in peacetime exercises meant that "definite conclusions as to the potentialities of army and navy forces to attack and/or defend in this sort can not be drawn." They only admitted that the army fliers could hit the target "under unfavorable visibility conditions."[21]

Secretaries Woodring and Swanson made no comment about the ability of the GHQ Air Force to navigate in bad weather. Since their report stated that the navy found and tracked the *Utah*, the GHQ Air Force had little to show for its efforts. The service responsible for aerial defense of the United States had to demonstrate its ability to seek out an attacking force in any weather. Otherwise, an enemy could simply wait for bad weather and approach the coast undetected and unscathed by the defending planes. Unaware of the "mistakes" made by the navy in reporting the location of the *Utah*, all Roosevelt could have inferred from this report was that navy planes had shown the army the way to their target as in the *Mount Shasta* exercise years earlier. Although the photographs clearly demonstrated that the army bombers could hit a moving target, Andrews and his men had a long way to go to win the president's unqualified support.

Sometimes Arnold had trouble remembering to put aside his personal emotions for the good of the Army Air Corps, and Andrews had to remind him of their ultimate goal. Such an occasion arose after the Cleveland National Air Races of 1937. The Air Corps personnel participating in the air race felt that the sponsors had provided inadequate housing and other facilities. To make matters worse, some of the local papers reported that the army fliers had threatened a "fly-away-strike" until they each received a ten dollar bonus. Incensed and feeling that the army fliers were being taken for granted, Arnold suggested that the Army Air Corps never send planes to the Cleveland races again. "Everyone who attends these races," he complained to Andrews, "cannot help but see that if the Army and Navy participation were eliminated there would be little attraction for the crowd."[22] Andrews calmed Arnold by explaining that the president of the Cleve-

13. Air races always provided the army fliers with an opportunity to perform for the public. Here, a formation of Army Air Corps aircraft spells out "A C" at the Cleveland Air Races in 1931. *Courtesy U.S.A.F.*

land Air Race Association and the editor of the *Cleveland News* had apologized. Andrews had been upset also, until he spoke to fliers who had been at Cleveland. They reported that 160,000 people had attended the last day of the races, and the cars in the airport parking lot had license tags from every state in the Union. Furthermore, most of the spectators had come to see the exhibitions by the two services. "I am inclined to think that we don't do enough advertising with the taxpayer," Andrews reasoned, "so I don't think that we should pass up this opportunity to sell ourselves to a pretty good cross section of the country."[23] Andrews's cooler head prevailed, and Arnold forgot his suggestion. But the Army Air Corps was a small organization, and word of the poor treatment received at the Cleveland Air Races would have spread quickly. To counter any bad feelings among Army Air Corps personnel, Ira Eaker wrote an article for the *Air Corps News Letter* about the problems encountered in Cleveland. Announcing that the

14. The "Skylarks," a precision flying aerobatic team from Maxwell Field, Alabama, demonstrated their flying skills at the National Air Races, at Cleveland, Ohio, in September of 1937. The "U.S. Army" painted on the underside of their Boeing P-12E aircraft was standard for all army airplanes, but at the air races, it served as a billboard. *Courtesy U.S.A.F.*

sponsors of the air race had apologized, Eaker informed the Army Air Corps that the matter was closed.[24]

Andrews's readiness to accept the apologies made sense. The free publicity afforded by the air races outweighed the poor treatment; and, denied the opportunity to publicize the Joint Air Exercises, he refused to throw away an annual opportunity to impress so many people. Arnold's willingness to forget the matter demonstrated his ability to put aside personal feelings for the good of the Army Air Corps. However, Andrews and Arnold's discussion of the problem indicated an important point. The General Staff's efforts to maintain control over the Air Corps and the GHQ Air Force by physically splitting them had failed. Officers of the Air Corps and the GHQ Air Force maintained contact with each other. As a result, they were able to meet challenges to the Army Air Corps and air power with coordinated efforts. One of their greatest challenges came from the reactions to the wars in

Spain and China. Since the World War, fliers had argued that aviation would be the decisive factor in any future war, but their contention had not been proved in Ethiopia, Spain, or China. The poor results achieved by aviation in those wars gave the War Department evidence that air power was not the decisive factor claimed by the fliers, threatening future appropriations for the Army Air Corps.[25] As they had after the Cleveland Air Races, officers in the Air Corps and the GHQ Air Force discussed the situation and worked together to remedy the problem.

In mid-September, 1937, General Arnold asked Col. Hugh Knerr for his recommendations on how to counter the adverse publicity coming out of Spain and China. Putting aside his personal hatred for Arnold, Knerr asserted his absolute confidence in both the ability of air power to dominate the battlefield and the technological superiority of the United States over the rest of the world. He recommended convincing the War Department that the failures experienced overseas resulted from a lack of bomb sights, and he suggested that Arnold should mention "this fact" in any public statements. Knerr offered the same recommendations to Andrews to forestall the agitation against air power "before it gains any more headway."[26]

General Westover addressed the problem of Ethiopia, Spain, and China in a different manner. Speaking to a Reserve Officers convention, he stated that military teams in all three wars had proved successful, but he emphasized "that there have been no modern Air Force operations attempted in either of these three theaters." By "Air Force operations," the chief of the Air Corps meant large units of bombers "employed far beyond the influence of ground arms against strategic centers such as great cities, important commercial arteries, manufacturing centers and fleets of surface craft." He asked the audience to prevent others from drawing false conclusions about air power, but he warned them against criticizing the War Department. Pointing to orders for over a thousand new planes as proof, Westover said that Secretary of War Woodring and Assistant Secretary Louis Johnson had "the interest of military aviation close at heart."[27]

Arnold, addressing an audience composed of officers from all branches of the army, argued that the war in Spain offered no real lessons about air power. The heterogeneous foreign legionary pilots flying in Spain did not make up a true air force, and the other nations involved in Spain were only testing tactics and weapons. In the Far East, the Chinese lacked the long-range bombers, such as the Flying Fortress or the Russian four-engine bombers, needed to carry the war to Japan's industrial centers. Ineffective Chinese air operations proved nothing, because all Chinese military operations were ineffective. If the Chinese had possessed an air force as well trained as the GHQ Air Force, the Japanese probably would not have attempted to land troops. The Japanese air force offered a stark contrast to the Chinese. While they unwisely terrorized civilians with their long-range bombers, the Japanese also attacked "proper air force objectives": shipping, aviation factories, and airfields. "It is important," said Arnold prophetically, "and it must never be forgotten. There is a first rate air power which knows how to use its air strength." Ground officers, citing the overseas conflicts as evidence, had told Arnold that airplanes were only useful for bombing area targets. Because the Army Air Corps had adopted a doctrine of precision bombing, Arnold had to rebut those claims. Following Colonel Knerr's advice, Arnold demonstrated with a slide presentation that American bomber crews could hit targets accurately.[28] In their eagerness to dispel the negative reports coming from the foreign wars, Arnold and other Army Air Corps officers blinded themselves to the lessons they should have learned. The visual image provided by photographs showing bombs accurately exploding on targets far below was too compelling. They discounted the importance of defending fighters, clouds obscuring the target, and anti-aircraft fire on the accuracy of bombing attacks. All they could see was the accuracy of their bomber crews, which allowed them to dismiss easily the failures of foreign air forces. They accepted without question the Army Air Corps's superiority.

The efforts of Westover and Arnold to dispel doubts about the importance of air power went for naught. The War Department put more credence in reports coming from overseas than the arguments of the Army Air Corps. In his annual report for 1937, General Craig said that events in Spain and the Far East had proved that the infantryman still achieved the decisive results in warfare. Referring to airplanes and tanks, Craig reported that the "new arms can aid him; they cannot replace him." More important, Secretary of War Woodring stated in his annual report that once the Army Air Corps reached its authorized level of 2,320 airplanes, only 500 replacements would be purchased each year.[29] His announcement exacerbated the split within the Army Air Corps over the long-range bombers. Westover and Arnold wanted to work within the system to form a balanced program of air power, but the other side, represented by Andrews and Knerr, wanted to commit the Army Air Corps to a long-range bomber program. This small number of 500 planes a year left little room for compromise between the two factions, and the *New York Times* reported that the two "schools" differed widely on the question.[30]

The differences between Andrews and Westover were more apparent than real. Reviewing the GHQ Air Force's activities in 1937 for the *Air Corps News Letter*, both Andrews and Westover praised the capabilities of long-range bombers in separate articles. But neither mentioned the twin-engine B-18s that would soon make up the bulk of the Army Air Corps's bombers.[31] Westover gave further evidence of his agreement with Andrews in a speech to the first National Aviation Planning Conference meeting at Cleveland, Ohio, on January 11, 1938. After calling for a balanced program of aircraft purchases, Westover demanded that a large "proportion of these must be the best Bombing planes obtainable," and he referred to the Flying Fortress as the best bomber available.[32] Andrews and Westover differed over the method of obtaining more Flying Fortresses. Westover wanted to work within the War Department, but Andrews was impatient. Willing to do whatever it took to get his planes, Andrews went outside the regular military channels and made an indirect appeal to President Roosevelt.

On November 2, 1937, the GHQ Air Force and the navy held a minor, joint exercise off the Virginia Capes. As with the *Utah* exercise, four YB-17s attacked the navy's target vessels with great success. To ensure that Roosevelt learned of these results, Andrews bypassed the War Department and sent a memorandum to Col. Edwin "Pa" M. Watson, President Roosevelt's military advisor. Somehow, Andrews obtained copies of confidential navy memorandums that detailed the accuracy with which the YB-17s had bombed the target vessels. Passing them on to Watson, Andrews commented that the exercise provided "a further illustration of the tremendous power of the GHQ Air Force in national defense."[33] While there is no guarantee that Watson passed Andrews's memorandum on to the president, it is highly likely. Roosevelt had expressed interest in every other navy maneuver, so it is probable that Watson told him about the memorandum.

Adm. Harry E. Yarnell, commander of the United States Asiatic Fleet, definitely influenced President Roosevelt's strategy for the Far East. Two weeks before the Virginia Capes exercises, Admiral Yarnell sent Chief of Naval Operations Adm. William D. Leahy a letter that had a great impact on future American responses to Japanese expansion in the Far East. After reading the letter, Admiral Leahy presented a copy to President Roosevelt with the comment that both "the Navy and the Army are already thinking along some of the lines indicated by Admiral Yarnell."[34]

Yarnell believed that the United States might be forced into a general war with Great Britain and France against Germany, Italy, and Japan. While Britain and France held Germany and Italy in Europe, the United States would play a predominant role in the Pacific, with the tacit support of Russia and Holland. To avoid another economic dislocation like the one following the World War, the United States had to fight an economic war against Japan. Because the United States and her allies controlled 90 percent of the world's iron, coal, and oil reserves, and a major portion of the other raw war materials, the United States could wage an economic war with a "reasonably early" victory. "Such an economic, and therefore economical war, must be one of strangulation, in short, *an almost purely naval war in the Pacific as far as we are concerned,*" wrote Yarnell. With the British and French fleets controlling the Atlantic, the United States Navy could concentrate its forces in the Pacific. Together with the Dutch East Indian forces and the Russian submarine and air forces at Vladivostok, the United States Navy would outnumber the Japanese navy. Japanese communications could be cut by forces operating from Dutch Harbor, Hawaii, Guam, the Philippines, Java, and Singapore. Envisioning an inexpensive war, Yarnell said that the only reason for sending the Battle Fleet west of the Hawaiian Islands would be to recapture Manila or Guam. He saw no reason for sending American troops to stop Japanese expansion. He preferred sending American officers and equipment to China and letting the Chinese be cannon fodder. To fight his "naval war of strangulation," the navy needed to build vessels for destroying enemy commerce and retaining command of the air along the line of bases. "*Naval* air force, submarines and light forces with cruising endurance and dual purpose batteries," he suggested, "should be concentrated upon at the expense of increasing the battleline." In addition, anti-aircraft equipment would be "vital."[35]

Yarnell worried about how the American people would react to his economic war. Naval wars of strangulation took time and had few spectacular naval battles. The people might become frustrated and lose interest. But by showing that the conflict was waged economically and with few American casualties, the American people could be dissuaded from sending a large expeditionary force to achieve a quick victory. To prepare for Yarnell's type of war, the State, War, and Navy departments had to work together. The State Department needed to ensure that the United States would not be left "to fight such a war alone." The War Department had to give up its plans for mobilizing millions of men and build a small force capable of being deployed rapidly. And the Navy Department had to provide the "necessary means and training" to carry out such a war, "keeping clearly in mind the part that aviation and submarines will play in future naval operations."[36]

Yarnell's ideas about military strategy for the Far East matched the president's ideas about projecting American air power into the Pacific. Writing to Admiral Leahy on November 10, Roosevelt said that Yarnell "talks a lot of sense" and expressed the same views he had held since the early 1920s. Moreover, Roosevelt explained that Yarnell's suggestions went "along with that word 'quarantine' which I used in the Chicago speech last month."[37] On October 5, 1937, Roosevelt had said that peace-loving people had to make a concerted effort to "quarantine [those] creating a state of international anarchy and instability." Afterward, Cardinal Mundelein claimed that Roosevelt did not have a military or naval plan or a plan to impose sanctions, but rather a policy of severing ordinary communications with an aggressor nation. When asked to explain the meaning of his speech, Roosevelt told reporters that he had no specific plan but was looking for one.[38] In Yarnell's letter, FDR found the program he was seeking. It was a program similar to his earlier plan for blockading Germany. The president showed that he knew a blockade would work by reminding Admiral Leahy of "an example of successful strangulation — when the United States, without declaring war, strangled Tripoli."[39] Roosevelt remembered his blockade or "quarantine" when faced by German aggression in 1938 and Japanese aggression in 1941. Furthermore, Roosevelt was in earnest during the 1940 presidential campaign when he told audiences that their sons would not be sent into foreign wars.

By the end of 1937, President Roosevelt wanted to find a way by which large areas in the Pacific could be patrolled. Taking notice of Yarnell's emphasis on airplanes, Roosevelt asked Leahy if the navy had thought about stationing a merchant ship, equipped with eight or ten seaplanes, at a fixed location. Using the ship as a floating base, the seaplanes could fly reconnaissance missions far beyond the range of aircraft stationed at an island. In addition, Roosevelt wanted to know whether the merchant ships could be armed for warding off small air attacks and sinking lightly armed merchant ships.[40] He had something in mind similar to the German transatlantic flying boat service. Their Dornier flying boats lacked the range to fly the Atlantic nonstop. So, the Germans stationed supply ships at fixed points in the Atlantic, where the Dornier flying boats would land for refueling. This procedure enabled the Germans to fly across large tracts of water with short-range airplanes. During the following year, General Andrews's men demonstrated that the B-17 had the potential to patrol large areas.

The influence of Yarnell's letter on Roosevelt was demonstrated after Japanese planes sank the American gunboat *Panay* on December 12, 1937. FDR sent the Japanese a strong protest. To ensure that the Japanese paid full compensation, he instructed Secretary of the Treasury Morgenthau to look into seizing all Japanese assets in the

United States. Roosevelt also considered taking military action against Japan. On December 16, he told the British ambassador, Sir Ronald Lindsay, that he wanted the United States Navy and the Royal Navy to begin a "systematic exchange of secret information" and to draw up plans for a joint blockade of Japan after the "next grave outrage."

At a cabinet meeting the next day, Secretary of the Navy Swanson called for firm action toward Japan. Swanson urged a declaration of war against Japan, or at least sending the fleet to Hawaii. Less bellicose, Roosevelt told the cabinet that he had the power to place an embargo upon Japan. Demonstrating Yarnell's influence, the president explained that the United States and Great Britain could blockade Japan along a line from the Aleutians to Singapore and force Japan to capitulate within a year. After mentioning staff talks between the United States Navy and the Royal Navy, he announced plans to offer Congress a naval budget larger than originally thought necessary. Reminding the cabinet how Japan and Italy fought undeclared wars to achieve their goals, Roosevelt suggested doing the same thing by using economic sanctions without declaring war. "We don't call them economic sanctions," he said, "but call them quarantines. We want to develop a technique which will not lead to war. We want to be as smart as Japan and Italy. We want to do it in a modern way." FDR saw a naval blockade as the modern way to stop Japanese aggression while avoiding a declaration of war. Following the cabinet meeting, Roosevelt backed away from his aggressive posture. He decided not to impose sanctions, and he also chose to send a naval officer to London for technical discussions only. After the Japanese apologized, offered to pay for all damages, and promised to protect the rights and interests of Americans in China, the *Panay* incident ended peacefully.[41]

A naval blockade of Japan would have resulted in shooting on the high seas. When Roosevelt reminded Leahy that "the United States, without declaring war, strangled Tripoli," he knew that the United States Navy and Marines had fought the Tripolitan pirates.[42] But if he had to fight, the president preferred a cheap naval blockade. When he said that Japan would collapse after a year of blockade, Roosevelt showed his belief that Japan's economy was fragile and dependent upon its sea communications, as Billy Mitchell had claimed. Acting on that belief, Roosevelt proceeded with his plans to expand the navy. At a press conference on December 28, Roosevelt announced that he would ask Congress for additional ships. Asked by the press if additional funds would be requested for the army, Army Air Corps, or Naval Air Ser-

vice, Roosevelt said no. Given no specifics, the nation waited throughout the month of January to see what armaments Roosevelt would
seek. In the meantime, the press learned of Roosevelt's plans to
blockade Japan and to send a naval officer to London. Capt. Royal E.
Ingersoll, Chief of the War Plans Division of the Office of the Chief
of Naval Intelligence, went to London for ten days, and reporters asked
Chief of Naval Operations Leahy and the State Department about the
purpose of Ingersoll's trip. Leahy claimed that Ingersoll was ascertain-
ing how the British figured tonnages in building their new ships, and
State Department officials denied the rumors of Anglo-American naval
cooperation in the Far East. "We are not that crazy," they said. Secretary of War Woodring, upon learning of the larger naval budget, tried
to get increased funds for the army, but Roosevelt refused to spend
much on the army. In his national defense message, Roosevelt requested a large sum for the navy, but little for the army.[43]

The president's defense program caused consternation among the
advocates of air power. Representative Wilcox publicly announced his
full support for the president's program. Yet privately, Wilcox told
Colonel Knerr that if Hoover had advocated such a program, he would
have "run out of names to call him." Wilcox suggested to Knerr that
a public exposition of how the War Department had neglected the
Army Air Corps would get wide support in Congress. Knerr, impressed
by what Wilcox had told him, sent notes of their conversation to Andrews. Quoting Wilcox, Knerr said that opposition to a big navy program only needed "some nucleus" and a "convincing argument in favor
of Air Forces" to ensure the growth of a more reasonable navy program. "However," Knerr continued, "somebody will get hurt if handled by the Air Corps, because it will make the President mad."[44]
Knowing what had happened to Billy Mitchell, Knerr did not want
Andrews to be the one to get hurt.

The national defense budget offered by President Roosevelt frustrated the supporters of air power. Another year had passed, and
nothing had seemed to change. Funding for the Army Air Corps remained small, and it appeared that the navy got everything it wanted.
Their growing frustration manifested itself in new movements to separate the Army Air Corps from the army. As Wilcox's conversation with
Colonel Knerr demonstrated, a number of the supporters of air power
were ready to return to the methods employed by Billy Mitchell. However, they were unaware that President Roosevelt had found a program whereby he could stop Japanese aggression: the joint air-sea
blockade proposed by Yarnell. It remained for the commanders of the
Army Air Corps to prove that their men and planes possessed the ca-

pability to carry out the aerial half of the blockade. Gen. Frank Andrews (temporarily promoted to from lieutenant colonel to brigadier general in 1935) grew frustrated at the War Department's refusal to purchase more B-17s, but he never lost sight of what he had to do. Throughout 1938, he, Westover, and Arnold continued their efforts to win their superiors' support.

VI. The Wings of Democracy

The GHQ Air Force had proved that it could quickly reinforce either coast in an emergency. The range of the Boeing B-17 gave it the capacity to reach points quickly in Latin America or reinforce Hawaii. However, the first service performed by the Flying Fortress for the Roosevelt administration was countering German and Italian political and economic threats in Latin America. While meeting these menaces, the GHQ Air Force proved that it could meet distant military threats.

The *Panay* bombing plagued President Roosevelt even after the crisis had passed. The ambassador to Costa Rica, William H. Hornibrook, sent Roosevelt a disturbing report about reactions to the bombing. Latin Americans appeared unable to understand the patience of the Americans and British to Japanese aggression. For that reason, Hornibrook applauded the president's firm demand for an apology and compensation from the Japanese. Hornibrook feared that the perception of a weak United States would allow German and Italian propaganda to "obtain political, cultural and economic domination in this section of the world."[1] Hornibrook had reason to be worried. By 1938, the Italians were spreading their propaganda throughout Latin America with free news service to newspapers, daily radio broadcasts from Rome, and frequent visits of prominent Italians. To win the popular support of the South Americans, a squadron of Italian aerobatic fliers attended the Pan-American Aviation Conference at Lima, Peru, in 1937. After the conference, the fliers toured Chile, Argentina, and Brazil. Everywhere, they won the favor of the crowds. Few South Americans knew of the conference, but most heard about the Italian fliers. Impressed by the Italian fliers, the Peruvian Army hired Italian pilots to train its fliers on Italian-made planes.[2]

Americans had already become apprehensive about the future of democracy in Latin America. Of great concern was the possibility that Getulio Vargas, president of Brazil, would make his country a fascist state. On November 14, 1937, the *Washington Post* ran an editorial cartoon of a Brazilian coffee cup steaming up fascism. Two days later, the *Post* ran an editorial warning of the danger.[3] Italian aerial successes in South America created consternation in the United States. As sales of Italian aircraft and flight instruments increased, the American aviation industry became alarmed.[4]

The growing Italian encroachment into Latin America, which many U.S. citizens thought was reserved for the United States, forced some people to reconsider their views on America's defensive needs. On February 2, 1938, Chief of Naval Operations Adm. William D. Leahy told the House Naval Affairs Committee that "at our door nothing stands in the way of the possible exploitation or seizure of the republics of Central and South America except the Monroe Doctrine, backed by such naval forces as the United States may have and the use of that force if the necessity should arise." An editorial on February 3 in the *Washington Post* agreed with Leahy, stating that the United States had to rely upon a "hemispherical" defense system instead of isolation. The *Post* was advocating what later would become a cornerstone of the Roosevelt administration's defense policy: hemispheric defense. However, the *Post* believed the United States Navy's ships would play the "dominant role" in upholding the Monroe Doctrine. The newspaper had an excellent reason for putting its faith in the navy. That same day, two navy patrol planes crashed near San Pedro, California, killing eleven sailors. Noting the "high fragility" of airplanes in an editorial the following day, the *Post* stated that "war planes, particularly in times of emergency, must fly as strategy commands." The uncertainty of an airplane to fly through bad weather made it an "uncertain quantity" on which military strategy could not be based.[5] Soon, the Army Air Corps showed the *Post* had made the correct assessment of the course American defenses should follow but had underestimated the role of air power.

When Bruno Mussolini led a flight of three Italian bombers from Rome to Rio de Janeiro across Africa and the Atlantic in late January of 1938, Americans responded. Probably acting at the suggestion of General Andrews, William A. Wieland of the Associated Press's Latin American Section spoke with Assistant Secretary of War Louis Johnson on January 24. To foster good will in Latin America and counteract Italian and German propaganda, Wieland proposed dispatching a flight of army bombers to Buenos Aires for the inauguration of President Roberto M. Ortiz. Besides offsetting Mussolini's flight, the flight would increase the sales of American aircraft in Latin America by displaying the high quality of American military aircraft. Furthermore, it would demonstrate that the United States had the means to back up the Monroe Doctrine. Assistant Secretary Johnson asked Wieland to put his ideas into a letter. With a contrived statement that it had too many ramifications for him to understand, Johnson sent Wieland's letter to Stephen T. Early, secretary to the president.[6]

Johnson's contrived statement resulted from his sharp disagreement with Secretary Woodring over aviation's role in the military. Woodring saw long-range bombers as "aggressive" weapons and believed they had no place in the Army Air Corps. Woodring wanted to purchase fighters and light bombers for ground support and coastal defense. Furthermore, he opposed the purchase of a few B-17s when more twin-engine planes could be bought with the same money. Arnold later said that "the superiority of one B-17 to two B-10's . . . was a mystery to Secretary Woodring and his people."[7] Johnson, on the other hand, strongly advocated the purchase of more B-17s, and he openly criticized Woodring's refusal to procure more heavy bombers. Knowing that Woodring would reject the proposal, Johnson went over his head by sending the letter to Early.

Observers in Argentina had reported that the election of Roberto Ortiz signalled a reorientation of that nation toward the United States.[8] By sending army bombers to Argentina, the Roosevelt administration could take the initiative in Latin American diplomacy. Early discussed the idea with Roosevelt and Marvin H. McIntyre, secretary to the president. Both Early and McIntyre approved of the proposal. On February 4, McIntyre informed Roosevelt that Sumner Welles had requested three of the new army bombers to be sent to the inauguration. The Argentine government had expressed a keen interest in the idea, and the State Department believed it would offset Italian propaganda in Argentina. Complaining about Woodring's opposition to it, Welles wanted Roosevelt to order the flight.[9] Roosevelt consented, and the next day Chief of Staff Craig told Andrews to make preparations. However, Craig ordered Andrews to keep all plans and preparations secret with "no publicity whatever."[10] Denied the opportunity to release any information beforehand, Col. W. H. Frank, chief of staff of the GHQ Air Force, knew that the press would give considerable coverage to the flight. He instructed the GHQ Air Force personnel involved to stress "the accomplishments of a typical unit of *the GHQ Air Force*

. . . rather than the accomplishments of individuals. . . ." Frank wanted the American people to believe that any unit of the GHQ Air Force could make the flight, if it had the equipment.[11]

The State Department announced the flight on February 9, calling it a gesture of good will. Six days later, six YB-17s under the command of Lt. Col. Robert Olds flew from Langley Field to Miami. From there, the army fliers made a nonstop, 2,844-mile flight to Lima, Peru, in fourteen hours and thirty-five minutes. The following day, five of the six bombers flew southward to Santiago and then crossed over the high Andes to Buenos Aires. Delayed by propeller trouble, the sixth plane flew directly from Lima to Buenos Aires and landed in the midst of a rainstorm, clearly proving the reliability of airplanes. After participating in the inauguration, the army fliers returned to the United States. On the last leg of the journey, they flew nonstop from Albrook Field, Panama, to Langley Field.[12]

Everywhere Olds and his fliers landed in Latin America, they were greeted by large, enthusiastic crowds. The flight succeeded in the United States as fully as in South America. Both *Time* and *Newsweek* magazines praised the army fliers. *Newsweek* noted the speed with which the planes reached Argentina: "The New York–Buenos Aires sea route takes up to seventeen days, and Pan-American Airways Clippers take five — but the Army men . . . arrived [from Langley Field] in 34 hours."[13] The Los Angeles *Times* carried a photograph taken of Olds's airplane at Lima, and the caption noted that "the stop at Lima was the only one on [the] 5000-mile trip. . . ."[14] A *New York Times* editorial quoted a Latin American newspaper to show how much the people of South America appreciated the good will flight. This newspaper, said the *Times*, "summed up the spirit of the flight very appropriately in an eight-column headline reading 'Welcome to the Wings of Democracy.'" Impressed by the "feat of these flying monsters," the *Times* noted that the six bombers made the 5,225-mile trip from Miami to Buenos Aires in only twenty-four hours and four minutes flying time, at an average speed of more than 185 miles per hour. Recognizing the speed and range of the Flying Fortresses, the editorial stated that "it is plain that these 'wings of democracy' bear their twenty-ton loads lightly."[15] In the guise of good will, Andrews had demonstrated the performance capabilities of the B-17 and how rapidly they could reach a distant trouble spot.

The Argentina flight influenced the Chicago *Daily Tribune*. On February 16, the same day that the newspaper first mentioned the flight, an editorial stated that the British kept the ports and coasts flanking their "sea routes to South Africa and to the east via the Mediterranean" in friendly hands because of the "addition of aircraft to the

15. Secretary of War Harry H. Woodring presenting the Mackay Award for 1938 on November 7, 1938, to Lt. Col. Robert Olds, who led the flight of six B-17s to Argentina in February 1938. Hap Arnold is standing to the left. *Courtesy U.S.A.F.*

machinery of destruction." Following the British example, the editorial recommended that the "first plank in America's foreign policy now ought to be for the acquisition of foreign bombing bases off our shores and along the lanes of our naval maneuvers." It proposed having the nations that defaulted on their World War debts give their possessions in the Western Hemisphere in payment.[16]

Olds and his fliers certainly impressed the *Washington Post.* Writing for the *Post,* Barry Sullivan stated that the aerial forces of the United States should not be overlooked. The flight, he said, "will have the effect of quieting fears, expressed during the past few months, that aggressive actions against the United States would first be made in the form of assaults against Latin-American nations, although such thrusts would violate the traditional policy of the Monroe Doctrine. In any case, the flight clearly shows that United States air power can assist in preventing armed intervention in the American continents if such prevention is to continue to be the policy of the Government."[17] The long range of the B-17, demonstrated on this flight, forever altered America's defensive planning. Henceforth, force projection over ever-increasing ranges became a key feature in American military planning. The ultimate expression of that feature was the intercontinental ballistic missile.

Rep. Dow W. Barter sent his congratulations to General Andrews, who used the opportunity to advertise the B-17. Writing back, Andrews explained that the flight illustrated the effectiveness of our training" and demonstrated the "value of the type of bombardment airplane which the GHQ Air Force has advocated for its equipment." To show the B-17's greater flexibility for defensive air operations, Andrews told Barter that the 31st Bombardment Squadron had recently been dispatched to Hawaii by ship. If that squadron had been equipped with B-17s, he said, "it could have been flown to Hawaii and then when required elsewhere, flown there also." The larger bombers were "more economical per ton of bombs delivered" than small bombers.[18]

Forced to allow the Argentina flight, the War Department opposed making further long-distance flights with the B-17s. Hoping to include them in maneuvers scheduled for March, the commander of the Hawaiian Department asked the General Staff to fly some of the B-17s to the islands. The army fliers welcomed the chance, but the chief of staff turned down the request. Only intervention from higher civilian authorities had made possible the flight to Buenos Aires, and a flight to Hawaii lacked the necessary civilian support. Disappointed at being denied the opportunity to prove that his B-17s could reinforce Hawaii, General Andrews found the Argentina flight an adequate substitute. He told Gen. Delos C. Emmons that it proved anything that a flight to Hawaii would have proved.[19]

The General Staff refused to let the Army Air Corps capitalize on the publicity surrounding the flight to South America. Besides ordering Andrews to keep the preparations secret, General Craig refused to let General Westover hold a big reception for the returning airmen. Craig told Andrews that the returning airmen would "get a more favorable reaction if they return to their station and the country gets the impression that this is a normal routine flight which our Air Corps is prepared to put on without any hullabaloo at any instant." Agreeing with Craig, Andrews said that "the impression we want to leave with the country is that the flight was not a stunt. . . ."[20] He wanted to convince the American people, as did Colonel Frank, that the GHQ Air Force could repeat the flight, with B-17s, whenever circumstances required it. Despite the cancellation of formal festivities, five thousand spectators welcomed the army fliers back to Langley Field. General Andrews told the crowd that the flight was not a stunt flight performed by specially selected crews. Each plane was manned by its regular crew, and any Flying Fortress crew in the GHQ Air Force could have done the job.[21] The *Washington Post* certainly felt more confident when it reported that the "flight . . . was the Army's graphic means of showing that the United States can aid any invaded South American republic in jigtime."[22] By treating this spectacular feat as an everyday occurrence, Andrews quietly built trust in the Army Air Corps and added validity to the spectacular claims about air power.

After receiving a letter of congratulations from the Secretary of State, General Andrews believed that the GHQ Air Force would receive more B-17s. Thinking that the flight would silence all opposition to the purchase of more Flying Fortresses, Andrews told a fellow officer that "everybody is climbing aboard the band wagon."[23] Comments by President Roosevelt before the Argentina flight had bolstered Andrews's confidence. Asked about his increase in the navy, Roosevelt had told reporters that the consensus among those who knew the most about national defense was "that we cannot rely on the single defense in one ocean, that there must be more defensive possibilities than mere defense in one ocean. . . . We have to consider the possibility of defense on both sides."[24] Andrews believed that the B-17s could defend either coast, and his expectation of receiving more B-17s was reinforced by Colonel Olds's visit to the White House upon returning from Buenos Aires. Delivering a message of friendship from President Ortiz, Olds told FDR that the six B-17s had proved themselves superior to any other airplane for defending the United States. After the meeting, Olds informed reporters that Roosevelt had been unusually familiar with the details of the flight and the country over which the flight was made.[25] Olds's surprise at the president's knowledge was understandable. Because Roosevelt loved ships, most people assumed that he had little knowledge of airplanes.[26]

Andrews confused the president's knowledge of airplanes with support for them. Although interested in the Argentina flight, President Roosevelt remained unconvinced that airplanes alone could control the seas or defend one of the coasts. Asked by reporters whether the battleship had lost any of its effectiveness, Roosevelt said his recent decision to add two new battleships to the navy showed his faith in them. FDR, to clarify his meaning, pointed out that torpedo boats, submarines, and Civil War Monitors had all been called supreme naval weapons, but an "antidote" for each had been found. The same held true for airplanes, in that anti-aircraft guns and defensive planes were antidotes for air attack. Roosevelt emphasized that no one weapon was supreme.[27] By avoiding a simple yes or no answer to the battleship question, he demonstrated a concern that airplanes might be the antidote to battleships. Roosevelt had held this concern since 1919, when he told the Senate Military Affairs Committee that "aviation might make surface ships practically impossible to be used as an Arm."[28] Saying that no one weapon was supreme, the president displayed flexibility and a broad grasp of the changing world. Roosevelt loved the sea, but his ability to draw on the past to put the present into perspective allowed him to see the potentialities of naval and air power working in conjunction, as Admiral Yarnell had suggested. Soon, Roosevelt demonstrated his appreciation of air power as a military and naval defensive weapon.

Andrews also misjudged the War Department's support for more Flying Fortresses. During a War Department meeting about aircraft purchases for the 1939 fiscal year, Andrews discovered that Secretary Woodring had not climbed aboard the B-17 bandwagon. Woodring announced that just enough planes would be purchased over the next three years to bring the Army Air Corps up to its authorized level of 2,320 planes, including only 12 B-17s. Ignoring objections from Assistant Secretary Johnson and General Andrews, Woodring refused to alter his plan. Before Woodring could submit his proposal to the White House, Johnson made a personal appeal to Roosevelt. The president informed Johnson that neither the army nor the Army Air Corps would receive increased funding at that time. Roosevelt approved Woodring's proposal, referred to as the Woodring Program, and Congress appropriated $37 million that spring for the purchase of 450 planes. Johnson acquiesced to the president's wishes, and he publicly supported the Woodring Program in a series of speeches.[29] Questioning the soundness of Woodring's program, *Time* magazine quoted Eddie Rickenbacker as saying that the United States needed 100,000 pilots and 30,000 airplanes immediately and another 500,000 pilots and 100,000 airplanes within five years.[30]

The Air Corps wanted a balanced air force, which included B-17s. Arnold did not want a lopsided ratio of pilots to planes. Fearing that Assistant Secretary Johnson might support Rickenbacker's plan, General Arnold protested that it was unrealistically expensive. He referred Johnson to an Air Corps study calling for 3,627 officers, 24,988 enlisted men, and 740 flying cadets "to provide a balanced personnel organization for the 2320 airplanes." Arnold would have liked a larger number of airplanes, but he thought it wise to remember that an air force must be a balance of airplanes, personnel, and ground facilities.[31] Both Arnold and Westover advocated this goal publicly. In the spring of 1938, Metro-Goldwyn-Mayer released the movie *Test Pilot* starring Clark Gable, Myrna Loy, and Spencer Tracy. As part of the ceremonies for the Hollywood premier showing, Arnold promoted the movie with a radio address. Noting that the Flying Fortresses used for the movie were identical to the planes used on the Argentina flight, he quietly educated the public about the superiority of one expensive B-17 to two cheaper B-18s. Repeating what he had told Assistant Secretary Johnson, Arnold supported the Woodring Program because it provided the three essential ingredients of a "successful, modern air force—Airplanes, Airmen, and Air Bases."[32] General Westover stated the same ideas a few days earlier in a speech to the Southeastern Aviation Conference at Montgomery, Alabama. Like Arnold, Westover praised the Woodring Program, saying that "the only thing that now stands in the way of providing an adequate air component for the Army is shortage of funds."[33] Since Ira Eaker wrote the public addresses made by Westover and Arnold, the commanders of the Air Corps had adopted a single plan of action. They would support the Woodring Program and avoid antagonizing the president, the Congress, or the War Department.

In March, 1938, Adolf Hitler achieved his first foreign policy success: the Anschluss with Austria. Before then, Charles Lindbergh had warned the War Department and President Roosevelt about the Luftwaffe. Lindbergh was widely regarded as an expert on aviation; during his trips to Germany in 1936 and 1937, the Nazis had convinced him that they had built the Luftwaffe into a very powerful air force. The Lone Eagle told British and French leaders that their air forces were no match for the Luftwaffe, and they believed him.[34] Together with Maj. Truman Smith, the American military attaché in Berlin, Lindbergh prepared a report for the War Department warning of the Luftwaffe.[35] Through Joseph P. Kennedy, he warned President Roosevelt that the Germans had the capacity to produce more airplanes than the United States. Impressed, Roosevelt sent copies of Lindbergh's warning to General Craig and Admiral Leahy.[36]

Following the Anschluss, President Roosevelt received the first of many requests for American-built planes. On April 15, George Norton Northrop, headmaster of the Roxbury Latin School in West Roxbury, Massachusetts, sent Roosevelt a letter from an Englishman who wanted the president to give Great Britain five hundred bombers. If the planes were sent as a gift, Hitler could be bluffed into thinking that the United States and Great Britain had an alliance.[37] Roosevelt rejected the suggestion, but unknown to him, the British government was considering the United States as a source of bombers. On May 1, Sir Thomas Inskip, minister of defense, asked Lindbergh about the production potential of the United States's aircraft industry. Apparently impressed by the Argentina flight, Inskip also asked if the large bombers could be flown across the Atlantic in an emergency.[38]

In the spring of 1938, expanding the navy concerned President Roosevelt more than getting bombers to England. At a press conference, he stated that the navy needed to be large enough to defend America's Pacific possessions, including the Philippines. But the navy also had to be large enough to prevent a European power from sending arms and airplanes to a fascist revolution in Latin America. Venezuela, said Roosevelt, "is only four hundred miles [from the United States], it is an hour and a half by some of these modern planes, an hour and a half further than Cuba." Emphasizing that airplanes had made everybody a potential target, FDR told a story about a Chinese village far from the fighting. Calling it the "Iowa of China," he said that Japanese planes killed three hundred people there, "and two minutes later they were gone." He then referred to documents captured after the World War, indicating that the Germans "were building a Zeppelin with the perfectly definite objective of sending her out in the spring of 1919 by way of the Great Circle Route, over Iceland, Greenland and down to New York, to drop a cargo of bombs on New York City." Since German Zeppelins had flown that route commercially, he was implying that Germany might try to do it again. Asked how the United States could defend itself from Maine to the Philippines, Roosevelt said that one enemy would be no problem. However, two enemies in different places required Americans "to be a bit shifty" and defeat one first, then the other.[39] Roosevelt's answer later emerged as the "Germany First" strategy adopted by the United States and Great Britain.

Even as President Roosevelt discussed the possibility, the Army Air Corps was preparing to test the ability of the armed forces to meet simultaneous attacks on both coasts. Lt. Col. Ira Eaker played a key role in publicizing the maneuvers. With a Bachelor of Arts in journalism from the University of Southern California, he had served as the assistant chief of the information division and had been promoted to chief of the Air Corps's public relations section. In April, he attended a short course in news photography at the University of Oklahoma. Upon his return from Norman, Oklahoma, Eaker used his training as a journalist to publicize the upcoming maneuvers.[40]

Colonel Eaker believed in using publicity to establish cordial relations with the public. Most of all, the Army Air Corps had to impress upon the public the importance of the GHQ Air Force to each American. Eaker told the Chief of Staff of the GHQ Air Force to send B-17s, which had not lost their "sex appeal with the public," to out-of-the-way places. More Americans could see the planes and would be more willing to spend their tax dollars on them. By deliberately using phrases like "'skeletonized' squadrons" in press releases, the public would be gently reminded that the Army Air Corps needed more planes. For the upcoming maneuvers, he suggested the exploitation

16. Maj. Gen. Frank M. Andrews and Brig. Gens. Arnold N. Krogstad and Delos C. Emmons outlining plans for the maneuvers of May, 1938. *Courtesy U.S.A.F.*

of personalities, greater coordination between staff officers on press releases, and the use of a final review on the last day of the exercises.[41]

The scenario for the May maneuvers supposed that the United States was at war with a Black Force, a coalition of European and Asiatic powers. While an Asiatic fleet held the navy in the Pacific, a European fleet of aircraft carriers, battleships, cruisers, and destroyer-escorted troop transports attacked New England. To meet the second Black fleet, all three wings of the GHQ Air Force gathered at temporary bases in New York, New Jersey, Connecticut, Massachusetts, Pennsylvania, and Maryland. Since the navy had not assigned ships to cooperate with the GHQ Air Force, General Andrews made no plans for the B-17s to participate in the exercises. The maneuvers would have taken on an unrealistic atmosphere as planes searched for nonexistent ships. The Los Angeles *Times* referred to it as a "mythical" enemy fleet. Eaker added a note of realism and showed the range of the B-17 in a very flashy exercise. He publicized a real search for a real ship by a flight of B-17s. Knowing that the *Rex*, an Italian ocean liner bound for New York, would be about 700 miles out when the maneuvers started on May 12, Eaker asked the ship's owners to participate. They quickly agreed because of the free publicity. Eaker had the three YB-17s assigned for the flight stationed at Mitchel Field on Long Island, where the New York City reporters had easy access to them. To record the interception, the bombers carried Maj. George Goddard, the Air Corps's best photographer; an NBC radio announcer, who gave a live broadcast from one of the bombers; and other reporters, including Hanson Baldwin. Heading out to sea, they encountered thunderstorms and turbulence that slowed them down, but the army fliers spotted the *Rex* right on time for the scheduled broadcast. The NBC commentator described the interception for his audience, and Goddard took pictures that the Air Corps distributed across the country.[42]

Hanson Baldwin was impressed. He reported that the three Flying Fortresses "reared through line squalls, hail, rain and sunshine . . . in a 1,300-mile overwater flight, unprecedented in the history of the Army Air Corps." Many people, he wrote, believed that the flight showed "the utility of aviation in the defense of our coasts and it also proved, the army air force believes, that army fliers as well as navy fliers can navigate over water out of sight of land." Although not totally convinced that airplanes could defend the coasts, Baldwin grudgingly admitted that "a nice problem in navigation was solved."[43] Goddard's photograph appeared on the back page of the Chicago *Daily Tribune*, a page devoted to photographs that referred the reader to stories contained within the paper. Its caption read: "It is evidence of their success in spotting the 'foe,' the innocent Italian liner Rex."[44] The GHQ Air Force pilots had proved they could navigate over water and in rough weather. Never again could the navy claim otherwise.

The maneuvers continued with simulated bombing raids on New York City, attacks on simulated aircraft carriers and mock air battles. Claiming that most nations recognized the vulnerability of aircraft carriers, Andrews announced that the GHQ Air Force had put five of the Black fleet's carriers "out of action." General Andrews also told the press that the GHQ Air Force had demonstrated a great improvement in its efficiency. Following Eaker's recommendation to publicize the "skeletonized" condition of the GHQ Air Force, other officers pointed out that only 222 airplanes had been available for the maneuvers. They stressed that the army did not have a real air force, only the beginnings of one. The attack on New York City reminded

17. As an unscheduled part of the 1938 maneuvers, YB-17s intercepted the *Rex*, an Italian ocean liner bound for New York, 776 miles at sea. Maj. George Goddard, the best photographer in the Army Air Corps, recorded the event on film, and his photographs were distributed to newspapers throughout the United States. *Courtesy U.S.A.F.*

Americans that they needed more planes to adequately defend their cities.[45]

On the night of May 16, Black bombers raided the Seversky and and Grumman aircraft factories at Farmingdale, Long Island, in a test of blackout procedures. The GHQ Air Force asked for voluntary participation in the blackout, and the residents of the area cooperated. With no lights to guide them, the bomber pilots never found their targets. NBC carried live reports of the blackout, and Arnold addressed the radio audience afterward. As Eaker had suggested, Arnold stressed the importance of the GHQ Air Force to the American people. "These national defense exercises demonstrated in a manner quite realistic," he said, "just what we might expect if invaders came within striking

distance of our shores. They have brought home with a bang the terrifying roar of hostile planes . . . the thrilling sight of aerial combats
. . . and the deafening crack of our antiaircraft guns. But, fortunately
we have been spared the sickening whine of dropping bombs, with
the death-dealing crash of their explosions."[46] For anyone remembering the German bombing of Guernica a year earlier, Arnold's comments held a poignant message. Without the Army Air Corps's protection, Farmingdale or any other American city could be another
Guernica. *Life* magazine made the point very clearly. It carried three
pages of photographs taken during the Farmingdale "air raid," and an
accompanying photographic essay detailed an actual Japanese air raid
on the Chinese city of Hankow.[47] Statements such as Arnold's did
not result in a public outcry for more airplanes, because Americans
still felt secure. But when they recognized a threat, the American people had been conditioned to respond to it by supporting the purchase
of more airplanes.

The day following the Farmingdale raid, the GHQ Air Force held
a final review. The planes assembled over West Point and flew to
Mitchel Field, where General Andrews and his staff watched them
fly overhead. From there, the planes dispersed to their permanent stations. After the aerial review ended and the skies were cleared of any
distractions, the Army Air Corps put its new Boeing XB-15 bomber
on display. For the officers gathered at Mitchel Field, spokesmen described the plane as the latest development in long-range bombardment, and they promised it would have an even greater range of reconnaissance than the YB-17s had achieved on the *Rex* flight.[48]

Eaker pulled a fast one on the navy by arranging to intercept the
Rex at sea. For years, the navy had argued that ships were necessary
because airplanes could not find enemy ships in bad weather, and with
Congress discussing the president's naval expansion bill the navy could
not afford any adverse publicity. The *Rex* flight embarrassed the navy,
which responded quickly. Somebody spoke to General Craig, and the
next day, he verbally ordered the Army Air Corps to stay within one
hundred miles of the coast.[49]

Nevertheless, Eaker's carefully orchestrated publicity campaign
documented the Army Air Corps's dependability. During the 1930s,
Americans suspected newspapers of being servants of special interests,
but they trusted radio broadcasts and photographs. Radio broadcasts
made listeners feel as if they had witnessed an event firsthand, giving
it added reality and plausibility. Largely through the efforts of the Farm
Security Administration's photographs and such books as Erskine Cald-
well and Margaret Bourke-White's *You Have Seen Their Faces*, photographs had become a valid type of documentary evidence for Ameri-

cans. NBC's radio program gave listeners the feeling that they were on board the YB-17s intercepting the *Rex*, and Goddard's photographs of the army bombers flying over the Italian liner gave viewers undeniable proof that the Army Air Corps could fulfill its promises.[50] When Andrews told the press that the GHQ Air Force had "theoretically" put five Black Force aircraft carriers out of commission, people believed that the GHQ Air Force could do it. The Army Air Corps had just proved itself by sending six bombers on a spectacular flight to South America and followed up that feat with the interception of the *Rex*.

Prevented from sending his planes out to sea, Andrews could still send them on flights to celebrate the inauguration of South American presidents. The GHQ Air Force planned to follow the Argentina flight with one to Bogota, Colombia, for the inauguration of President-Elect Eduardo Santos, but a disaster almost forced Andrews to cancel the trip. On July 24, 1938, the 155th anniversary of Simon Bolivar's birthday, the Colombian Air Force dedicated a new airfield near Bogota, and over 50,000 visitors swarmed to the field. As part of the festivities, a military pilot put on an aerobatics exhibition. He lost control of his plane, however, and smashed into the crowd, killing over sixty people and barely missing Santos in the reviewing stand. The GHQ Air Force fliers expected their flight to be cancelled, but it went on as planned. Flying from Miami to Bogota, on August 3, three YB-17s made the trip in eight and a half hours. Undeterred by the recent tragedy, enthusiastic crowds met the American bombers. Presenting a wreath paid for out of their own pockets, the airmen participated in the memorial service held for those killed on the airfield. Following Santos's inauguration, the three bombers returned to the United States by way of Panama.[51] Once again, the army fliers had demonstrated the remarkable range of the B-17, and the navy could not prevent it.

Ira Eaker tried to make the entire Army Air Corps conscious of public relations. Throughout the summer of 1938, Eaker used his position as chief of the Air Corps's public relation section to advocate a number of his own ideas, which included having Army Air Corps officers establish personal contacts with members of the press. While warning other officers about the dangers of giving personal interviews, he advised the timely release of photographs and stories to local newspapers from army airfields. General Andrews, before submitting an article for publication, asked Eaker to critique an outline he had written, and Eaker used the opportunity to influence the general. Eaker suggested using an informative and entertaining style, rather than a controversial article, to attract readers. He recommended that George Kenney and Beirne Lay write the article, emphasizing Lay's personal

18. The crewmen of the three YB-17s that flew to Bogota, Colombia, in August of 1938, posing in front of one of their aircraft. Standing sixth from the left is Maj. Harold L. George. Third from the right is 1st Lt. Curtis E. LeMay, future Chief of Staff of the United States Air Force. *Courtesy U.S.A.F.*

connections with the *Saturday Evening Post.* To let more people see what they were paying taxes for, Eaker arranged for a YB-17 to be displayed at the San Francisco Fair. At the 1938 Cleveland Air Races, he gave photographs of the participating planes and pilots to the press. Insuring that he had an experienced staff acquainted with the press, Eaker arranged for Beirne Lay to accompany him to Cleveland.[52]

As part of his duties, Eaker dealt with the unfavorable reports about air power coming from Spain and China. From the Command and General Staff School at Fort Leavenworth, Col. Lewis Brereton asked him in October for information on air operations in Spain and China to show "the value of *air force* operations—as opposed to tactical." Eaker sent Brereton some speeches containing the requested data, and he asked the General Staff for any pertinent information. The General Staff did not respond until March of 1939. Eaker suspected the General Staff intentionally kept any useful information from Brereton, but he refrained from making accusations. Instead, Eaker recommended to Brereton that he send an Air Corps officer stationed at Fort Leavenworth to get the necessary information from the General Staff's files.[53]

The General Staff matched its reluctance to provide information supporting the claims of the advocates of air power with its reluctance to provide more long-range bombers. In May, Deputy Chief of Staff Stanley D. Embick rejected an Air Corps request for more long-range bombers. Embick cited four reasons: the policy of the United States was defense, not aggression; the defense of the seas, except for the coastal zone, was the navy's duty; the B-17 had not proved itself superior to the three smaller planes that could be purchased for the same money; and there appeared "to be no need" for a plane larger than the B-17. A month later, the assistant secretary of war announced that the funds allocated to purchase two B-15s and another experimental, long-range bomber would be spent on twin-engine bombers. In July, the secretary of war told General Westover that no B-17s would be purchased during the 1940 fiscal year. To control the B-17's supporters in the GHQ Air Force, General Craig informed Andrews in February that, henceforth, the General Staff would chose the GHQ Air Force's staff members.[54]

By the end of summer, the Army Air Corps's hopes for obtaining more B-17s appeared crushed, but by Christmas, the outlook had improved after a change in the General Staff. In May, Brig. Gen. George C. Marshall became the new chief of the War Plans Division. Everybody in the War Department knew that Marshall would soon receive a more important position. After serving as the chief of the War Plans Division for only three months, Marshall was promoted to deputy chief of staff. At his new position, Marshall was groomed to replace Craig as the chief of staff.[55]

Marshall's selection as the future chief of staff proved most fortunate for the Army Air Corps. Marshall had been no stranger to the development of airplanes as weapons of war. While at the General Staff School in 1908, Maj. George O. Squier, the head of the signal corps, had startled Marshall by stating that the Wright brothers had built a successful airplane. Marshall had seen nothing about the Wrights in the newspapers, and Squire's comment had a profound impact on him. A year later, Marshall stopped at Fort Meyer to spend the night with a friend, Lt. Benjamin Foulois. While there, he watched the Wrights demonstrate their airplane to the army, President Taft, and thousands of onlookers. In March, 1911, the army held maneuvers on the Mexican border and Marshall served under Major Squier. All of the army's planes and pilots were also there. After seeing one plane crash into a horse and buggy, Marshall got out of bed before the planes took off at 5:30 each morning. The planes barely cleared his tent on takeoff, and he took no chances. Marshall survived the harsh Texas winter and primitive airplanes. Over the following twenty-five years, he continued his steady climb in the army, but his connections with aviation differed little from any other ground officer until 1937. On June 17, three Russian fliers left Moscow on a nonstop flight over the North Pole to Oakland, California. After sixty-three hours in the air, the Soviet plane had engine trouble and made an emergency landing at the CCC camp at Vancouver Barracks, Washington. As the camp commander, Marshall found himself responsible for the Russians, who had flown over 5,000 miles but could not speak English. When Marshall put them up in his own home, the press and other dignitaries invaded his house. To top things off, a radio broadcast was made from the Marshall home. Only after the Russian fliers left did the general and his wife return to their normal routine.[56] But Marshall had learned that airplanes could span vast distances.

Marshall's promotion to chief of the War Plans Division did not go unnoticed in the Army Air Corps, but Marshall had already caught Hap Arnold's attention in 1914. On maneuvers in the Philippines, Marshall and Arnold were assigned to the same side. Marshall, made the chief of staff, impressed Arnold. Afterward, Arnold told his wife that one day Marshall would be the chief of staff of the United States Army. When Marshall joined the General Staff, General Arnold already knew the man had great capabilities. In his memoirs, however, Arnold explained that Marshall still had to be won over to the side of air power.

> "The best efforts of Malin Craig, when he was chief of staff, the ups and downs of Secretary Woodring's understanding, never changed the basic conviction of the [War] Department that allocation of the skimpy funds it had for the purchase of airplanes should be put into medium bombers and other ground-support planes. Even when George Marshall first took over in 1937 [sic], he needed plenty of indoctrination about the air facts of life. The difference in George, who presently was to become one of the most potent forces behind the development of a real American air power, was his ability to digest what he saw and make it part of as strong a body of military genius as I have ever known."[57]

The "indoctrination" started as soon as Marshall arrived in Washington, D.C.

General Andrews asked the new chief of WPD to accompany him on an inspection tour. Ignoring opposition to the trip within the War

Department, Marshal and Andrews visited Army Air Corps facilities across the nation and aircraft factories along the West Coast. Westover carefully arranged the ten-day trip. Given guided tours at the aircraft factories by the chief engineers, Marshall learned a great deal about the problems encountered in the construction of aircraft. At the army airfields, Marshall discovered that the airmen needed better representation on the General Staff because they were starting to take their complaints to Congress again. Westover had coordinated the trip so well that Marshall did not have time to contact friends at the places he visited, but Marshall later told General Pershing that it was "a very interesting trip professionally and a most magnificent one personally."[58]

Besides exhibiting some of the Army Air Corps's problems, Andrews tutored Marshall on the advantages of long-range airplanes. To avoid the expense of garrisoning Hawaii and Panama with enough planes to meet any situation, Andrews proposed building air bases there. Then, long-range bombers stationed in the United States could be flown overseas in case of attack. Marshall listened carefully, and Andrews discovered one of Marshall's strengths: a desire to make decisions based upon all the evidence. Afterward he told Claire Egtvedt, president of the Boeing Aircraft Corporation, that Marshall would "occupy an important position" in Washington. Andrews also stated that the firsthand knowledge Marshall had gained on the trip would "be of value to him in future War Department decisions in which he will have a hand."[59] In Marshall, Andrews found a potential friend of air power.

The trip affected Marshall. Upon his return to Washington, Marshall took steps to remove one of the major difficulties he had seen. Too many trained specialists, such as weathermen or mechanics, who were trained at great expense, chose not to reenlist or purchased their discharge to take a more lucrative civilian job. Marshall wanted the men reporting for special training to be discharged and immediately reenlisted for three years. That way, they would still have two years of service left after completing their training, but by that time they would have reached a sufficient rank to keep them from wanting to buy their discharges. General Craig thought Marshall had a good idea, but he never carried it out. Nevertheless, Marshall had shown a greater interest in the condition of the Army Air Corps than any other member of the General Staff.[60]

At the state convention of the West Virginia chapter of the American Legion, Marshall demonstrated that he understood the problems involved in aircraft production. He told the legionnaires that aviation had "progressed with such leaps and bounds, such unbelievable advances in speed and distance, in altitude, and in size, that it staggers the imagination. . . ." This rapid advancement, however, had made it difficult to choose the type of planes needed. Designing and building a prototype took five years, and it took another year to put the plane into production. By that time the airplane's "obsolescence is becoming apparent." However, Marshall still failed to see the superiority of large bombers over smaller ones. Addressing the Air Corps Tactical School at Maxwell Field, he said that pilots flying smaller planes required less training than those flying large planes. He also believed that smaller planes would be better in a theater of operation lacking modern airfields. Marshall asked the army fliers to become acquainted with the needs of the entire army because the "War Department needs Air experts who understand the Army, for we must have a team."[61] His desire to foster team spirit matched that of Andrews, Westover, and Arnold.

As Arnold noted after the Second World War, Marshall "needed plenty of indoctrination about the air facts of life." However, Andrews had shown Marshall the realities involved in aircraft production and made him aware of many of the difficulties faced by the Army Air Corps. Unlike other ground officers, Marshall actually listened to the fliers and changed his mind if the evidence warranted a change. His willingness to listen to the airmen played an important role in shaping America's military planning for the Second World War. By the time the United States entered the war, Marshall was convinced that strategic bombing played an important role in the army team.

VII. Roosevelt and the Munich Crisis

When the Second World War began in September of 1939, President Roosevelt told the American people that he could not ask them to "remain neutral in thought."[1] As the conflict overseas intensified, FDR moved from thoughts to action. In a fireside chat in December of 1940, he stated that the United States "must be the great arsenal of democracy,"[2] and following the adoption of the Lend-Lease legislation, he said on March 15, 1941, that "our country is going to be what our people have proclaimed it must be—the arsenal of democracy."[3] These policies, enunciated under the pressure of war, had their foundations in the Munich Crisis of 1938.

Throughout the spring and summer of 1938, Hitler pressured Czechoslovakia to surrender the Sudetenland, but the Czechs refused to succumb. A war seemed likely, since France was willing to fight if Germany invaded Czechoslovakia, but the French overestimated the Luftwaffe and feared the Germans would control the skies. To remedy the situation, the French government embarked upon an aerial rearmament program in early 1938. The Neutrality Act of 1937 required shipments of American-built planes to France stopped if a war broke out, but the French, encouraged by a movement in Congress to repeal or amend the law, believed the United States would be another source for combat planes.

By January, 1938, many Americans recognized that the Neutrality Law had treated aggressors and victims similarly in the Spanish Civil War and the Japanese invasion of China. Bills were introduced in Congress to repeal the act or allow the president to apply discriminatory embargoes against aggressors. In March, Roosevelt gave his unofficial support for revision, but when the House Foreign Affairs Committee voiced unanimous opposition to revision, he withdrew his support. Legislation to repeal the embargo on arms shipments to the Spanish Republicans received more support. Most Americans realized that the embargo hurt the Republicans more than the Fascists. Others wanted the United States to follow its traditional policy of supporting the established governments, which was in this case the Spanish Republicans. Still others, disgusted by the Fascist air raids on Republican-held towns, feared a Fascist victory. President Roosevelt favored the Spanish Republicans, but he refused to intercede. The recent economic backslide absorbed his attention, and the failed attempt at packing the Supreme Court had weakened him politically. FDR contemplated lifting the embargo but decided against it. After a meeting with congressional Democrats, he told Harold Ickes that lifting the embargo would lose every Catholic vote in the fall elections, because the Spanish Republicans opposed the Catholic Church.[4]

Congressional reconsideration of the Neutrality Law convinced the French that Americans would not remain idle in case of a war with Germany, and President Roosevelt strengthened their misconception. On January 12, 1938, Amaury de la Grange, a French senator and old friend of the president, asked FDR to sell France one thousand planes like those flown by the Army Air Corps. Roosevelt said that the Neutrality Law would "hinder" French purchases in wartime, but he expressed a desire to help. Senator de la Grange left the White House believing that Roosevelt had offered to help France reinforce its air force during peace or war. Uncertain of Roosevelt's ability to help, the French minister of defense, Edouard Daladier, asked Ambassador William Bullitt to make further inquiries. In February, Bullitt and Jean Monnet, a French industrialist, visited Roosevelt in Washington. Roosevelt explained that he had been trying to change the Neutrality Law to allow discriminatory embargoes, and he promised to push the necessary legislation through Congress if war broke out. He told them he would get around the Neutrality Law by sending planes through Canada. With this assurance, the French initiated efforts to buy planes from the United States, but neither Secretary of State Hull nor Secretary of War Woodring knew what Roosevelt had pledged. In March, Daladier, now the premier, and his minister for air, Guy La Chambre, sent Jean Monnet back to Washington to discuss aircraft purchases with Roosevelt. At that time, Roosevelt still intended to have the arms embargo removed and told Monnet so.[5] Roosevelt later changed his mind about the embargo and thought better of circumventing the Neutrality Law, but the French never took notice. They only remembered the president's willingness to lift the embargo.

After inspecting America's aircraft industry and planes, the French decided to purchase the Curtiss-Wright P-36, but Curtiss-Wright could supply only one hundred planes during the upcoming year. Monnet wanted to buy the plane, despite the small number. Furthermore, the Air Ministry questioned the P-36's ability to stand up to the German planes. The French sent a test pilot to fly the plane and make the decision, but the War Department refused to let him fly the plane. Two years earlier, Roosevelt had approved an anti-espionage policy that prohibited representatives of a foreign power from flying an American military plane until a year after the second production plane had been received. Ignoring his own order, on March 10 Roosevelt gave the French test pilot permission to fly the P-36 with "utmost secrecy." The president also instructed the Air Corps to remove anything secret from the plane before the flight.[6]

On May 11, La Chambre told Ambassador Bullitt that the Armee de l'Air, the French air force, required at least 2,600 first-line airplanes to fight Germany, but it only had 1,500. Although French aircraft manufacturers could produce only forty-five planes a month, La Chambre had promised the French General Staff that he would make up the 1,100-plane deficit by the following spring. Bullitt was shocked to learn that the French still believed Roosevelt would find a way to circumvent the Neutrality Law, and he could not convince them otherwise. Ignoring his protests, La Chambre asked Bullitt to arrange for two of the Army Air Corps's P-36s to be sent to France for inspection before the others arrived. Bullitt reported his conversation to the president, but Roosevelt seemed unconcerned about the French shortages. In a reply drafted by the State Department, FDR said that even with the forty-five planes produced each month and the 100 P-36s on order, the French would be 750 planes short. Roosevelt wanted to know where the French thought they would get them. Unless the French immediately placed more orders, the American aircraft factories, "which already have almost as many orders as they can handle," could not deliver that many planes in time. Roosevelt rejected the request for two of the army's P-36s because of the political risk involved. If the French were upset about the slow delivery of planes, it was the result of their "dilatory methods of doing business and not to any lack of reasonable cooperation on our own part." Furthermore, President Roosevelt assured Bullitt that he would not violate the Neutrality Law.[7] Since they had ordered only one hundred planes while professing to be short 750, Roosevelt believed that the French were not too worried. They could have been trying to involve America in another war. By the end of the Munich Crisis, however, Roosevelt knew that the French were truly worried, and he increased the productive capacity of the American aircraft industry.

As the possibility of war in Europe grew, Roosevelt received alarming reports from his ambassadors. Bullitt informed him that the French General Staff believed the Germans would hold the Siegfried Line with a third of their army, overwhelm the Czechs with the other two-thirds, and destroy Paris with the Luftwaffe. Anticipating that an outbreak of hostilities would result in a repetition of the World War, they planned to hold the Germans with the Maginot Line while a British naval blockade strangled Germany. Gen. Gustave Gamelin, the French chief of staff, thought that two years of blockading would deplete Germany's oil supplies. With the German airplanes and mechanized units paralyzed by a lack of fuel, the Allied armies would march into Germany as easily as they had in late 1918. Despite Bullitt's protests, the French thought that the United States would enter the war as it had in 1917. Bullitt told FDR that the war would destroy Europe and that the United States had to stay out of the war. Somebody had to remain strong enough to pick up the pieces and "keep alive whatever human beings may remain alive in Europe."[8] Roosevelt replied, "May God in His infinite wisdom prove that you are wrong."[9] Hugh R. Wilson, the ambassador to Germany, became interested in the German productive capacity after speaking to his military and air attachés and American aircraft manufacturers visiting Europe that summer. They convinced Wilson that the Germans were producing six or seven thousand planes annually, giving them the best and largest air force in the world. His attachés complained that Washington ignored their reports, and Wilson turned to Roosevelt. Unaware that the Germans had shown the attachés selected units of the Luftwaffe to intimidate them, Wilson told Roosevelt that the Germans had been "consistently willing to show our people about and give them the widest kind of knowledge." He asked the president to send someone to Germany with "sufficient influence to carry conviction" to learn their production methods.[10]

Roosevelt's main concern that summer was purging the Democratic party of its conservative members. By the middle of August, however, he wanted the European democracies to take a firmer stand toward Hitler. Learning that Hitler would use the Nuremberg Nazi Party Congress in September to rally German support for an attack on Czechoslovakia, Roosevelt and Secretary of State Hull indicated publicly that America would support the democracies in case of war. Roosevelt hoped to intimidate Hitler and Mussolini by allowing France and Great Britain to deposit gold in the United States for purchasing war materiel. Secretary of the Treasury Morgenthau opposed the idea, and Secretary Hull advised Roosevelt that he was taking steps the American people would not support. Roosevelt dropped the plan, but he continued his efforts to embolden the French and British. Sir Ronald Lindsay, the English ambassador to the United States, told London that Washington supported a strong stand toward the Germans, and Roosevelt told a French visitor that France could count on the United States for everything but "troops and loans."[11]

President Roosevelt took concrete steps to meet the German menace after hearing Hitler's Nuremberg speech on September 12. He sent Harry Hopkins to the West Coast to survey the aircraft industry with a view toward expanding the production of military aircraft. FDR had decided that war would inevitably come within five years. Echoing Bullitt's belief, he told William Phillips, the American ambassador to Italy, that the United States had to be in a position to pick up the pieces of European civilization and save the "remains of the wreck." If the American people thought the European dictators were threatening America, however, the United States might "wade in with everything we have" to support the Allies. Postulating that, unlike 1914 when Americans tried to be neutral in thought, 90 percent of Americans were now anti-German and anti-Italian, Roosevelt said, "I would strongly encourage their natural sympathy while at the same time avoiding any thought of sending troops to Europe."[12] This is what Roosevelt did when World War II started one year later.

On Friday, September 16, 1938, Chamberlain flew to Berchtesgaden to discuss the surrender of the Sudetenland to Germany.[13] The submission of France and Great Britain to German pressure disgusted President Roosevelt. He told his cabinet that Chamberlain was for peace at any price and that the French and British would sell the Czechs out to the Germans and then "wash the blood from their Judas Iscariot hands." The following day, Roosevelt told Harold Ickes that the French could not penetrate the German frontier; the attempt would cost France over a million men. But the Germans could not breach the Maginot Line either. Totally discounting the British army, Roosevelt believed the Russian army could not strike Germany effectively through Romania. Roosevelt explained that he would fight a defensive war. First, he would inform the German people that no nation had designs on German territory, to calm their fears and undermine their morale. Second, he would blockade Germany; third, he would make it principally an air war. With Great Britain, France, and Russia pounding Germany from the air, Germany would be unable to defend itself, and the German civilians would crack before the French and

British. Roosevelt said that an air war would cost less, have compara-tively fewer casualties, and be more likely to succeed than a tradi-tional land and sea war. Conveniently, Roosevelt left Italy out of his strategy, but Mussolini still had a stake in keeping Germany from get-ting too powerful.[14]

Like the French General Staff, President Roosevelt assumed a gen-eral war in Europe would be a repetition of the last war. His comments to Ickes echoed William Bullitt's reports of a stalemate on the Franco-German border and a naval blockade. However, Roosevelt's ideas about the results of an air war did not echo those of the French General Staff. Like the Luftwaffe, the Armee de l'Air was designed for ground sup-port, and the French army generals put little faith in strategic bomb-ing. Roosevelt's assumptions about civilian morale and the low cost of an air war came from the advocates of strategic bombing, such as Billy Mitchell. In *Skyways*, Mitchell had written:

> Should a war take place on the ground between two industrial nations
> in the future, it can only end in absolute ruin, if the same methods
> that the ground armies have followed before should be resorted to.
> Fortunately, an entirely new element has come into being, that of air
> power. Air power can attack the vital centers [population and produc-
> tion centers] of the opposing country directly, completely destroying or
> paralyzing them. Very little of a great nation's strength has to be ex-
> pended in conducting air operations. A few men and comparatively
> few dollars can be used for bringing about the most terrific effect ever
> known against opposing vital centers.[15]

Roosevelt knew that a blockade and an air war would bring starva-tion and death to German civilians, but the bombing of Germany would not be in retaliation for the bombing of Paris and London. Like the advocates of strategic bombing, Roosevelt anticipated millions of casualties and the complete destruction of European civilization in a repetition of the World War. When viewed that way, Roosevelt's plan for defeating Germany seemed the more humane approach.

Once the Czechs agreed, under Anglo-French pressure, to sur-render the Sudetenland on September 21, Roosevelt believed war might be averted. However, fresh demands from Hitler once again increased the chances of war. The French continued mobilizing, prepared to evacuate Paris, and packed up the art treasures of the Louvre for safe storage against German bombs. The British issued gas masks to civil-ians and dug air raid trenches in London's parks. At a cabinet meet-ing, Roosevelt repeated his ideas on fighting a defensive war, but he still hoped to prevent the conflict. On September 26, FDR appealed to the Europeans to avoid a war in which "the lives of millions of men, women and children in every country involved will most certainly be lost under circumstances of unspeakable horror." Hitler remained unmoved. The next day, Roosevelt asked Mussolini to help negotiate a peace. Then, Hitler changed his mind and invited the leaders of Great Britain, France, and Italy to Munich, where they worked out a settlement. Hitler signed a joint declaration that Great Britain and Germany mutually desired never to go to war, and Chamberlain returned to England to proclaim "that it is peace for our time." During the crisis, Bullitt explained the situation: "If you have enough airplanes you don't have to go to Berchtesgaden."[16] It was a moral that Roosevelt remembered.

Before learning that Hitler had invited Chamberlain, Daladier, and Mussolini to Munich, Bullitt prepared for Roosevelt an estimate of the European air forces. France had 600 combat planes, to be supplemented by 240 British light bombers. French military intelligence mistakenly estimated that the Germans had 6,500 combat planes, two-thirds of them bombers, and that the Italians had 800 pursuit planes and 1,200 bombers. To overcome the German and Italian superiority, Minister for Air La Chambre suggested bypassing the Neutrality Law by building aircraft factories in Canada and letting Americans work there. He also asked for airplane parts, motors, and machine tools. Bullitt believed that the American people would be willing to send airplanes to the French after the Luftwaffe destroyed Paris, and he wanted to let the Allies purchase anything, provided they could pay for it. After learning of the Munich conference, Bullitt urged Roosevelt for a quick reply about exporting planes, motors, and machine tools. "Unless France and England can manufacture in this way and on this scale," he warned, "the time will come again when Hitler will issue a ukase, and make war when it is not obeyed by France and England."[17] Through Bullitt's warnings, Roosevelt learned that an increase in the French air force was vital.

Even though the Czechoslovakia crisis had been resolved at Munich and the threat of war abated, Roosevelt went out of his way to facilitate French purchases of American planes. On September 26, a French air mission requested permission to inspect the various planes being built for the United States Navy. Discovering that the navy prohibited trial flights of its airplanes without presidential approval, they sought the aid of Cordell Hull. He assured the president that the planes carried no secret devices and asked him to approve the flights.[18] Chief of Naval Operations Admiral Leahy suggested the president withhold his official approval because it would form a precedent. If the president wanted to let the French fly the planes, Admiral Leahy recommended giving informal approval to avoid the risk of another nation demanding the same privilege.[19] President Roosevelt faced a greater risk of antagonizing the isolationists in Congress should they learn that he had allowed the French to fly navy planes. By October, 1938, President Roosevelt's conviction that the democracies needed more planes to halt Hitler outweighed his misgivings about antagonizing Congress. On October 4, Roosevelt gave the French air mission his approval.[20]

Throughout the Munich Crisis, Harry Hopkins had toured the West Coast aircraft factories, accompanied by Col. Arthur R. Wilson, the liaison officer between the army and the Works Progress Administration. Hopkins told Wilson that the army and navy were "sitting pretty to get a lot of money in the next relief bill for the national defense *if* they can sell the idea to the President." Hopkins wanted the War Department to present a big program for modern armaments and airplanes. This program would create full employment and get the arsenals going at top speed. Saying that Hopkins "has the ear of the President," Wilson reported Hopkins's remarks to the General Staff with a recommendation that the chief of staff or the deputy chief meet with Hopkins to formulate a plan. Seldom aggressive in seeking funds beyond those appropriated by Congress, the War Department hesitated to seek funds from the WPA, and Hopkins criticized their lackadaisical efforts. Informing Marshall of Hopkins's comment, Wilson suggested that Marshall see Hopkins himself. After Christmas, Marshall told Hopkins about the weak condition of the army and the Army Air Corps. Shocked by the information, Hopkins recommended that Marshall visit Roosevelt personally, but Marshall refused, not wanting to go outside the proper channels. However, he convinced Hopkins to spend several million dollars of WPA funds secretly on machine tools for the manufacture of small arms ammunition. When the British ammunition shortages became desperate in 1940, the production of ammunition had been gearing up for almost a full year. A year delay then would have been disastrous for the British, but more importantly, Marshall started seeking funds in a more aggressive manner. This meeting with Hopkins proved very important to Marshall's career. They became close friends, and Hopkins helped persuade Roosevelt to name Marshall the chief of staff in 1939.[21]

On September 21, Gen. Oscar Westover died in an airplane crash, and Hap Arnold became the chief of the Air Corps. Returning to Washington from his tour of the West Coast factories, Hopkins met with Arnold to discuss aircraft production. In Harry Hopkins, Arnold also found a friend. Concluding that productive capacity needed to be greatly expanded, Hopkins suggested using WPA funds to build more aircraft factories. Arnold, watching the events in Europe, realized that the Army Air Corps might have to expand rapidly. He remembered how foreign and domestic orders for aircraft had swamped the American aviation industry in 1917, and decided on a plan. By enlarging the American aircraft industry to supply the needs of Great Britain and France, the factories needed to expand the Army Air Corps would already be in place. One difficulty, however, was the unwillingness of aircraft manufacturers to invest capital into expanding their factories only to have them sit idle after the government orders were completed. Arnold called a meeting with representatives from all the aircraft manufacturers in the United States and persuaded them to expand their factories.[22]

On September 2, Roosevelt showed Ambassador Wilson's letter of July 11 to Secretary of War Woodring, who became increasingly worried about Germany's growing aerial powers. In early October, Woodring directed Arnold to prepare a plan for expanding the Army Air Corps by 4,000 planes. Calling together his staff, Arnold went around the table and had each officer write on an easel his estimate of the number of planes needed to meet America's worldwide requirements. Accustomed to thinking in terms of only a few planes, they estimated a total of only 1,500 airplanes. Dismayed, Arnold named each area they might have to defend and asked them to reconsider. Still, they came up with a total of only 7,500 airplanes. Thinking in terms of tens of thousands of planes, Arnold realized how difficult it would be to sell his vast expansion scheme if his own staff had such a narrow view. He left the easel in the conference room, and during the Second World War he would point to it as an example of small thinking.[23]

Soon after meeting with his staff, Arnold spoke with the aviation representatives in the Munitions Building. Making no promises, he told them that tens of thousands of planes would be needed. The aircraft manufacturers were used to negotiating for as few as six planes, but they were not shocked. They had also been following the events in Europe. Some of them balked, but most accepted Arnold's ideas for farming out the production of subassemblies to converted industrial plants. The meeting was successful and broke up with plans for more meetings in the future. Having won the support of the aircraft industry, Arnold submitted his expansion plan to the War Department on October 19.[24]

The American public first learned of Roosevelt's concern about the German and Italian threat when William Bullitt returned to Washington on October 13. FDR and Bullitt talked late into the night, and the next day Roosevelt told a press conference that the defense needs of the nation were under reevaluation. The reappraisal had been in progress for over a year but had "been forced to a head by events, developments and information received within the past month." A War Department spokesman announced plans to ask Congress for an increase in the Army Air Corps to more than twice the authorized level of 2,320 planes. Reporters asked General Arnold to name the types of planes under consideration. He explained that the Air Corps, concentrating on speed rather than size, would not order any more thirty-two-ton B-15s. Purchases would be limited to ground support bombers and seventeen-ton B-17s. The Flying Fortresses would be used to attack distant strategic objectives and to reinforce Hawaii, Panama, and Alaska.[25]

The supporters of air power saw in Roosevelt's reappraisal an opportunity to obtain a larger air force. On October 15, Johnson sent Roosevelt and the chief of staff a memorandum outlining America's aerial requirements in wartime and calling for a larger air force. In 1937, the United States had produced only 949 military aircraft of all types and had a shortage of 5,000 aircraft. Johnson argued that America had to build enough planes to meet its requirements at the outbreak of war plus sufficient reserves to replace wartime losses until production could be expanded.[26] Reading press reports that Roosevelt would ask Congress for 10,000 airplanes and a large increase in aircraft factories, General Andrews attempted to convince the General Staff that the bulk of the planes should be B-17s. Writing to Deputy Chief of Staff Marshall, he said that army fliers wanted the GHQ Air Force to consist of a larger percentage of long-range, heavy bombers. In addition to being "of inestimable value" in supporting the Monroe Doctrine, the long-range bomber was the best weapon for controlling the narrow waters around Singapore, the Mediterranean, and Panama. He also warned that purchasing large numbers of airplanes would strengthen the aircraft industry, without creating an air force. The GHQ Air Force needed personnel to operate the new planes. Great Britain and France did not fear Germany's potential air power. They were principally worried about the "German and Italian airplanes sitting on their airdromes with trained combat crews, ready to go." Andrews's appeal to Marshall had little effect. Scheduled to end his tour as commander of the GHQ Air Force in early 1939, Andrews was left out of the planning for the president's expansion program. Nevertheless, Andrews had done his part by instructing George C. Marshall about the problems involved with aircraft production.[27]

In a meeting on October 25 with Bullitt, Secretary Morgenthau, and Jean Monnet over ways to enlarge the Armee de l'Air, President Roosevelt said that the American aircraft industry could supply France with one thousand pursuit planes and one thousand bombers. Roosevelt moved to fulfill his commitment. Later that day, FDR told Assistant Secretary Johnson that he wanted to expand the Army Air Corps and the production of aircraft. Placing him in charge of a three-man committee, which included Aubrey Williams, the deputy administrator of the WPA, Roosevelt instructed Johnson to report on ways to increase the monthly production of military aircraft. Unhindered by presidential restrictions, the committee submitted a plan on October 28 to produce 31,000 planes within two years and increase production capabilities to more than 20,000 planes annually. Private industry would be called on to increase its annual production capacity from 2,600 to 11,000 planes. Meanwhile, government-owned factories would be built with the capacity to produce 20,000 planes a year. They anticipated the plan would cost $855 million.

However, Johnson was not the only official working on an expansion program. Realizing that Secretary Woodring's plan for purchasing 4,000 airplanes fell short of what the president would want, General Arnold submitted a new plan. Less ambitious than Johnson, Arnold proposed expanding the Army Air Corps to 7,000 planes and increasing production capacity to only 10,000 planes annually.[28]

The 14,000-plane difference between the plans submitted by Johnson and Arnold demonstrated that Arnold had failed in March to convince the assistant secretary of war of the need for a balanced air force. The disparity also showed the influence of Harry Hopkins, Aubrey Williams, and the other liberal New Dealers, who hoped to reduce the economic peak and boom periods by increased government spending during hard times and increased taxes during prosperity. Since the first of the year, these New Dealers had tried to convince Roosevelt to move away from the idea of a balanced budget to a more Keynesian approach. They wanted a multi-billion-dollar spending program. Secretary Morgenthau opposed them, but when the stock market crashed again on March 25, 1938, Hopkins and Williams convinced the president to support their spending program. On April 14, Roosevelt asked Congress to authorize a large-scale spending program, and Congress gave him $3.75 billion. Johnson's expansion program was another victory for the Keynesian New Dealers. Williams exploited Johnson's enthusiasm for a large air force and created another way to pump money into the economy. Roosevelt realized what would happen. After all, Roosevelt knew that Williams favored expanded government spending and that Johnson favored an expanded air force.[29] The president might have wanted to increase spending or expand the Army Air Corps, but his main concern was producing enough aircraft to deter Hitler through a show of force.

During the second weekend of November, Roosevelt invited key military and civilian leaders to a White House meeting on November 14. When the conference gathered that Monday afternoon, Roosevelt had before him Secretary of the Treasury Henry Morgenthau, Jr., Assistant Secretary of War Louis Johnson, Administrator of the WPA Harry Hopkins, Solicitor General Robert Jackson, General Counsel of the Treasury Herman Oliphant, Chief of Staff Gen. Malin Craig, Deputy Chief of Staff Gen. George Marshall, Chief of the Air Corps Gen. Hap Arnold, Executive Assistant to the Assistant Secretary of War Col. James Burns, the President's Military Aide Colonel Watson, and the President's Naval Aide Capt. Daniel Callahan. The president did most of the talking. The defenses of the United States were very weak and needed a heavy striking force of army planes. The navy also needed more planes. Any production plans adopted by the army had to leave sufficient facilities for naval aircraft production. Congress should amend procurement bills to allow the use of cost-plus and fixed-fee contracts. Roosevelt wanted to assure the manufacturers that they would receive adequate returns on all investments in expanding their factories. The government would assign construction to any available factory suited for the design. Mass production would flow from the assembly lines, which would not be halted to incorporate alterations. Manufacturers delivering planes below cost estimates and ahead of time could earn a premium. Late delivery dates and excessive costs would incur a penalty.

After Arnold described Britain and France as inferior to Germany and Italy in numbers of airplanes and productive capacity, Roosevelt said that the United States needed an air force large enough to protect the western hemisphere. America must not repeat its 1918 failure to provide airplanes. Since Congress would provide only half of the 20,000 planes and capacity to produce 24,000 planes annually, the War Department had to present an "acceptable" two-year program for 2,500 trainers, 3,750 combat planes and 3,750 reserve combat planes. One-fifth of the 10,000 planes would be built in new government factories, and the rest would come from existing commercial facilities. The WPA needed to construct seven new factories, two building the government's portion of planes and the other five remaining idle until needed for a larger air expansion program.[30]

The president's strong stand on aviation startled most of the men attending the conference, but not Johnson, Burns, Hopkins, or Arnold. Having discussed the expansion beforehand, they had already agreed on a plan. After the meeting, Arnold and Burns gave General Craig what Arnold called a "get-rich-quick course" on how to build an air force. This time, he found Craig to be a "very apt pupil." Arnold left the White House feeling that the Army Air Corps had finally "achieved its Magna Carta." With the president's support for a larger air force, Hap Arnold had the power to create the balanced air force he wanted. Later, Arnold wrote, "A battle was won in the White House that day which took its place with—or at least led to—the victories in combat later for time is a most important factor in building an Air Force. There is no substitute—five years to secure a plane after the designers get the idea, and one year to train personnel after they are inducted."[31] The airplanes with which the Army Air Forces devastated German and Japanese cities were available because of Roosevelt's actions in 1938. However, these same aircraft allowed the Army Air Forces to drive the Luftwaffe from the skies of Europe in 1943-44. Had the Luftwaffe not been defeated, the Normandy invasion might not have been successful, and Nazi tyranny on the European continent might have continued years longer.

President Roosevelt's decision to expand the Army Air Corps marked a significant reversal of his earlier efforts to reduce the Army Air Corps and reduce military expenditures. The events in Europe forced the reversal. With arms limitation a dead issue, the military threat to liberal government from overseas outweighed the threat of being "wrecked on the rocks of loose fiscal policy."[32] However, FDR's willingness to increase spending did not indicate a shift from the First New Deal. He had opposed monopoly by ordering the Army Air Corps to carry the mail, and his expansion program also embodied the idea of controlling business. Government-owned factories, like the TVA, would ensure increased production while providing a "yardstick" to gauge the prices charged by the aircraft industry. Similar to the defunct NRA's codes, the government would assign construction so that no plants remained idle. Also reminiscent of the relief measures of the PWA under the NRA, the WPA would provide increased spending.

Many people believed that Roosevelt really wanted the planes for the British and French rather than the Army Air Corps. The *New Republic* found it "difficult to avoid the suspicion" that behind the president's "desire for a huge air force is a desire to give some measure of support to the British position vis-a-vis Germany; in other words, to build up here the British air reserve which Britain cannot build herself."[33] The absence of Secretary Woodring and General Andrews from the conference on November 14 substantiates that supposition. Woodring was not invited because he opposed expanding the Army Air Corps without a commensurate increase in the rest of the army.[34] Furthermore, if the president had wanted to build a strike force of army planes to defend the western hemisphere as he said, then Andrews, who commanded the strike force of the Army Air Corps, should have been present. Instead, only Arnold, who controlled the procurement of aircraft, attended the meeting. Roosevelt said nothing about airfields or personnel, making it clear that the production of large numbers of planes, not their tactical usage, concerned him. Leaving tactics to the British and French, FDR dealt with the production of airplanes.

Roosevelt told the press that he would ask Congress to defend the western hemisphere by expanding the Army Air Corps.[35] Privately, FDR indicated that he really desired aiding the British and French. Soon after the November 14 conference, he suggested to Arthur Murray ways that the Allies could match the German and Italian air programs. Roosevelt also described methods, outside the Neutrality Law, by which the United States could help them build an overwhelming aerial superiority. Murray relayed the information to Chamberlain.[36]

Despite the president's explicit desire to concentrate on the production of airplanes, his military advisors drew up plans for creating a balanced ground force to go along with the airplanes. General Marshall asked Gen. John J. Pershing to lobby Roosevelt for increased funding of the ground forces. Assistant Secretary Johnson instructed Chief of Staff Craig to prepare a two-year budget for 10,000 planes and seven government-owned aircraft factories, but going far beyond Roosevelt's instructions, Johnson told the General Staff to include the necessary provisions to prepare for a much larger ground force. Under pressure to finish its plans for inclusion in the president's January address to Congress, the General Staff used Air Corps officers to prepare the aviation requirements.[37] Rather than planning for the 10,000 airplanes Roosevelt wanted, they planned for a balanced air force. In addition, the War Plans Division presented its own plan for a ground force capable of rapidly taking control of potential air bases in the western hemisphere.[38]

On December 1, Johnson sent Roosevelt his rearmament program. It included $1.3 billion for an air program, $421 million for supplies to equip the Protective Mobilization Plan Army, and $122 million for industrial preparedness. Roosevelt called his military advisors to another meeting and sharply explained that Congress would not approve more than $500 million. Roosevelt complained that he had asked for airplanes but was being offered everything but airplanes. Less compliant than two weeks before, his advisors replied that the 10,000 planes would become obsolete before they could be used. To this he said that the British could use the planes if the army could not. Clearly intending to use airplanes as a deterrent, Roosevelt explained that planes, not "barracks, runways and schools for mechanics," would influence Hitler. But by the end of the meeting, his advisors changed Roosevelt's mind. The president agreed to ask Congress for $500 million. Of that sum, $320 million would go to the ground forces, leaving $180 million to purchase 3,000 airplanes. On January 12, 1939, Roosevelt asked Congress for the agreed-upon numbers.

Roosevelt had political reasons to scale down his 10,000-plane program. Between November 14 and December 1, Johnson had publicly spoken of the need for a large air force, and Sen. Bennett Clark from Missouri criticized it as a cover for a pump-priming, spending program. Senators George Norris, Gerald Nye, David Walsh, and William Borah expressed the same suspicions, and many newspapers across the nation opposed the building of a huge air force. Had the public greeted Johnson's remarks more favorably, President Roosevelt might not have been so compliant. The aviation program that Roosevelt finally accepted was based on the program Woodring had asked Arnold to prepare back in October. Later known as the Woodring Plan, the plan called for a 5,500-plane Army Air Corps by the middle of 1941. Passed by Congress and signed by Roosevelt on April 26, 1939, the Woodring Plan raised the strength of the Army Air Corps to 6,000 planes, 3,203 officers, and 45,000 enlisted men.[39]

Roosevelt's speech to Congress initiated new calls for long-range bombers. Three days after the speech, the *New York Times* printed a graph showing the range of the B-17: with five tons, it could fly from New York City to Washington and back, a 300-mile radius; with three tons, it could make a round trip to Cincinnati, a 900-mile radius.[40] The inference was obvious; if a B-17 could fly 900 hundred miles westward over the United States, it could as easily fly the same distance eastward over the Atlantic. Although not credited to the GHQ Air Force, the graph looked like something made by Andrews and his men, but Andrews was blunter than that. On January 17, he warned the National Aeronautic Association that air power could not be created by purchasing airplanes. To possess real air power, the United States needed trained crews and long-range bombers to meet any emergency.[41]

Like so many others, General Andrews thought that FDR only wanted to strengthen the Army Air Corps. However, the American people discovered that was not necessarily the case. After meeting with Roosevelt on October 25, Monnet had convinced Premier Daladier to place a large order for American planes. Warning of the need for absolute secrecy, Daladier told his defense council on December 5 that France might receive one thousand of the United States Army Air Corps's latest planes, and Monnet returned to Washington to purchase them. Aware that Woodring, Craig, and Arnold would oppose the sale of American planes to the French, Roosevelt had Monnet deal with Secretary Morgenthau, who favored aircraft sales to the Allies. Roosevelt justified his decision by claiming that the procurement division of the Treasury Department was more experienced in handling large scale purchases than the War Department. Woodring learned of Monnet's mission when the Frenchman asked to see the newest army planes. The secretary of war objected, but the president had made up his mind. Calling France America's first line of defense, Roosevelt gave Morgenthau a note granting the French permission to inspect and purchase the planes.[42]

Negotiations with the French had been confidential, but the press learned of Monnet's mission when a bomber carrying a French inspector crashed on January 23. General Arnold was testifying before the Senate Military Affairs committee when the senators heard about the crash. Under questioning, Arnold admitted knowledge of the Frenchman's presence to Senator Clark but tried to explain that the plane carried no secret devices. Clark asked who had permitted the Frenchman to see the plane, and Arnold said that permission came from Secretary Morgenthau. Later, the committee forced Secretary Woodring to admit that Roosevelt had authorized the inspection. Chairman Morris spoke to Roosevelt and reported that there was nothing to worry about. Still skeptical, the whole committee called upon the president. FDR explained that he wanted the American people to gradually realize the danger of world domination by Germany, Italy, and Japan. A series of Pacific islands defended by the navy, army, and Army Air Corps formed America's first line of defense, but England and France acted as America's first line of defense in the Atlantic. If the Axis destroyed the British and French air forces, "their factories, including their airplane factories, which, of course, are in a very small area—you could put the whole of England into the State of New York and you could put France very easily into the area of New England— would be put out of commission in short order." Without planes and other implements of war, France and England would be defeated and forced to cede their African colonies. The rest of Europe would fall under Hitler's domination. Next would be the Nazi domination of Latin American countries by controlling their commerce with Europe or inciting fascist revolutions. A Nazi foothold in Latin America would threaten the United States. From Venezuela, he mistakenly claimed, their planes could fly to Miami in two hours and fifty-five minutes, and planes from Colombia could reach the Panama Canal in fifty minutes. Also incorrectly, Roosevelt said that Germany had 1,500 bombers capable of flying from Germany to Colombia within forty-eight hours. The United States had "about eighty that can go down there." To prepare for such an emergency, Roosevelt wanted to achieve the mass production of airplanes through large orders. Since French and British orders furthered that goal, the president welcomed them. Moreover, foreign orders would reduce unemployment in America and strengthen France. He promised to make the Allies pay cash for the planes and protect America's only real military secret, the Norden bomb sight. Despite pledging to keep the meeting secret, someone on the Military Affairs Committee told the press that Roosevelt regarded France as America's frontier. Roosevelt called it a "deliberate lie," but the public controversy did not abate until Monnet purchased 555 planes and returned to France in March.[43] By then, the American people knew that Roosevelt planned to sell planes to the Allies. His intention to make America the arsenal of democracy was clear long before he formally announced it.

Roosevelt's use of New York and New England as examples to the Senate Military Affairs committee showed that the army fliers had influenced the president. The GHQ Air Force's highly publicized cold-weather and Farmingdale blackout tests had studied ways to defend the area. Warnings about the area's vulnerability to air attack had impressed him. Furthermore, the president's comparison of the vulnerability of the British and French aircraft factories to those in the New York–New England area would not have been lost on the senators. Because of the B-17 flights to Latin America, nobody could ignore Roosevelt's warning about 1,500 German planes in South America.

Monnet's air mission influenced President Roosevelt's decision to compromise on his 10,000-airplane plan.[44] Monnet's arrival with the money and the authority to buy American planes suggested that more foreign orders would follow, having the same effect on America's aviation industry as would increased orders from the Army Air Corps. Factories would be expanded, and American productive capacity would grow. Also, when war had seemed imminent in September of 1938, Ambassador Bullitt had told Roosevelt that "the horror and hatred evoked by German bombings will be so great that the people of the United States . . . will not feel inclined to prevent planes purchased before the outbreak of war from being sent to defend whatever may be left of France from further German bombings."[45] Should war break out, Roosevelt knew that he would have less difficulty in shipping planes bought beforehand than shipping planes designated for the Army Air Corps. Between the opposition from his military advisors, the threats from isolationists, and the prospect of increased French orders, Roosevelt had every reason to agree to a smaller, but balanced, Army Air Corps.[46]

The Neutrality Law would not have hindered the shipment of American planes to France. Roosevelt had gotten around it for half of 1938. By not declaring the Sino-Japanese conflict a war, Roosevelt allowed American arms manufacturers to sell weapons, but the Roosevelt administration ensured that only the Chinese received American arms. In June, Secretary of State Hull publicly condemned the bombing of civilians and discouraged American manufacturers from selling bombers to countries practicing that form of warfare. Since Japan was bombing civilians in China, the manufacturers understood what Hull meant. To further that policy, Hull warned that the State Department would issue "with great regret" licenses authorizing exportation of airplanes, parts, or bombs to countries "making use of airplanes for attack upon civilian populations." Aircraft sales to the Chinese were not prohibited, because they were not bombing Japanese civilians.

Secretary Hull stopped the sale of aircraft and aircraft parts to Japan with the president's approval. After seeing an article about markets for airplanes and parts in Asia, Roosevelt asked Under Secretary of State Sumner Welles if aviation sales to Japan might be cut further. Welles gave the president a copy of the letter sent to the manufacturers and reported that, with the exception of the United Aircraft Corporation, most had cooperated. Sales of airplanes and parts to Japan had dropped from $1,710,049 in June to only $7,215 in October. To force United Aircraft to cooperate, Welles planned on publicizing the company's "failure to conform to the Department's policy. . . ."[47] Since Roosevelt did not object, he approved the State Department's actions. A year later, on December 2, 1939, FDR formally suggested to manufacturers that they refrain from selling airplanes to belligerents who bombed civilians.[48] The National Munitions Control Board reprinted Secretary Hull's letter in its annual report to Congress, and a *New York Times* editorial pointed to it as evidence of Roosevelt's skirting the Neutrality Law by declaring that a war did not exist. The *Times* supported Roosevelt's actions because in this case the Neutrality Act did not represent the opinion or serve the interests of the American people.[49]

The *Times* and other Americans did not know how far the president would support the Chinese and oppose the Japanese. Chief of Naval Operations Admiral Leahy sent Roosevelt a memorandum containing parts of another letter on policy from Admiral Yarnell. Motivated by a lack of raw materials, Japan wanted to turn China into another Manchukuo. Since China lacked oil, iron ore, rubber, wool, and other necessities, Japan would "extend her domination over the Philippines, Netherlands Indies, and any other lands containing the necessary items." If the United States chose to oppose the Japanese, it had to make a joint announcement with the other signatories of the Nine Power Treaty that no Sino-Japanese agreement would be recognized unless it maintained Chinese independence and territorial integrity. The signatories could not make loans or ship war materials to Japan. The United States had to strengthen its defenses in the Philippines, Guam, and Hawaii. Yarnell specifically recommended an "increase of Army and Navy aviation in the Philippines." Japan depended upon sea communications for supplies and to supply its troops in China. "Any threat against these lines of communication," wrote Yarnell, "will have a profound effect on her attitude of mind regarding the settlement of the present controversy."[50] As relations with Japan deteriorated in 1941, President Roosevelt remembered Yarnell's proposal to threaten Japan's supply lines as a way to halt Japanese aggression.

However, Yarnell's recommendations had a more immediate effect. When the seventy-sixth Congress met in January, the first document filed was the report of the Naval Board, headed by Rear Adm. Arthur J. Hepburn. Among other places, the board recommended the construction of air and submarine bases at Guam, Wake, Johnson, Palmyra, Canton, and Rose islands. Establishing a base at Guam would assure the practical immunity of the Philippines to a major attack, simplify the defense of Hawaii and the West Coast, and allow the United States Fleet greater freedom to operate in the Atlantic Ocean should an emergency arise. Fortifying Guam meant a major extension of American naval power into the Western Pacific. A strong base at Guam, which was located in the middle of the Japanese Marianas and only 1,353 miles from Yokohama, threatened Japan's predominance in the area. *Kokumin*, a newspaper that expressed the views of the Japanese army and ultranationalists, warned the United States against establishing fortifications on Guam or Wake Islands. Rep. Carl Vinson introduced legislation to implement the Hepburn Report, and Roosevelt supported it. The House passed the Naval Appropriations Bill but deleted the provision to improve the harbor and seaplane facilities at Guam.[51]

The roots of President Roosevelt's Far Eastern policy in 1941 came from Admiral Yarnell and the Hepburn Report. Yarnell suggested that threatening Japan's sea communications would force them to stop their aggressive behavior. The Hepburn Report declared that the establishment of a base at Guam would assure the practical immunity of the Philippines to a major attack, simplify the defense of Hawaii and the West Coast, and allow the United States Navy greater freedom to operate in the Atlantic Ocean should an emergency arise. The destruction of the French navy in 1940 created that emergency. When the Japanese threatened to move into the Dutch East Indies in 1941, Roosevelt combined Yarnell's recommendations with those of the Hepburn Report. Deterrence became the cornerstone of America's foreign policy toward Japan.

VIII. Strategic Planning and the Army Air Corps

Despite Hap Arnold's appointment as the assistant chief of the Air Corps, officers in the Air Corps and GHQ Air Force continued to struggle for dominance. The General Staff realized that the divided command was unworkable and reorganized the Army Air Corps. Effective March 1, 1939, the adjutant general placed the GHQ Air Force under the command of the chief of the Air Corps "to meet the difficult problems relating to personnel and training due to the augmentation of the Air Corps." Believing the primary task of the Army Air Corps was an orderly expansion, General Arnold once again opposed efforts to form a separate air force. In February, 1939, Arnold warned the Senate Military Affairs Committee that any drastic organizational change might hinder the rearmament program.[1] However, many officers within the GHQ Air Force objected to being placed under the chief of the Air Corps. Lt. Col. Russell L. Maxwell, who had been transferred to the War Department, expressed the GHQ Air Force's view to General Marshall. Since the Air Corps took care of materiel and aircraft development, Maxwell explained, the GHQ Air Force was free to develop tactics and train personnel. If the chief of the Air Corps took control over the GHQ Air Force, materiel and personnel assignments might become more important than leadership, tactics, and bombing. Furthermore, the division of the Army Air Corps created a "healthy growing condition" that suppressed the clamor for a separate air arm.[2] Despite Maxwell's objections, Arnold convinced Marshall that the expansion program required clear lines of authority, and the reorganization proceeded.[3]

By 1939, the General Staff trusted Arnold enough to give him command of the air arm, but the vocal advocates of long-range bombers lost their leaders. Gen. Delos C. Emmons replaced Andrews, who became the air officer of the Eighth Corps Area. When Billy Mitchell had lost his job as the assistant chief of the Air Service, the army had sent him to the Eighth Corps Area. The meaning of Andrews's assignment could not have been missed. Also, Lieutenant Colonel Knerr was forced to retire.[4]

Like Billy Mitchell and General Fechet before him, Knerr did not remain silent after leaving the army. Unfettered by superiors, Knerr did something he would never have dared if still in uniform. Somehow, possibly through Edwin Watson, Knerr got a paper entitled "Air Power for the United States" into the hands of President Roosevelt. This paper contained the usual claims made by the advocates of air power: air power had become the most powerful "instrument" available for national defense, offense, or "diplomatic threat"; national policies had to be backed up with air power; air power could greatly augment a small military force and ensure greater freedom of action to the navy; and the inertia of military conservatism had hindered air power. Placing the GHQ Air Force under the command of the chief of the Air Corps, who always placed "convenience of administration . . . over efficiency in operation," was a mistake. By taking experienced personnel from tactical units to fill supply and administrative functions, the chief of the Air Corps had made the operations of the tactical units "unduly hazardous." To correct the situation, the paper recommended the creation of a chief of staff for air, who would report directly to the secretary of war. President Roosevelt became angry after reading the paper, and once General Arnold learned about it, he became furious. Suspecting Knerr, Arnold sought proof that he had written it. One of the president's cabinet members warned Knerr, and he quickly covered his tracks.[5]

The reason for Arnold's anger was understandable. He, Westover, and Andrews had worked hard at convincing the General Staff and the president that the Army Air Corps was made up of reliable team players, who no longer used the antagonistic methods of Billy Mitchell. For the first time, Arnold had the authority and the funds to build the balanced air force he sought, and Knerr had jeopardized his plans. However, Arnold was angered by the way Knerr acted, not by what he said. With the exception of the complaint about military conservatism, Knerr expressed ideas that reappeared in 1941 as reasons for sending B-17s to the Philippines.[6]

The expansion program occupied most of Arnold's attention, but he continued to publicize the abilities of the Army Air Corps with well-staged feats. On August 2, 1939, the thirtieth anniversary of the purchase of the army's first airplane, the Army Air Corps celebrated with a nationwide event. Upon a signal from President Roosevelt in Washington, over 1,500 army planes simultaneously took to the air from airfields across the nation. Between thirty and fifty million Americans witnessed the army planes flashing through the skies. At Wright Field, Arnold informed several hundred listeners that the Army Air Corps had broken a number of aviation records over the past four days, and he stressed that the fliers had used standard army equipment.[7]

Sending up 1,500 army planes on his signal must have had a special significance for President Roosevelt. In February, he had observed naval maneuvers in the Caribbean. The exercises presumed that a European nation had sent troops to aid a revolution in South America. These attackers planned to occupy a base in the Windward Islands, from which their bombers would weaken the United States fleet enough for the attacking fleet to defeat it. After the maneuvers, Roosevelt said he had no idea that, for seven days straight, the United States could launch six hundred planes from airfields, cruisers, and aircraft carriers without losing a single plane. Still, he remained unconvinced that airplanes alone could stop a fleet. The attacking force managed to send planes, submarines, and cruisers into the Windward Islands, where they theoretically destroyed several bases. Discussing the maneuvers with the press, Roosevelt expressed his apprehension that bombers based in Latin America could attack the United States. To make all Americans aware of the threat, he said that bombers from Tampico could reach Kansas City in three and a half hours. FDR claimed that the Axis powers had about 1,500 aircraft that could leave their countries that night, be in the Cape Verde Islands the following morning, and be in Brazil that afternoon. Reiterating that the Axis had the airplanes, Roosevelt said that the United States had only "eighty planes that could get there in time to meet them. They have 1500."[8] Roosevelt overestimated the capabilities of the Axis air forces, but his concern about air attacks from Latin America demonstrated the influence of the Army Air Corps. Over the previous five years, General Andrews had repeatedly stated that one of the GHQ Air Force's primary missions was to keep "nests" of enemy bombers out of range of the United States. The B-17 flights to South America a year earlier had shown Roosevelt that long-range bombers could be rushed there to meet an enemy attack. By the spring of 1939, the Army Air Corps had convinced President Roosevelt that the GHQ Air Force could defend the United States with enough long-range bombers. His conversion came about not as a result of rancor and wild claims but from clear-cut demonstrations of the Army Air Corps's abilities.

Roosevelt had not forgotten the frightening role of bombers in modern warfare. The war in China would not let him forget. On July 6, the American ambassador to China complained that the Japanese were still indiscriminately bombing civilian targets and had almost hit American property. In response, Roosevelt sent the Japanese ambassador a personal protest and asked for an informal reply. Ambassador Kensuke Horinouchi dismissed the charges, saying that the Japanese military commanders in China had orders to avoid injuring persons or property of other nations. Ten days later, Horinouchi gave Secretary Hull two informal statements from the Japanese government. Hull said they were unsatisfactory but advised the president to drop the subject. Roosevelt continued to pressure the Japanese. When the Japanese forced the British to acknowledge Japan's responsibility for maintaining order in occupied areas, Roosevelt announced the abrogation of a 1911 trade agreement with Japan. The bombing of Chinese citizens continued, but the Japanese feared pushing the United States into taking harsher measures.[9]

The possibility of a war in Europe grew after the Nazi-Soviet non-aggression pact of August 23, 1939, cleared the way for a German attack on Poland. This time, the British and French refused to submit to German aggression. The German armies swept into Poland on September 1, the same day that George C. Marshall became chief of staff. France and Great Britain declared war on Germany two days later, and the European war, dreaded for so long, had begun.

The European war brought President Roosevelt reminders of the accuracy and range of America's bombers. In preparation for war, Prime Minister Chamberlain asked Roosevelt to provide Norden bomb sights for the RAF. Chamberlain claimed that the Norden sight's accuracy would increase British power more than any other weapon available. Promising to attack only legitimate military targets and avoid indiscriminate bombing of civilians, Chamberlain said that "air bombardment accuracy and humanity really go together." Roosevelt refused the request, but it reminded him of the accuracy claimed by the GHQ Air Force's bomber crews. FDR had only a vague notion of the performance characteristics of the Flying Fortress. In late September, Roosevelt discussed with Sen. Sheridan Downey, a California Democrat, the importance of long-range bombers to national defense. Downey asked what the range of the planes was, but Roosevelt did not know. Watson overheard their conversation and telephoned General Arnold for the information. Without bombs, the B-17 had a range of 3,000 miles and a radius of 1,000 miles. With a maximum bomb load of 8,800 pounds, it had a range of 1,000 miles and a radius of 400 miles. The normal load was 4,000 pounds, giving the plane a range of 1,800 miles and a 750-mile radius.[10] Roosevelt's inability to recite the range of the B-17 was not as important as his perception of the B-17 as a long-range weapon. The long flights to South America had influenced the president.[11]

Roosevelt's plans to expand the Army Air Corps initiated a new debate within the army about the mission of the Army Air Corps. To settle the question, Chief of Staff Craig created a board on March 23, 1939, to study the strategic and tactical use of the Army Air Corps in accordance with national policies. General Arnold presided over the air board. Acting on the advice of Lt. Col. Carl Spaatz, chief of the Air Corps Plans Division (ACPD), Arnold convinced the other members to expand the scope of the study to include the mission, doctrines, and composition of the forces required by the Army Air Corps. Submitting its report on May 7, the air board made two basic assumptions. First, the primary function of the armed services was to defend United States territory by deterring or defeating an invasion. Second, an enemy would establish a series of ever-closer bases from which attacks on the vital centers of the United States would be launched. Defining air power as "the measure of a nation's capacity to wage air warfare," the air board stated that air power could be effective only if the combat units operated as a single force. Since the mission of air power was offensive, an enemy's air force could be defeated only by attacking its air bases. Neglecting defensive fighters, the air board called for bombers with a range greater than an enemy's bombers, enabling American bombers to attack enemy bases sooner than the enemy could strike. The air board wanted most production devoted to bombers. The President's Aviation Expansion Program, completed on June 12, adopted the recommendations of the air board. Of twenty-four groups, thirteen were to be bomber groups—five heavy bomber, six medium bomber, and two light or attack bomber groups— and only nine were to be fighter groups.

When he submitted the air board's report to Secretary Woodring on September 1, General Marshall made a significant addition. Earlier, Marshall had read a memorandum written by Col. J. W. Anderson in the War Plans Division. Anderson stated that the army must be prepared for quick, limited operations in the mid-Pacific, Caribbean, Latin America, and possibly Europe. Once these needs were met, there might not be a need for large armies. Instead, the Army Air Corps could conduct "active and aggressive" defensive operations beyond American territory, but to carry out these operations, the United States required advanced bases to deepen the defensive zone around its vital areas. General Marshall suggested incorporating Anderson's ideas into the report. In particular, Marshall wanted to protect America's vital installations through "the wise strategic location of our Air Bases" and an "adequate radius of action of our airplanes." Woodring approved the report with Marshall's suggestions. For the first time, the Army Air Corps had a clearly defined mission.[12]

The General Staff accepted the ideas expressed in the air board's report and incorporated them in official correspondence. President Roosevelt received a letter calling for airplanes with a range equal to the navy's ships. In an emergency, these planes could be flown to an overseas base. Roosevelt asked the WPD to comment on the letter. Like the president, the WPD did not believe that air power alone could stop an enemy fleet. Rejecting the call for such long-ranged bombers, the WPD said that the Army Air Corps only needed planes with a radius greater than an enemy's bombers. This requirement could be met by the "wise strategic location of our Air Bases" and with an "adequate radius of action of our airplanes." The 2,000-mile-radius bomber already authorized for construction would be sufficient. Denouncing the proposal to fly bombers to critical areas in an emergency, the WPD stated, "Reinforcement of Panama by heavy and medium bombardment and of Hawaii by heavy bombardment is not possible without recourse to staging points in territory not under our jurisdiction." This remark was foolish. General Andrews's planes had already flown non-stop from Miami to Panama and further. The president had a better understanding of the range of modern airplanes than the WPD did. Nevertheless, the air board's report had become the official doctrine for employment of the Army Air Corps, codified in Field Manual 1-5, *Employment of the Aviation of the Army*, on April 15, 1940.[13] The readiness of the General Staff to adopt the air board report with little criticism indicated that the General Staff no longer held the deep suspicion and resentment of the airmen it once had.

Unlike the president and the WPD, the Army Air Corps believed that airplanes could stop an enemy fleet. To determine the requirements for implementing the air board report, Arnold instructed Lieutenant Colonel Spaatz to make studies based upon five strategic areas: the Far East, Expeditionary Forces, the Pacific, the Atlantic Coast, and the Caribbean. Spaatz's first plan, "Strategically Offensive Operations in the Far East," estimated the composition and the general method of employment of airplanes in operations against Japan. This plan embodied the army fliers' belief in air power, but it also included ideas similar to Admiral Yarnell's about fighting Japan. The ACPD saw three ways of forcing Japan to acquiesce to American demands: invade Japan, institute a naval blockade, or conduct a sustained air attack on the critical elements of Japanese industry. Since Japanese land-based airplanes could prevent the first two methods, the Air Corps planners favored the third. The ACPD reasoned that Japan, with its industries and population concentrated in relatively small areas, was extremely vulnerable, and a sustained air attack could probably force Japanese acquiescence. However, the "mere existence of a land-based striking force, based within effective operation radius of Japan, would probably be sufficient to restrain Japan from open and active opposition to our national policies." These operations required a secure base near Japan. Obtaining a base in Chinese, British, or Russian territory involved unwanted political encumbrances. The planners saw Luzon as the most viable location, but they knew that the Japanese could occupy it before reinforcements from America could arrive. Yet, if an air base was prepared beforehand, a strike force, using islands as stepping stones, could fly across the Pacific at the outbreak of hostilities, "establish an air defense zone about the Island of Luzon and prevent its seizure by Japan by interdiction of its overseas expedition." This strike force could hold Luzon until more units arrived to conduct the air campaign against Japan. To stop an invasion fleet and prevent the Japanese from initiating "counter air force operations," the strike force required two groups of heavy bombers, two squadrons of long-range reconnaissance planes, three groups of medium bombers, three squadrons of medium-range reconnaissance planes, and two groups of interceptors. The ACPD stated that the strike force needed this many units just to defend the island. To conduct strategic operations against Japan, the strike force had to have six more groups of heavy bombers.

If the Philippines were to be fortified, the Air Corps planners suggested a four-step procedure: first, expand the air base facilities on Luzon without increasing the size of the Air Corps units stationed there; second, form the initial defense force in the United States; third, and only after the first two phases had been completed, dispatch the total defense force to Luzon; and fourth, maintain in the United States the additional force needed to conduct a sustained strategic offensive against Japan. General Arnold forwarded all five of the ACPD's plans to the WPD, but the War Department ignored the Far East plan.[14]

The War Department placed little faith in the ACPD's plan and refused to fortify the Philippines, lest the Japanese consider it a challenge. Earlier, the War Department had joined with the State Department to oppose the navy's plans to improve facilities on Guam. The fear of provoking the Japanese stemmed from a belief that the Philippines could not be defended. Since the Great War, the Joint Army and Navy Board had prepared plans for war with any number of adversaries, with each potential enemy designated by a color. Under War Plan ORANGE, which was a war with Japan, the American garrison in the Philippines would fight holding actions until the main battle fleet relieved them. American and Japanese naval officers anticipated a great, Jutland-style naval battle to decide the outcome of the war, but U.S. Army officers doubted the ability of the small Philippine garrison to hold the Bataan Peninsula and Corregidor until the fleet arrived. Even navy officers had their doubts, because the fleet would need a secure harbor in the Far East to operate effectively. These doubts were incorporated into the army's war plans. The 1928 and 1938 versions of ORANGE expected the Japanese to mobilize and transport an overwhelming number of troops to the Philippines within thirty days.

By April, 1939, the Joint Army and Navy Board recognized that the possibility of cooperation between Germany, Italy, and Japan had made the color plans obsolete. Therefore, the joint board instructed each service to consider fighting a coalition of enemies in a variety of different situations. The result was a set of five new plans, called RAINBOW plans, indicating various coalitions of enemies. RAINBOW 1 planned for the United States to defend North America with no major allies. RAINBOW 2 envisioned the United States allied with Great Britain and France. Under this second plan, the United States would conduct offensive actions in the Pacific while Great Britain and France fought in Europe. RAINBOW 3 was similar to RAINBOW 2, except that the United States received no help from the British and French. RAINBOW 4 had the United States defending the entire Western Hemisphere without allies. RAINBOW 5 called for the United States to fight a defensive war in the Pacific while conducting major offensive operations with Britain and France in Europe. Once the Axis had been defeated in Europe, RAINBOW 5 planned for a major attack on Japan. Despite the different scenarios envisioned, one premise did not change in the new RAINBOW plans. The army still believed that the Philippines were indefensible.[15] By the middle of 1941, however, the War Department had revised its appraisal.

Like Yarnell, the ACPD planned for an economic war against Japan. Both pictured Japan's industrial strength as its weakness. Whereas Yarnell believed a naval blockade would cripple Japanese industry by severing its vital supply lines, the ACPD proposed crippling it through air attacks on the factories themselves. The weakness of Yarnell's plan was his presumption that the French and British fleets would control the Atlantic, freeing the United States Navy to concentrate most of its forces in the Pacific. The strength of the ACPD's plan was its indifference to the navy. When Germany conquered France and threatened to defeat Great Britain in 1940, the United States had to keep a large part of its fleet in the Atlantic, and Yarnell's plan became irrelevant. The events of 1941 seemed to validate the ACPD's plan.

While the War Department ignored the ACPD proposal to fortify the Philippines, the General Staff concurred with the idea of using the GHQ Air Force to stop an enemy assault. On October 30, 1939, Chief of WPD Gen. George V. Strong, who had sat on the air board, told General Arnold and officers of the ACPD how the Army Air Corps would be employed. General Strong considered the GHQ Air Force a strategic weapon that should be kept intact. Under the RAINBOW plans, Natal, Hawaii, and Alaska were the critical defensive points, and the quick reinforcement of those points required more long-range bombers. Then, Strong recognized one of the prime tenets of the advocates of air power: airplanes could defend the coasts against enemy fleets. If the United States were on the defensive in the Atlantic and the offensive in the Pacific, the GHQ Air Force would have to operate in lieu of naval forces.[16] Finally, the General Staff trusted the army fliers enough to rely upon them to defend the coasts and incorporated that reliance into its planning. The Army Air Corps offered proof that the General Staff's trust was warranted. On November 26, army fliers proved that they could quickly reach an endangered area in South America. Carrying ten Brazilian army officers, six B-17s flew non-stop from Maracaibo, Venezuela, to Bolling Field, a 2,100-mile trip.[17]

The General Staff's willingness to provide more B-17s for the Army Air Corps ran counter to Roosevelt's plans to provide the Allies with American-built airplanes. Throughout the summer of 1939, the French and British had ordered planes and other war materiel from American manufacturers. To prevent chaos and facilitate foreign orders, Roosevelt directed the Army and Navy Munitions Board on July 5 to coordinate French, British, and American military purchases. At first, the Clearance Committee, appointed by the munitions board, successfully assigned orders to American manufacturers, which sped up foreign contracts and helped build up America's war industries, but when Congress replaced the arms embargo provisions of the Neutrality Laws with "cash and carry" on November 3, a tidal wave of orders swamped the Clearance Committee. Roosevelt formed the President's Liaison Committee on December 6 to process all foreign orders. To keep from bidding against themselves for American war materiel and raising the prices, the Allies formed the Joint Anglo-French Purchasing Commission the same day.

Airplanes and airplane engines were the most pressing needs of the Allies, which placed the Allies in direct competition with the Army Air Corps's expansion program. Remembering how Secretary Woodring had opposed the sale of aircraft to France, FDR placed Secretary Morgenthau in charge of aircraft sales. Morgenthau wanted to divide the aircraft produced in America fifty-fifty with the Allies, but Woodring and Arnold objected, creating a split within the Roosevelt administration. The president, seeking to expand the productive capacity of the aircraft industry through sales to the Allies, sided with Morgenthau.

In March, 1940, the press learned that Woodring and Arnold were opposing Morgenthau's efforts to release the army's newest planes to the Allies, but President Roosevelt had made his decision. When Congress started asking questions, Roosevelt warned Arnold to "play ball" or be sent to Guam. Arnold feared that the president's warning signaled his replacement as the chief of the Air Corps. Instead, Roosevelt left him out of important conferences at the White House. On March 19, Roosevelt publicly announced that every type of American-built military plane would be released to the Allies. That evening, he told Woodring that anybody opposing his policy faced "drastic" action. Acceding to the wishes of the commander in chief, Woodring, Marshall, and Arnold devised a plan to sell the Allies the latest models while giving the army improved models later. Roosevelt approved the plan. Woodring publicly supported the plan, but he privately hampered it. Eventually, Woodring's obstructionism cost him his job.[18]

In 1939, the Army Air Corps lacked modern airplanes. Arnold should have opposed the president's release of army planes to the Allies; he was responsible for the condition of the Army Air Corps. But the chief of the Air Corps quietly acquiesced. As a soldier, Arnold thought that he had to defer to his commander in chief, but he also had to worry about Roosevelt's threat. Having been exiled after Billy Mitchell's court martial, Arnold believed that Roosevelt would send him to Guam. Arnold had worked too long and too hard for the cause of air power to throw his career away when he had gotten in a position to advance the cause.

After the fall of Poland, the most likely scenario was that envisioned in RAINBOW 2, the United States conducting offensive actions in the Pacific while Great Britain and France fought in Europe. The army and navy agreed to conduct joint maneuvers off the West Coast in February, 1940, to simulate the conditions of RAINBOW 2. General Marshall realized that the Army Air Corps was unprepared because the expansion program had disrupted the training of the tactical units. He tried to reschedule the maneuvers, but the navy could not change the date because of previous commitments. The press found out about the exercises and portrayed them as a test between the navy's carrier pilots and the GHQ Air Force. Although the navy planes outnumbered them two to one, the army fliers bragged that they would deny information to the navy scouting planes, ward off "bombing attacks" on vital military centers, and destroy the aircraft carriers.[19]

Much to the chagrin of the army pilots, the navy fliers won the day. From press reports and a careful monitoring of army radio frequencies, the navy fliers knew the exact location of the defending army planes. On the day before the exercises, eight B-17s secretly flew from Langley Field to Reno, Nevada, from where they planned to attack the Black fleet. But the navy learned of the Flying Fortresses' arrival and location from a routine warning announcement issued by the Civil Aeronautics Authority. On the first morning of the exercises, navy planes left their carriers seventy-five miles out to sea and caught the concentrated army planes on the ground. Afterwards, the GHQ Air Force fliers sheepishly said that the expansion program had handicapped them. They also considered themselves lucky not to have had any accidents, since many of the pilots had never flown together in formation.[20] Their excuses were true, but the navy pilots had a good laugh. When the Japanese did the same thing to army airfields in December of 1941, however, more than pride was damaged. Despite the poor showing of the GHQ Air Force, General Marshall was pleased with the maneuvers, calling them "the most realistic affair in the air and on the ground, in my military experience, short of war." He knew from experience that any expansion program entailed disruptions in training and coordination.[21]

If General Marshall's confidence in the army fliers was shaken, it was soon restored. After the maneuvers, he made a tour of American installations throughout the Caribbean and Canal Zone. By flying in a B-17, he cut what would have been a long trip to just ten days. Generally satisfied by what he saw, Marshall was very impressed by the Flying Fortress. During the trip, one of the engines quit. The pilot pointed out the problem to Marshall, but he assured the general that the plane could easily make its destination on the other three engines. He explained that a twin-engine plane could not. Afterwards, Marshall proudly told friends about having set a new speed record on the flight from Puerto Rico to Miami and of his plans to fly in a B-17 on an inspection trip to Hawaii. The general flew from Washington to San Francisco in a B-17, but problems at the last minute forced him to make the round-trip to Hawaii in a Pan American Clipper. Marshall's readiness to fly to Hawaii in a Flying Fortress showed his appreciation of the range of the airplane. Furthermore, he trusted the plane enough that he was ready to make the hazardous, over-water flight in it. During the last few months preceding America's entry into the Second World War, that trust influenced Marshall's decisions.

While inspecting the facilities in Panama and Hawaii, Marshall discovered that the local Army Air Corps commanders were making derogatory statements about the navy. Since Chief of Naval Operations Admiral Stark was cooperating with the army, Marshall wanted the fliers to cease their provocative actions, but he reacted in a mild manner. Ordering the commanders of the Canal Zone and Hawaiian Department, "when the opportunity casually arises," to inform the army fliers of his wishes, Marshall wanted it done "in a tactful way."[22] Only a man with great patience and trust could have acted in that manner. Marshall trusted the men of the Army Air Corps as much as he trusted their Flying Fortresses.

The Luftwaffe played a critical part in the German military victories of 1939–40. In September, 1939, it destroyed the Polish air force. With complete air superiority, the Luftwaffe turned on the Polish armies and finally destroyed Warsaw. German artillery participated in the bombardment of the Polish capital, but the Luftwaffe received most of the credit. On April 9, 1940, German troops crossed the border into Denmark, crushing all organized resistance within a few hours. Meanwhile, other German troops, hidden in coal and iron barges, attacked the seaports of Norway, and German paratroopers captured the airfields and radio stations. The Norwegians put up a stiff resistance but were no match for the Germans. Slowly, the Allies responded to the German assault and landed troops in northern Norway. At Narvik, the British Royal Navy defeated the German navy; but, using Norwegian airfields, the Luftwaffe kept German supply lines open and land-based planes close to the action. With command of the air, the Luftwaffe forced the Royal Navy to withdraw. The Allied supply lines were broken, and their position in Norway became untenable. German air superiority played a large part in forcing the Allies to pull their troops out of Norway in early May. The loss of British ships off Norway incited a new round of airplane-versus-battleship arguments in the United States. This debate intensified when the Luftwaffe and the Royal Air Force attacked each other's naval bases.[23]

The war in Europe changed the opinion of one important American journal. In April, 1940, a *New Republic* editorial stated that "the Norwegian war has already shown the enormous importance of air supremacy, not only in a contest with sea power, but in all aspects of military strategy." Two weeks later, the *New Republic* strongly supported the airplane in the airplane-versus-battleship argument. The Norwegian campaign convinced the magazine's editors. They wrote, "One thing which the German High Command seems to have demonstrated ought to reassure those protecting our shores. An invading expedition is at the mercy of a superior air force based on nearby flying fields, even though it is backed by a superior navy. So forewarned, we ought to be able to vanguard North and Central America from any possibility of aggression."[24] Only fifteen months earlier, the *New Republic* had decried President Roosevelt's building of a large air force as "a grave overbalancing of our defensive mechanism, an overemphasis on air power which might have very serious results. . . ."[25]

Besides influencing an important American magazine, the war in Europe created international problems in the Far East. To prevent Iceland from falling into German hands, the British occupied the island. Citing the British action as justification and anticipating a German attack on Holland, Japan threatened to occupy the Dutch East Indies. The United States reacted by stationing its fleet, which was on maneuvers in the Pacific, at Pearl Harbor. When the commander of the fleet asked why, Admiral Stark said it was "because of the deterrent effect which it is thought your presence may have on the Japs going into the East Indies." However, navy spokesmen told the press that the fleet would stay in Hawaiian waters to perfect anti-aircraft lessons learned from the Luftwaffe attacks on the Royal Navy at Scapa Flow. Since Secretary of the Navy Edison had admitted earlier that the German airplanes had caused the Royal Navy trouble off Norway, the press accepted the navy's story.[26] The deterrent effect of basing the fleet in Hawaii soon wore off. Furthermore, the effect was lessened when surprises on the European battlefields forced the navy to move some of its vessels to the Atlantic.

German troops invaded Holland and Belgium on May 10. That evening, Winston Churchill replaced Chamberlain as prime minister, and he promised "to wage war by sea, land and air, with all our might and with all the strength that God can give us." But Churchill's brave words were not enough. German armies swept through the Low Countries and, avoiding the Maginot Line, into France. As in Poland, the German fliers won air superiority. Panzer forces, supported by the Luftwaffe, quickly crushed the French and British. Only over the beaches of Dunkirk did the Royal Air Force defeat the Luftwaffe, and the British pulled what was left of their shattered expeditionary forces out of France at the end of the month. On June 22, the French surrendered, and all that stood between Hitler's armies and Great Britain were the English Channel, the Royal Navy, and the Royal Air Force. With most of its equipment left in France, the British army was no match for the Germans. Furthermore, the English Channel was not the formidable barrier it had been in the past. If Germany took the French navy as part of the peace settlement, it could be used to carry German troops to Great Britain. Since the Luftwaffe had swept all its opponents from the skies of Europe, the RAF seemed to have little chance of saving Great Britain.[27]

Americans, expecting a long repetition of the First World War, were stunned by the German victories. Against the British and French navies, the highly touted Maginot Line, and the industrial potential of the democracies, the Germans appeared to have little chance of victory, and Congress had been considering cutting the defense funds requested by the administration. Before the French surrender, Roosevelt concentrated on acquiring more aircraft and excluded the ground forces. On April 15, General Marshall asked for $25 million to purchase critical items, but Roosevelt only gave him $18 million. The president was more interested in increasing the size of the Army Air Corps than the size of the army. On May 13, Arnold asked for $80 million to purchase two hundred B-17s and $106 million for pilot training, and Marshall asked for 15,000 additional troops. Roosevelt rejected Marshall's request but approved Arnold's. When Assistant Secretary Johnson warned that aircraft were being delivered too slowly and recommended increasing purchases to expand the production of aircraft to 19,000 a year, the president went much further. Roosevelt asked Congress on May 16 to raise the army and navy air arms to a total of 50,000 planes and expand the capacity of the aviation industry to 50,000 airplanes annually. Alarmed by the German victories, Congress cooperated and provided half a billion dollars more than FDR had requested.[28]

Army planners, as anxious as Congress over Axis successes in Europe, feared that the Germans and Italians would capture the British and French fleets and join the Japanese. On May 22, they gave Marshall a memorandum explaining that, single-handedly, the United States possessed sufficient resources to defend only the western hemisphere, Alaska, and Hawaii as envisioned in RAINBOW 4. Later that day, Marshall presented copies of the memorandum to President Roosevelt, Chief of Naval Operations Admiral Stark, and Under Secretary of State Sumner Welles. All three agreed that the United States had to concentrate on South America and not become involved with Japan. RAINBOW 4 became the basis for WPD's planning.

FDR agreed that the army should contain its planning to the western hemisphere, but he disagreed with his military advisors on two major points. First, his advisors concluded that Great Britain would collapse, and they wanted to keep America's supplies to train and equip American troops. Roosevelt believed that the British would withstand a German assault, and he wanted to furnish munitions to Great Britain. Second, he wanted to dissuade the Japanese from making further moves in the Far East with a show of strength in the Pacific, but his advisors wanted to avoid moves that might start a war with Japan.[29]

Trouble between Roosevelt and his military advisors over the first point of disagreement arose as the Germans pushed across France. The British and French appealed for more weapons and materiel. On May 22, General Marshall told Secretary Morgenthau that the army could not afford to give the Allies any of its planes. The army only had 160 pursuit planes for 260 pilots and only 52 of the 136 heavy bombers it needed to defend the hemisphere. The requests were dropped, and for a time the problem faded. But in June, President Roosevelt brought up the idea of releasing twelve B-17s to the British. Again, Marshall prevented the White House from releasing the bombers, but when the destroyer deal of September 3, 1940, went through, five B-17s were included. Only an inadvertent omission in the official document kept the B-17s from being sent, but Roosevelt had had enough. The president told Marshall that he wanted an "even-Stephen" division of the bombers with the British.[30]

The Committee to Defend America by Aiding the Allies supported Roosevelt and made the dispatch of B-17s to Great Britain a public issue. On September 12, William Allen White demanded the release of twenty-five B-17s and twenty torpedo boats to the British; he stated that these weapons "may be the only things we can now send to Britain in time to be of major help in resisting destruction from air and invasion by sea." Isolationist senators Bennett Clark and Homer Holt denounced the giving of B-17s or torpedo boats to the British. Calling the B-17 "one of the greatest defense weapons" owned by America, Senator Holt of West Virginia charged that the administration was planning to declare twenty-five of them obsolete only to be able to send them to Great Britain. If the planes fell into German hands, they would be used in the "most vicious attack" ever made on the United States. With the 1940 presidential election approaching, Roosevelt could not ignore such powerful opposition to providing weapons to Great Britain, and he told Marshall to find a legal way to release the planes. In a memorandum, carefully worded with help from the attorney general, Marshall proposed releasing a few B-17s to the British for combat tests. The United States would benefit by learning what improvements should be incorporated into later models. Arnold and Maj. Gen. George Brett approved the idea. To obtain valid test results, Arnold and Brett advised releasing a minimum of twenty planes. None of the three generals was pleased about releasing the planes, but Brett hoped that giving the British a few planes might prevent the need to split production with them.[31] However, Brett underestimated the president's willingness to aid the British.

The ever-changing course of world events forced the United States to reevaluate its strategic plans. On June 10, the Soviets and Japanese settled their differences over the Manchurian border with a peace agreement. With the French defeated, the British on the ropes, and their northern flank secured by an agreement with the Soviets, Japan was free to press its claims in the Far East. Japan forced Great Britain to close the Burma Road, one of the supply lines for the Nationalist Chinese. The United States responded by restricting the export of oil and scrap metal to Japan, but the Japanese were not deterred. On September 27, 1940, Japan signed the Tripartite Pact with Germany and Italy, becoming a member of the Axis.[32]

The Royal Air Force defeated the Luftwaffe in the daytime skies over Great Britain, forcing the Germans to concentrate on night raids on London. Throughout the Battle of Britain, Edward R. Murrow made his famous live broadcasts from London, and Americans became aware of the savagery of the German "Blitz," as the attacks on London came to be known. More importantly, Americans realized that the British would survive. By the end of October, the threat of a German invasion of Great Britain in 1940 disappeared. Convinced that the British could survive at least six more months, the General Staff concluded that the United States had at least a year before the Germans and Italians could launch an attack on the western hemisphere.

Navy planners also responded to the new situation by proposing four feasible lines of action. Admiral Stark converted them into a memorandum, and he recommended the fourth line of action, Plan D or Plan Dog, which was similar to the army's RAINBOW 5. Fighting simultaneous Atlantic and Pacific wars was unwise, and the Pacific war would reduce the aid available to Britain. If the Philippines and Guam were fortified, the situation would be different, but "Japanese armed opposition" might be precipitated if the United States tried to fortify its Far Eastern possessions. Stark opposed the establishment of a blockade around Japan because it would lessen the number of ships available for the Atlantic. In case of war, Stark argued, the United States had to remain on the defensive in the Pacific and prepare for full-scale land operations across the Atlantic. When presented with "Plan Dog," the army planners recommended using it as the basis for a joint army-navy study. On November 13, the "Plan Dog" memorandum and the army recommendation were sent to Roosevelt. Although Roosevelt never gave his formal approval to the plan, he authorized conversations with the British about Stark's recommendations.

On January 17, 1941, Roosevelt discussed with Admiral Stark, General Marshall, and the secretaries of state, war, and navy the possibility of a sudden war with Germany and Japan. In the event of such an emergency, Roosevelt instructed his military advisors to be realistic and avoid plans that could be carried out only after several months had passed. They had to be ready to fight with what was available. The president was concerned by the possibility that Japan, acting in concert with Germany, might disrupt the flow of American supplies to Great Britain with a Pacific war. Roosevelt wanted to be able to assure Churchill that supplies to Great Britain would not be seriously curtailed. At the close of the meeting, Roosevelt gave his advisors a general directive as to how the United States would meet the world situation and not jeopardize the flow of supplies to Great Britain. In the Pacific, the United States would stand on the defensive with the fleet based in Hawaii. The commander of the Asiatic Fleet would have the discretionary authority as to how long he could remain in the Philippines and as to his direction of withdrawal—to the East or to Singapore. There would be no naval reinforcement of the Philippines. The navy should be considering bombing attacks against Japanese cities. In the Atlantic, he wanted the navy to prepare for convoying ships to Great Britain and for maintaining patrols off the coast. Roosevelt instructed the army to avoid commitments to aggressive action until they were fully prepared; keep its plans conservative until its strength had been developed; and be prepared to give moderate assistance to Latin American countries fighting Nazi-inspired fifth column movements. Then, Roosevelt reiterated that every effort should be made to continue supplying Great Britain. Primarily, he believed that continued succor would foil Hitler's principal objective of involving the United States in a war at that time, but he also judged that it would "buck up England."[33]

Significantly, Roosevelt wanted the navy to consider the bombing of Japanese cities. Throughout the previous month, efforts had been made to provide the Chinese with American bombers for attacks on Japanese cities. In October, 1940, Claire Chennault returned from China, where he had been training Chinese pilots, with T. V. Soong and Gen. P. T. Mow to seek American aid. On November 30, Soong presented to Secretary Morgenthau a plan whereby a 500-plane force, supplied and maintained by the United States, would drive the Japanese out of China and neutralize the Japanese navy. Based only 650 miles from Tokyo, these planes would conduct air raids against the Japanese capital.[34]

Sending bombers from China to attack Japan was not a new idea. On February 23, 1938, Chinese bombers had attacked the Japanese on Formosa. Two days later, Kyushu (the southwestern island of Japan proper), the main island of Honshu, and Formosa had been thrown into a panic by reports of Chinese bombers approaching from the China Sea. The Japanese spent four hours terrified by a nonexistent specter of Chinese bombers. News of the panic was relayed to the United States by the Associated Press. "In Tokyo, much of the reaction dwelt on the fact that Vladivostok, Russian Siberia, where a huge Soviet air fleet is concentrated, is almost as close to the capital as Formosa is to China."[35] Armed with American-built bombers capable of striking Tokyo, the Chinese could have presented as great a threat as the Soviet air forces.

Realizing that sending any bombers to China would decrease those available for Great Britain, Morgenthau asked Lord Lothian, the British ambassador, on December 3 about bombing Tokyo and other Japanese cities. At first, the British were enthusiastic, but their interest waned as they considered the diversion of planes from Great Britain. Following a luncheon with President Roosevelt on December 8, Morgenthau told Soong that giving the Chinese so many bombers would be impossible until sometime in 1942, but the secretary of the treasury did not drop the matter. He mentioned it to Secretary of State Hull. Expressing enthusiasm for the idea, Hull said that he would love to see 500 American planes "start from the Aleutians and fly over Japan just once." Hull also thought it would be nice "if we could only find some way to have them drop some bombs on Tokyo." Morgenthau told Soong about Hull's comments, and immediately, Chiang Kai-shek started cabling Roosevelt for bombers.

Just before Christmas, Morgenthau discussed the idea of sending bombers with Soong, Mow, and Chennault. Saying that the president wanted to dispatch some B-17s to China, he asked for specifics. Chennault proposed sending an indeterminate number of B-17s with crews, released from active duty in the Army Air Corps, to serve with the Chinese. From airfields protected by 200 fighters, the B-17s could attack Tokyo, Nagasaki, Kobe, and Osaka. Asking Chennault about the methods used to bomb these cities, Morgenthau suggested using incendiary bombs, since the cities were built of wood and paper. Chennault replied that a lot of damage could be done that would justify the loss of a few Chinese bombers. When Morgenthau broached the plan to Secretary of War Stimson, Secretary of the Navy Knox, and General Marshall, the chief of staff strongly opposed diverting any bombers from Great Britain. He was willing, however, to divert some pursuit planes to the Chinese. Roosevelt approved that idea. Eventually, these pursuit planes were used by the American Volunteer Group, better known as Chennault's Flying Tigers.[36]

When Roosevelt told his naval advisors to plan air attacks on Japanese cities, the idea was fresh in his mind. The surprising aspect of
this episode was Roosevelt's directive to begin planning air raids on
Japanese cities with no mention of precision bombing or attacking
industrial targets. Throughout his presidency, Roosevelt had denounced the use of bombers and had even tried to get them abolished.
Suddenly, he changed his course and started calling for plans to implement what he had opposed. The reason for the president's abrupt
change rested in the conduct of the war overseas. The Italian air attacks on Ethiopia, the Japanese air attacks on China, the Russian air
attacks in Finland, and the recent, indiscriminate night bombing of
London by the Luftwaffe had demonstrated how the war would be
fought. Perhaps Roosevelt had only come to a pragmatic decision that
this was how modern war would be conducted, or, in what should
serve as a warning to all civilian leaders, perhaps he had become cal-
loused by the war. In any case, the Roosevelt administration seriously
considered the bombing of Japanese cities at the end of 1940. Why
the army was not instructed to plan the same thing was obvious; the
navy had a way to get its planes to Japan—on aircraft carriers. As he
had told his advisors on January 17, Roosevelt wanted them to be realistic and avoid plans that could only be carried out after several months
had passed. He wanted them to be ready to act with what was available, and in early 1940, aircraft carriers were available.

IX. The Best-laid Schemes of Mice and Men

The survival of Great Britain became the cornerstone of Franklin Roosevelt's foreign and military policies in 1941. Maintaining an uninterrupted stream of supplies to the British took precedence over other considerations. Therefore, a conflict with Japan had to be avoided because it would threaten the shipments to Great Britain. During the first half of 1941, however, the Roosevelt administration's plans turned from avoiding a war with Japan to deterring a war. This shift was due to events in the European war and to a growing faith in the army's air arm and its planes.

Throughout the summer of 1940, army officers opposed the release of American planes and surplus war materiel to the Allies, but they remained silent after Roosevelt warned General Arnold to "play ball" or be sent to Guam. Word of the president's warning soon spread throughout the army and muted any further objections from that quarter. When he acceded to Roosevelt's wishes, Arnold made the right decision—not only for himself, but for the Army Air Corps as well. By continuing as the chief of the Air Corps, he provided the experience and the political acumen necessary to see the army air arm through a very difficult period of transition.

Convinced that the army should have first priority, Secretary of War Woodring continued voicing his opposition to sending war goods overseas. Roosevelt was reluctant to remove Woodring because they were friends, because doing so would anger congressional isolationists, and because he needed Woodring's support at the Democratic convention. But Woodring finally pushed Roosevelt too far when he opposed the release of ten B-17s to the British. On June 19, Roosevelt

asked for Woodring's resignation. It gave Roosevelt a free hand to re-
form his cabinet.

Hoping to unite the country behind him during the war emergency, Roosevelt created a coalition by placing prominent Republicans in the cabinet. In May, Secretary of the Navy Charles Edison had
resigned to run for governor of New Jersey, and Roosevelt decided on
Republican Frank Knox to fill that post. Supreme Court Justice Felix
Frankfurter recommended Republican Henry L. Stimson for secretary
of war. Stimson had the proper qualifications: he had been Taft's secretary of war and Hoover's secretary of state. Moreover, Stimson agreed
with Roosevelt on foreign policy and aid to the Allies. Roosevelt accepted Frankfurter's recommendation but waited until just before the
Republican convention opened to announce the appointment of Knox
and Stimson. A great cry went up from the Republicans. Condemn-
ing the president for stooping to dirty politics, they talked of running
Knox and Stimson out of the party. The Republican charges backfired,
for by making the cabinet bipartisan, Roosevelt gave the appearance
of responding to a foreign threat by taking national defense out of
politics. Consequently, the Democrats successfully argued that the
Republicans were more interested in politics than national defense.[1]

The large sums of money spent on expanding the Army Air Corps
failed to produce airplanes as quickly as Roosevelt had hoped. Bottlenecks hampered the flow of mass-produced airplanes, and under public pressure, General Marshall restructured the army. In November,
Arnold became the deputy chief of staff for air and remained the chief
of the Air Corps. The General Staff retained control over the GHQ
Air Force, but Arnold was given control over production allocations
to prevent bottlenecks. This new arrangement satisfied the public
critics, but it proved to be impractical. Only the close relationship
between Marshall and Arnold prevented a complete breakdown of administration. Also, Arnold's new position meant nothing without the
support of the president. In September, Arnold gave Elliot Roosevelt
a captaincy in the Air Corps. By skillfully rebutting claims that it was
a political appointment, Arnold demonstrated that he could handle
embarrassing questions. Harry Hopkins and General Marshall convinced Roosevelt of Arnold's reliability, and Arnold received a position reflecting the increased importance of the Army Air Corps. Both
Secretary Stimson and General Marshall realized that a reorganization of the Army Air Corps was necessary to end the long-standing
squabbles between the combat and the supply units. Under their guidance, the Army Air Corps became the Army Air Forces on June 20,
1941. Divided into two branches—the office of the chief of the Air
Corps, and the Air Force Combat Command, formerly the GHQ Air

Force—the new organization was commanded by Arnold. Named the chief of the Army Air Forces, he also retained the position of deputy chief of staff for air.[2]

The reorganization effectively gave Arnold the command of an autonomous air force, but not all of the supporters of air power were pleased. Hugh Knerr, working for the Sperry Gyroscope Company after his retirement, had kept in touch with other advocates of a separate air force. Plotting to achieve total independence, Knerr won the support of a close friend of the president by suggesting that this unnamed friend would be made the new secretary of air. Knerr wanted Frank Andrews named the first air marshall, but when Arnold became the chief of the Air Forces, Knerr told Andrews it "looks like the old slicker is sitting pretty again." Andrews, who had been transferred to the Canal Zone, agreed with Knerr that the air force could not reach its full potential until it won its independence. He told Knerr and Alexander de Seversky that it left too much control with the General Staff. Marshall was a progressive thinker, admitted Andrews, but he could be replaced as chief of staff by a reactionary. However, Andrews disagreed about Arnold. Andrews said that Arnold would be "the best man available" to head up a separate air force because of his political skills. Fortunately, Knerr's plot failed. Arnold faced great problems in the middle of 1941, and he could not have afforded the distractions political infighting would have brought.[3]

By the end of 1940, the United States and Great Britain realized that their military and naval forces needed to plan for possible joint action against the Axis powers. Secretly meeting from late January to March of 1941, representatives at the American British Conversations (ABC) agreed to defeat Germany and Italy first, then deal with Japan. The Americans rejected a British request for aid in defending Singapore. They believed that the American fleet in the Pacific, actively threatening the Japanese flank, would keep Japan from conducting extended operations. The views of both sides were presented in a final report, ABC-1, on March 27. Then, allocations of aircraft were discussed, and an arrangement, ABC-2, was reached two days later. The Joint Army and Navy Board approved ABC-1 and directed that RAINBOW 5 be prepared with the defeat of Germany as the primary strategic objective. In the European theater, RAINBOW 5 called for putting economic pressure on the Axis, conducting a "sustained air offensive against German Military power," and building up the forces needed for the eventual offensive against Germany. In the Pacific, the army would remain on the defensive, while the navy destroyed the Axis sea lanes and diverted Japan from the Malay Barrier with attacks in the Marshall Islands. Army and navy forces in the Far East would not be reinforced and would have to defend the Philippines with what they had. Adding their approval, the secretaries of war and the navy sent RAINBOW 5 and ABC-1 to the president. Roosevelt read both plans but returned them unsigned on June 7. He wanted to wait until war broke out before signing them. General Marshall, unable to wait for war before building up the army, took the position that Roosevelt had tacitly approved RAINBOW 5. Marshall continued preparing the army for war.

With the approval of their superiors, military representatives from the American, British, Australian, Dutch, and New Zealand governments met in Singapore from April 21 to April 27, 1941. The American-Dutch-British (ADB) representatives formulated a military plan for the Far East. Calling the security of sea communications and of Singapore the primary objective, ADB recognized the importance of the Philippines. Submarines and airplanes from those islands would threaten the flank of a Japanese expedition against Malaya or the Dutch East Indies, and an economic blockade consisting of naval pressure and air bombardment would cause the collapse of Japan. The planners stated that the Japanese particularly feared air attacks and recommended that Luzon's defenses needed strengthening. Bomber forces there and in China were required to block Japanese communications with Thailand and Indochina. However, ADB's plans for strengthening the defenses of Luzon ran counter to RAINBOW 5, and in early July, General Marshall and Admiral Stark rejected ADB. As it had for twenty years, the army rejected any suggestion to significantly reinforce the Philippines. In February, the Air Corps had requested the General Staff to provide routes for flying heavy bombers across the Pacific to the Far East, but the General Staff refused, saying that there was no need to send heavy bombers there.[4] Within three weeks of rejecting the ADB report, however, the General Staff radically changed its opinion about reinforcing the Philippines.

On June 22, Hitler sent his armies crashing into the Soviet Union. Stunned and overpowered by the German Blitzkrieg, the Soviets reeled back toward Moscow. Hitler claimed that victory would soon be his, and few people doubted him. Although it was halfway around the world, the German attack still had a tremendous effect on the situation in the Far East. With Russia, their traditional enemy, engaged in a life-or-death struggle in Europe, the Japanese were free to move troops from the Soviet border for use elsewhere. At the same time, the General Staff concluded that the Philippines could be defended. This new attitude was due in part to optimistic reports from Gen. Douglas MacArthur, who had gone to the Philippines as a military advisor in 1935. Preparing the Philippines for independence in 1946,

MacArthur started building a Filipino army of 250,000 men, a balanced air force, and a navy consisting of high-speed torpedo boats. This force, he told Marshall, could "provide an adequate defense at the beach against a landing operation by an expeditionary force of 100,000, which is estimated to be the maximum initial effort of the most powerful potential enemy." If given more coastal artillery, MacArthur promised to defend not only Manila Bay, as called for in Plan ORANGE, but all of Luzon and the Visayan Islands. After being assured by the WPD that giving MacArthur some smaller caliber guns would not interfere with shipments to Great Britain or to the American forces under General Grunert in the Philippines, Marshall and President Roosevelt approved the shipment.[5]

Marshall wanted to send more aid to the Philippines, but he did not have enough equipment to arm Pearl Harbor, the Philippines, and the Panama Canal adequately. Protecting the fleet at Pearl Harbor remained his primary concern. He recommended to the president only minor increases in the Philippine Scouts and their officers. Marshall also wanted to publicize the reinforcement of the Hawaiian garrison with P-36s and P-40s. General Gerow in WPD agreed that releasing that information "may worry the Japanese a bit. At least it can do no harm."[6] Still considering a public disclosure, Marshall told the Senate Military Affairs Committee in a secret session, sometime after February 10, that additional P-36s and P-40s were being sent to Hawaii. On February 21, the *New York Times* printed the information in a front-page story.[7] From this episode, Roosevelt, Marshall, and the War Department learned that a shipment of aircraft to the Far East would be difficult to hide.

Still, Roosevelt and his military advisors sought ways to deter the Japanese without risking the flow of supplies to Great Britain. On February 26, the president thought about sending cruisers and destroyers to the Philippines on a "training cruise" to illustrate America's commitment to defend the islands. But at the suggestion of General Marshall and Secretary Stimson, he agreed to build a few airfields for pursuit planes instead.[8] The following day, the War Department announced that fifty planes were being sent to the Philippines.[9] The airfields and pursuit planes were for defense, but the idea of reinforcing the Philippines with more aircraft had been put into the heads of Roosevelt and his military advisors.

Passage of the Lend-Lease Act in March exacerbated the shortage of materiel available for the army and Army Air Corps, but it forced the army to coordinate demand with supply. Late in May, Marshall directed the WPD to prepare a rough estimate of the production requirements necessary to defeat America's potential enemies and to prepare a production plan. Roosevelt learned of the army plans, and he became concerned that the army, navy, and British might prepare competing programs instead of one overall program. On July 9, FDR directed the secretaries of war and the navy to formulate a joint plan for production requirements. Submitted to the president in September, the "Victory Program" called for an army of eight million men, with about a quarter of them allotted to the Army Air Forces. Consistent with RAINBOW 5, the Victory Program envisioned the defeat of Germany as the first objective while avoiding major military and naval commitments in the Far East.[10]

British war plans called for an intensive air offensive to destroy Germany's industrial capacity, which was a strategy the president supported. On May 5, Roosevelt released for publication a letter to Secretary Stimson stating that the "effective defense of this country and the vital defense of other democratic nations" required "a substantial increase in heavy bomber production." Believing that "command of the air by the democracies must and can be achieved," the president instructed Stimson to cooperate with the secretary of the navy and the Office of Production Management to achieve that increase.[11] In a private directive to Stimson the day before, Roosevelt had demonstrated his awareness of the importance of air power. "I know of no single item of our defense today," he wrote, "that is more important than a larger four-engine bomber capacity."[12] Since the ABC-2 agreement had allocated any increase in aircraft production for Great Britain, Roosevelt ensured that the production of heavy bombers was increased. The fall of France had not changed President Roosevelt's idea about fighting Germany with a blockade and an air war. Instead of striking Germany from airfields in France, the RAF would strike from British airfields with long-range bombers.

Not long after Roosevelt called for increased bomber construction, the war in Europe demonstrated the importance of air power in naval actions. Skipping over the Royal Navy's ships, the Germans attacked Crete on May 20, 1941, with paratroopers and gliders. British sea power was powerless to prevent them from gaining a foothold on the island, and German air power forced the British ships to retire. Without naval support, the British army was forced to evacuate Crete, as had happened in Norway. From Cairo, the American military attaché reported on May 27 that the situation in the Mediterranean was precarious. He wrote, "The British Navy is now certain that naval vessels cannot stand against shore based air superiority." Even at Alexandria, the Royal Navy was in danger because it had no place to avoid attacks from land-based planes. The attaché estimated that the strength of the Royal Navy had fallen "so low that the Italian fleet is likely to seek battle with it." Brig. Gen. Sherman Miles passed the report on to the president, the secretary of war, the chief of staff, the War Plans Division, the Office of Naval Intelligence, and General Embick, with the observation that "the British position in Crete is now definitely untenable and that the British fleet in the Eastern Mediterranean is unquestionably increasingly vulnerable to air attack, both at its bases and at sea."[13]

While the Luftwaffe mauled the Royal Navy at Crete, the German battleship *Bismarck* made its famous sortie into the North Atlantic. After sinking the vaunted British battleship *Hood* and damaging the *Prince of Wales*, the *Bismarck* ran for the protection of the land-based Luftwaffe. Before the German ship could escape, however, torpedo planes from the British aircraft carrier *Ark Royal* damaged its control system, allowing other British ships to sink the German battleship on May 26. When the navy called to inform Roosevelt that the *Bismarck* had gone down, the president hung up the receiver and exclaimed "She's sunk!"[14] Over the next few months the importance of air power, as demonstrated in the fight for Crete and the *Bismarck* episode, greatly influenced the Roosevelt administration and the United States Army.

The events of May reopened the airplane-versus-battleship question in the American press. In an editorial on May 26 entitled "Sea Power vs. Air Power," the *New York Times* said that a revolution had taken place in the conduct of war. The sinking of the *Hood* was dramatic, but it was not as important as the actions around Crete. There, the British losses had been much more serious and were brought about almost entirely by air power. The Luftwaffe had shown the supremacy of air power "in any place within its range." The editorial cited an article printed in the *American Mercury* before the Germans attacked Crete. The author, Alexander de Seversky, pointed to the Norwegian campaign as proof that fleets could no longer approach hostile shores guarded by first-class aviation. The *Times* expressed concern that "our own defense program is seriously lopsided in its expenditure on and plans for capital and other heavy ships compared with bomber planes."[15] This editorial signaled quite a switch for the *Times*. Only a year earlier it had held the battleship as almost sacrosanct. Roosevelt may have missed the *Times* editorial, but he knew about de Seversky's ideas. On May 26 Roosevelt received a memorandum written by de Seversky on American air power.[16] Over the following months, the Roosevelt administration showed that it accepted de Seversky's argument.

The Battle of the Atlantic forced a change in America's military plans. As German submarines sank merchant ships faster than they could be replaced, Britain's situation became desperate. On April 3, to ensure the continued delivery of American supplies, Roosevelt tentatively approved the transfer of three battleships, one aircraft carrier, four cruisers, and other vessels from the Pacific to the Atlantic for convoy duty. He soon gave up the idea of convoying ships, choosing to extend the area protected by American naval patrols. The extended patrol was announced on April 24, and Roosevelt emphasized that ships were not being convoyed. Fearing it might encourage Japanese aggression, Roosevelt hesitated to give final approval to the transfer of almost a quarter of the Pacific fleet. Roosevelt's concern intensified when the Soviets and Japanese signed a neutrality pact on April 12. After the Japanese demonstrated a willingness to continue diplomatic discussions, he approved the transfer in the middle of May. This action left the Pacific fleet inferior to the Japanese navy in every category of combat ship, but the president agreed to the transfer only after he had been assured that Hawaii's air defenses would make Oahu virtually impregnable. When completed, the defenses would include 35 Flying Fortresses, 48 light and medium bombers, and 150 pursuit planes. Furthermore, Oahu could be reinforced by heavy bombers flying in from the mainland.[17]

Since 1935, the Army Air Corps had claimed that Hawaii could be reinforced with long-range bombers flying in from the mainland. Led by Lt. Col. Eugene L. Eubank, twenty-one B-17Ds of the 19th Bombardment Group made the first massed flight of army bombers from California to Hawaii in May. Leaving their planes and fifteen instructors behind, the crews of the 19th sailed back to the mainland, having proved that Hawaii could be reinforced by long-range bombers.[18] Reporting on the transfer of ships to the Atlantic, Hanson Baldwin stated that they had been compensated for by the Flying Fortresses, "the most modern Army aircraft ever stationed in the islands — an aerial fleet capable of carrying great loads of bombs many long miles above the Pacific." Even Hanson Baldwin, a skeptic about air power, had changed his opinion by the summer of 1941.[19] Eubank's successful flight to Hawaii added validity to all the other claims about the potential of air power.

Now convinced of the importance of employing air power against sea power, the *New York Times* espoused a greater role for airplanes in national defense. The paper published reports and photographs of a British bomber successfully bombing an Axis ship off the Dutch coast. When the Dutch East Indies broke off trade discussions with Japan, a *Times* editorial stated that Dutch air power in the area forced the Japanese to acquiesce. The invasion of Crete and the torpedoing of the *Bismarck* showed that the Japanese fleet needed air cover to attack the Dutch East Indies, stated the *Times*, but the inferior Japanese air force could not provide it against the American, British, and Dutch land-based airplanes in the area. The editorial called for the United States to build up its pursuit and long-range bomber forces in the Philippines in order to maintain a potentially aggressive defensive.[20] On the day Hitler attacked Russia, the *Times* followed up its editorial with an article by Henry N. Dorris, who reported an increase in the air forces in the Philippines, the Dutch East Indies, and Singapore. Although no general understanding existed between them, said Dorris, the military commanders in the area believed that a strong air force could prevent a Japanese invasion of the Philippines or the Dutch East Indies. They believed that the lessons of the battle of Crete could be applied in the South Pacific.[21]

As long as a war in the Pacific could be avoided, President Roosevelt refused to jeopardize the peace. Earlier, Harold Ickes had asked him to cut off shipments of American oil to Japan, but Roosevelt refused because "every little episode in the Pacific means fewer ships in the Atlantic." When negotiations between the United States and Japan broke down in late June, the chances of avoiding war dwindled. The German invasion of Russia left Japan free to move against Russia or the South Seas. Roosevelt told Ickes that the Japanese were fighting among themselves over their future moves, but he did not know which way they were "going to jump." FDR waited for the Japanese to make the next move. On July 2, the Japanese Imperial Council decided to move into Indochina for its raw material and strategic location for attacks on China and further south. Unable to resist, the Vichy government allowed the Japanese to occupy French airfields and naval bases in Indochina. Finally knowing which way the Japanese were jumping, Roosevelt reversed his Far Eastern policy. On July 26, he froze all Japanese assets in the United States, closed the Panama Canal to Japanese ships, mustered the Philippine army into United States service, and named Douglas MacArthur the commander of the United States Forces in the Far East.[22]

The General Staff's unwillingness to fortify the Philippines disappeared between June and July. General Marshall approved a proposal to send tanks and antitank guns to defend Luzon. In his volume for the official history of the United States Army in World War II, Mark S. Watson suspected that the increased activity in the Philippines "came about not so much from alarms over the new threats [from Japan] as from a sudden awareness that in the newly developed B-17 heavy bomber, America at last had a weapon with which the Philippines could actually and effectively and for the first time be armed against such threats."[23] Watson was correct, as revealed by Secretary Stimson's comments toward the end of July, 1941. Replying to the navy's objections about the president's giving priority to the long-range bomber program, Stimson told Rep. Carl Vinson:

> While I do not pretend to know all of the considerations bearing upon the President's decision in this matter, I have no doubt that factors of common knowledge entered into the decision in addition to the special information of strategical and tactical character. We have all seen the devastating effect of long-range bombers, both against shipping and land objectives. We have recently had the dramatic incident of Crete in which land-based aircraft inflicted serious losses on the British fleet in the Eastern Mediterranean and made the Naval forces impotent to save the Island. The record of sinkings by German aircraft of both merchant and Naval vessels is most impressive. The development of long-range aircraft has reached the point where it is very dangerous for Naval craft to operate in waters which can be commanded by long-range bombing planes. The situation on the coast of France, in the channel and on the North Sea, and in areas as far West as the northern approaches of Ireland, give ample proof of the increasing role played by long-range bombers in attacking British sea lanes.[24]

This recognition of the effectiveness of long-range bombers against naval and land targets resulted in the dispatch of B-17s to the Philippines.

Stimson overestimated the influence of air actions around Crete on the president. Roosevelt had given the production of long-range bombers priority weeks before the Luftwaffe forced the Royal Navy to withdraw from Crete. For years, Roosevelt had seen the results of bombing tests like those conducted against the *Utah*, and he had recognized the potential effect of air power on naval warfare since his comments in 1919. The RAF's strategic bombing campaign against Germany was what Roosevelt had suggested in 1938, and he called for increased production of heavy bombers to aid that campaign.[25]

The fighting in Europe and China had greatly influenced Roosevelt, and he had moved away from the idea that a war could be fought humanely. At the Young Democrats' national convention, Rep. Lyndon Johnson read a letter from President Roosevelt: "Across both oceans, on the oceans, and above the oceans the struggle is one of armed forces, with the ghastly result of destruction and slaughter on a scale unparalleled in modern history. . . . Against naked force the only possible defense is naked force. The aggressor makes the rules for such a war; the defenders have no alternative but matching destruction with more destruction, slaughter with greater slaughter. . . ."[26] Roosevelt understood that modern war escalates to its most savage level and ends only when an enemy's will to resist is crushed. After the Germans, Italians, and Japanese had resorted to bombing civilian populations, Roosevelt decided that the Allies had to pursue the same methods. A weapon remains a deterrent until it is used; then it becomes just another weapon in a nation's arsenal. When the Japanese bombed Chinese civilians, the Italians bombed Ethiopian civilians, and the Germans bombed civilians in Warsaw, Rotterdam, and London, the prewar deterrence of bombers evaporated. The British, no longer having to fear a German retaliation if they bombed Berlin, made use of the weapons in their arsenal. By 1941, the rules of the Second World War had been laid out, and the savagery reached two of many peaks at Hiroshima and Nagasaki.

Knowing that the Japanese intended to move toward the Dutch East Indies, on July 16 General Marshall told Arnold that the Philippines had become strategically important as a naval and air base to threaten the flank of a Japanese movement southward. Arnold suggested that a striking force of heavy bombers would be necessary to ensure the defense of the Philippines. Concurring, the General Staff reversed an earlier rejection of an Air Corps request for ferry routes to the Philippines, and the War Department approved Arnold's suggestion to reinforce the Philippines. After the war, Secretary Stimson explained that the War Department had "decided that if a sufficient number of our bombing planes, which would be able to proceed to the Philippine Islands under their own power, could be gathered there, this would present a very effective nucleus of a defense against the advances of the Japanese Navy or convoys in South Asiatic waters." The General Staff approved the movement of four heavy bomber groups and two pursuit groups to the islands, but shortages of aircraft forced them to cut those numbers in half. Secretary Stimson approved the proposal in early August.[27]

Once he learned of the army's interest in strengthening Philippine defenses, Admiral Stark asked Marshall for more information. Marshall detailed what was being shipped, which included "six to nine of the super Flying Fortresses, B-24 type planes" in November. Marshall did not know that the nickname of the B-24 was the "Liberator," but his reference to it as a "super" Flying Fortress showed an awareness of its superior performance characteristics. "These planes will have an operating radius of 1500 miles," he told Stark, "with a load of 14,000 bombs, which means that they can reach Osaka with a full load and Tokyo with a partial load."[28] By the middle of September, the General Staff had decided not only to reinforce the Philippines with America's most modern planes, but it knew how those reinforcements would be used.

In spite of the War Department's increased interest in the Philippines, the defeat of Germany remained the top priority in all American plans. As commander in chief, Roosevelt made the avoidance of war with Japan a key part of his strategy. However, there were limits on what he would tolerate. While sailing to the Argentia (or Atlantic) Conference on board the U.S.S. *Tuscaloosa*, Roosevelt told Generals Marshall and Arnold that the United States would not be concerned if the Japanese moved into Thailand. However, FDR said that if the Japanese went into the Dutch East Indies, then the United States would be "vitally interested [and do its] utmost to get them out."[29] Unlike the president, the War Plans Division could not base its planning on Japanese actions. It had to work within the framework of ABC-1 and RAINBOW 5 and plan for a major American effort in Europe while maintaining a defensive posture in the Pacific. As they worked out the estimates for the Victory Program, the WPD planners kept these points in mind. Shorthanded, the WPD suggested that Arnold detail some officers from the Air War Plans Division to assist in drawing up the requirements for aviation. Upon hearing the suggestion, Lt. Col. Harold "Hal" George, chief of the Air War Plans Division, objected. He believed that AWPD should develop the plans because that was why it had been created. General Gerow in WPD concurred, asking only that the AWPD stay within the guidelines of ABC-1 and RAINBOW 5. Going beyond their instructions, the Air War Plans Division drew up a plan for the strategic bombing of Germany, named AWPD/1, and submitted it in the second week of August. The joint board approved AWPD/1 on September 11. In accordance with RAINBOW 5, AWPD/1 called for the defeat of Germany first through a strategic bombing campaign against German industry. For the defense of the Philippines, AWPD/1 assigned one pursuit and two heavy bomber groups.[30] This was substantially fewer planes than the two heavy bomber, two medium bomber, and two pursuit groups the Air Corps Plans Division had deemed necessary, in September of 1939, "for the initial defense of Luzon, pending the arrival of reinforcements from Hawaii or the mainland."[31] Furthermore, the army dispatched its planes to the Philippines in the piecemeal fashion the ACPD had warned against. These problems were easily overlooked. While the joint board studied AWPD/1, nine B-17Ds island-hopped from Hawaii to Manila.[32] This flight not only proved the feasibility of sending more bombers to the Far East, but it added validity to the other claims made by the army fliers.

The decision of the General Staff to let the AWPD draw up the requirements for aviation under the Victory Program surprised George and his officers. In part, the General Staff was under pressure to meet a deadline, but Gerow's cursory instructions to stay within the guidelines of ABC-1 and RAINBOW 5 showed that the General Staff trusted the fliers. If he had not trusted them, Gerow would have given them more specific instructions. Thus the efforts of the Army Air Corps to prove itself part of the army team had finally paid off. The Army Air Forces had won a degree of autonomy from and equality with the General Staff that would have been unimaginable when Roosevelt took office in 1933.

Maj. Gen. Lewis H. Brereton was given command of the new Far East Air Force. Before Brereton left for the Philippines, Marshall and Arnold briefed him on the status of the aerial reinforcement and said that two more squadrons of heavy bombers were being sent to the islands. Eventually, four bomber and four pursuit groups would be assigned to the islands, but the pursuit groups would not be there for several more months. Brereton pointed out that putting bomber forces into a sensitive area before establishing the fighter protection and an air warning system would be extremely hazardous. If the situation in the Far East became critical, the presence of unprotected bombers might incite an attack. The Japanese, said Brereton, "would have everything to gain by neutralizing our bomber force before the arrival of the units necessary for their protection." Brereton expressed a concern that only two airfields in the Philippines — Clark Field on Luzon and Del Monte on Mindanao — could support the operations of heavy bombers during the wet season. Concentrated on only two fields, the bombers would be more vulnerable to air attack. Without support units, the bombers presented too inviting a target. Marshall and Arnold explained that the risk was necessary because a strong force of heavy bombers in the Philippines would allow the United States to enforce its demands on Japan. Also, they said he could use airfields from China to Australia to disperse his bombers.[33]

On October 7, Arnold informed MacArthur about Brereton's assignment and explained that the primary function of the Far East Air Force was "opposing the advance of surface forces over water." The range of the bombers being sent to the Philippines allowed them to fly to Australian, British, and Dutch airfields for joint action against an invasion force while it was afloat and highly vulnerable to air attack. Arnold told MacArthur that efforts were underway in Washington to arrange for the joint use of airfields, and he asked MacArthur to accelerate or expand those plans at his end. One week later, Arnold told MacArthur that by using the airfields at Singapore, Darwin, Rockhampton, Rabaul, Davao, and Aparri, "the sea routes between Japan and Singapore, and Japan and the Dutch East Indies can be very well covered by B-17 and B-24 types of aircraft. Furthermore, B-24s operating out Aparri can cover the south section of the Japanese Islands as far north as Nagasaki." If the airfields around Vladivostok could be used, "operations from that point can cover most of the Japanese Islands."[34]

The General Staff believed that the air and ground units in or on their way to the Philippines had changed the strategic balance in the Far East. Using the threat of air power to deter Japanese aggressions became the center of the army's strategic planning for the Far East. With the concurrence of General Marshall, WPD sent Secretary Stimson a memorandum outlining its strategic concepts for the Philippines on October 8. The main concern of the army planners remained the avoidance of war with Japan because it would interrupt the flow of supplies to Britain and Russia. Army planners were particularly nervous about the supply line through Vladivostok; it handled 3,000 tons per day, compared to only 270 tons by the Persian Gulf route. When Marshall and Arnold briefed Brereton in Washington, they explained that Lend-Lease supplies would be shipped to Russia through Vladivostok, and they were worried that Japan might block the route. By placing heavy bombers in Manchuria to threaten Japan's northern flank, said Marshall and Arnold, the Dutch East Indies and the ships going to Vladivostok might be protected. WPD echoed Marshall and Arnold when it suggested to Secretary Stimson that the "present deterrents should be maintained and further strengthened by the provision of strong offensive air forces in the Philippines." The range of the heavy bombers would allow them to operate from bases in British possessions to the south and from eastern Russia."[35] The General Staff had accepted the idea of using long-range bombers as a mobile strike force that could rapidly go wherever it was needed, from Australia to Vladivostok. When the strike force was in the Philippines, the Japanese would be deterred from moving southward. Japan's lines of attack and supply would be exposed to naval and air assault. Should the Japanese attack the Russians and the United States enter the war, the Japanese home islands would be "open to aerial attack by U.S. and Russian heavy bombardment based in Siberia." Also, the army planners believed that the air power based in the Philippines made an attack on them a "hazardous military operation" because the Japanese would have to rely upon carrier planes and "intermittent support" from long-range planes from Taiwan for air support.[36]

Underlying the General Staff's Far Eastern strategy was the mistaken belief that the Japanese were inferior pilots, but the strategy had two other fatal misconceptions. First, it discounted the Japanese carrier planes. The General Staff overlooked the West Coast maneuvers of February, 1940, when the navy's carrier planes caught the GHQ Air Force's planes concentrated at Reno and "destroyed" them, remembering only the more recent battle of Crete. This misconception created a false sense of security in the Philippines and Hawaii. Japanese carrier pilots corrected that misconception in December. Second, the strategy assumed only "intermittent support" from the long-range planes based in Taiwan but expected the American long-range planes to maintain constant protection. This misconception was founded in the GHQ Air Force's successful flights to South America and the *Rex* interception in foul weather. Because the army pilots had proved that they could do these things, the army planners believed that they could do it every time. Overconfident, the army planners underestimated the threat from airplanes on Taiwan.

By the first week of October, 1941, the feasibility of air strikes on Tokyo had been impressed upon the State and War departments. Since the Army Air Corps had done what it had promised during the prewar years, the Roosevelt administration assumed the Army Air Forces could fulfill this plan. Secretary Stimson had recognized the strategic value of stationing heavy bombers in the Philippines before he received the WPD's memorandum. On October 4, he had sent Secretary of State Hull, by way of Stanley Hornbeck, a map of the Western Pacific to show him "the tremendous change which is being introduced by the new establishment of the heavy bombers in the Philippine Islands." Drawn on the map were concentric circles representing the radius of action of B-18s, B-17s, and B-24s flying out of Singapore, Manila, Vladivostok, Rabaul, Rockhampton, and Darwin. The circles overlapped and graphically demonstrated how most of the China Sea and the Coral Sea were under the protection of American air power. Just as important, however, the map also had lines drawn to show that the B-24s from the Philippines could fly over Tokyo and on to Vladivostok for a landing.[37]

The idea of using Vladivostok for attacks on Japan fired the imagination of the State Department. After Pearl Harbor, the State Department directly approached the Soviets. On December 11, Secretary Hull met with Soviet ambassador Maxim Litvinov and asked for two air bases, one on the Kamchatka Peninsula and the other near Vladivostok, which would allow American bombers to fly over the Japanese home naval bases, fleet, and cities. Litvinov accepted the idea of sending bombers over the Japanese navy, but in view of the experiences in Moscow, London, and other cities, he said that the bombing of cities would not necessarily settle the matter. Hull vainly argued that there was no substitute for the injury that American planes could and would inflict upon the Japanese if allowed to operate over all parts of Japan.[38] With German tanks at the gates of Moscow, the Soviets refused to be drawn into a two-front war to implement a dubious plan.

The Army Air Forces had proved that they could get their B-17s to the Philippines, but there was no assurance that they would have the planes to send. Roosevelt wanted the British and Russians to have as many B-17s as possible, but every plane sent to them meant one less for the Army Air Forces. American industry, still on a peacetime schedule, could not meet the growing demand for bombers. The only solution was to put American industry on a wartime schedule, but it took the Japanese attack on Pearl Harbor to force the United States into full production. Even then, it took another year before the production of aircraft was in full swing. In late September, Roosevelt had asked Secretary Stimson to estimate how many heavy bombers could be sent to other nations without endangering American defenses. Stimson attempted to dissuade the president from releasing any heavy bombers, because the United States lacked sufficient numbers to adequately meet its own defense requirements. Stimson explained that two groups of bombers in the Philippines were "the smallest force" that could have any influence in the Far East, and a larger force would be needed to retard Japanese aggression. Although Roosevelt agreed about the need for the heavy bombers in the Philippines and Hawaii, he instructed Stimson to divert planes bound for Newfoundland to Great Britain instead of the Philippines.[39]

General Arnold complained to Secretary Stimson about giving heavy bombers to Great Britain or Russia. Arnold was particularly opposed to releasing any B-24s to the British, because he believed they would not use the planes effectively. Furthermore, the range of the B-24s made it possible "to reach the interior of Japan, while the range of the B-17 brings only the southern tip of Japan within our bombing range." Spurred by Arnold, Stimson again pleaded with the president to keep America's bombers for the Army Air Forces. Stimson told FDR that a strategic opportunity of the "utmost importance" had arisen in the Far East. After being "impotent to influence events" in the Far East for twenty years, the United States was "vested with the possibilities of effective power." Sending bombers to Great Britain had limited the number available for the Philippines, but even this "imperfect threat" could stop Japan's southward march and secure the safety of Singapore. If the Army Air Forces were given the heavy bombers scheduled for Great Britain, they could fly from Alaska to Vladivostok; from there, they could fly over Japan and land in the Philippines. This threat would give the United States "control over the Western Pacific" and assure the Russians of continued American aid. Furthermore, Stimson argued, it might force the Japanese to quit the Axis.[40]

After the Japanese invaded Manchuria in 1931, Stimson had advocated stern responses to Japanese aggression. But the weak condition of America's defenses had made Hoover and Roosevelt reluctant to risk war in the Far East. Suddenly, American technology appeared to have dramatically altered the balance of power in the Far East. Stimson believed that with its long-range B-17s, the United States had negated the power of the Japanese navy and could force its will on Japan. The secretary of war was convinced that the Army Air Forces could fly their bombers the long route from Alaska to the Philippines over Japan. It had never been done, but he did not doubt that the army fliers could do it. As a consequence, Stimson took a less compromising attitude toward Japan.

Secretary Stimson was advocating the employment of America's technological superiority to further its foreign policy goals. Its numerical inferiority would be compensated for by superior weaponry. Thus, four years before the atomic bombs were dropped on Hiroshima and Nagasaki, the United States government was considering a policy of atomic diplomacy—without the atomic bomb. Deterrence had been advocated by the supporters of air power throughout the interwar years, and the atomic diplomacy practiced by the United States to deter Soviet expansion in the years following the Second World War was nothing more than an extension of an earlier, if only slightly less terrifying, application of air power.

In addition to everything else, there was a shortage of bombs in the Philippines. To remedy the situation, Chief of Air Staff Spaatz asked the General Staff to rush four hundred tons of various sized bombs to the Philippines "at the earliest possible date." Spaatz requested 2,000-, 1,000-, 500-, and 100-pound bombs, but no incendiary bombs.[41] However, the Army Air Forces soon rushed to send incendiaries as well. On a trip to Great Britain in April, 1941, General Arnold had been impressed by the effectiveness of British and German incendiary bombs. When he returned to the United States, Arnold instructed the Army Ordnance Department, Chemical Warfare Service, and the National Defense Research Committee to produce bombs equivalent to those used in Europe.[42] To clarify what was wanted, Dr. Roger Adams, a chemist at the University of Illinois and a member of the NDRC, asked Lt. Col. Max Schneider for exact details. Adams said that finding one incendiary equally capable of igniting evergreen woods, docks, or dwelling houses would be "almost out of the question." Schneider explained that the "major function of the small incendiary bomb requested was "to ignite structures built of burnable materials or containing burnable stores." All other uses were "secondary." Also, large numbers would be dropped to ensure that "some should find a burnable resting place." If enough were dropped to overwhelm the fire departments, "the desired results will be obtained, i.e. an un-controlled fire will sweep through the target area and either destroy the structures therein or so damage them as to materially reduce their economic and social value."[43]

Since it was common knowledge that Japanese cities were built of highly inflammable materials, there is no question about how the Army Air Forces intended to use the small incendiaries. It was what General Marshall had in mind when he told Admiral Stark that the B-24s had "an operating radius of 1500 miles with a load of 14,000 bombs, which means that they can reach Osaka with a full load and Tokyo with a partial load."[44] They planned to set uncontrollable fires in the Japanese cities.

In the last month before Pearl Harbor, the General Staff made hurried efforts to arm the Far East Air Force with bombs to carry out these plans. A shortage of magnesium hindered the production of incendiaries, but 100-pound chemical bombs filled with gasoline would work. In November, five thousand of these empty bombs were shipped to the Philippines. On December 1, with Marshall and Arnold's approval, army chemists told General MacArthur how he could adapt eight hundred white phosphorus bombs already in the Philippines. During the first week of December, twenty thousand more empty chemical bombs were flown to San Francisco from across the United States for shipment to the Philippines. Also, the Army Air Forces arranged to ship fifty thousand four- to six-pound incendiaries before New Year's Day. The Japanese attack on December 7 halted the shipments.[45] One should note that all of these secret preparations were made before Pearl Harbor incited hatred and demands for revenge from the American people.

When diplomatic relations between the United States and Japan deteriorated in the fall of 1941, people questioned the hard line the United States was taking toward Japan. In Tokyo, Ambassador Joseph Grew thought an embargo or blockade of Japan was being planned, and he warned the State Department that Japan would not collapse as a military power from an exhaustion of its economic and financial resources. The Japanese had successfully adapted to a loss of commerce, a drastic curtailment of industrial production, and a depletion of natural resources by integrating their national economy without regard to the capitalistic system.[46] On November 15, E. Ruffcorn Armstrong, a state senator in Montana, expressed his concern over America's relations with Japanese to United States Sen. Arthur Capper, a Kansas Democrat. Having just returned from a five-month stay in the Philippines, Armstrong warned that there were only 125 planes in the Islands. He asked, "WHY ARE WE TALKING SO STRONGLY TO

JAPAN WITH SUCH A WEAK SHOWING IN OUR AIR FORCE?" Senator Capper forwarded Armstrong's letter to General Arnold for his consideration. Lt. Col. William W. Dick answered for Arnold. Making Armstrong look like a crackpot, Dick explained to Senator Capper that the War Department had already answered other letters from Armstrong. He assured the senator that the General Staff was "completely cognizant of the military situation in the Philippines and that all necessary steps are being taken." Obviously, the War Department was afraid to let even a United States senator know about the changed situation in Far East.[47]

General Arnold almost revealed the secret during a speech at West Point on October 10. "Suppose it is necessary," he said, "to reinforce the Philippines immediately with several squadrons of Heavy Bombers. War Plans must figure out to the last detail how we can get them there safely and quickly." Catching himself, Arnold changed the subject and concluded his address.[48] War Department officials tried to keep the reinforcement of the Philippine Islands secret, but they knew word of the B-17s arrival would leak out eventually. Accordingly, they prepared a statement for use when the story broke. The press would be told that "as a routine initial strengthening of our Island outposts we are replacing obsolescent aircraft in the Philippines with modern combat planes." On Halloween, to prevent any contradictory statements, Secretary Stimson sent copies of the announcement to General Marshall and Secretary Hull.[49]

General Marshall, remembering how quickly the press had reported the shipment of a few pursuit planes in February, expressed amazement that the reinforcement of the Philippines had been kept secret, but he wanted the secrecy maintained until the defenses became truly effective on December 10. After that date, he believed, it would be advantageous for the Japanese to learn that the Philippines had been effectively reinforced. Admiral Stark also feared going to war with Japan before the navy was ready. He and Marshall met on November 3, and the next day, they set forth their views to Secretary of State Hull. On November 5, Marshall and Stark signed a joint memorandum for Roosevelt that stated: "By about the middle of December, 1941, United States air and submarine strength in the Philippines will have become a positive threat to any Japanese operations south of Formosa. The U.S. Army air forces in the Philippines will have reached its projected strength by February or March, 1942." Until that time, they warned, war in the Far East had to be avoided.[50]

To prevent the publication of any information about what the United States was doing in the Philippines, General Marshall asked the press for help. On November 15, Marshall met with key members of the press to keep their interpretations of current and forthcoming events from upsetting American military strategy. He said that anyone who did not care to share secrets was at liberty to leave. Nobody left. The United States and Japan were on the brink of war, said Marshall, but the United States had the advantage. Under great secrecy, the United States had built up the defenses of the Philippines to an extent unimagined by the Japanese. MacArthur was unloading ships at night, building air fields in the carefully guarded interior, and allowing no one within miles of military reservations. The United States was preparing for an offensive war, but the Japanese believed that America was only preparing for a defensive war. Without mentioning that Japan's codes had been broken with "Magic," Marshall said that a leak was informing the United States about everything the Japanese knew of American military preparations, and they were unaware of the build up in the Philippines. Moreover, the Japanese thought the Army Air Forces had only eighteen B-18s in the Philippines, but there were actually "35 Flying Fortresses already there—the largest concentration anywhere in the world." More planes, artillery, and tanks would arrive very soon.

Calling it a miracle that the Japanese had not found out about the B-17s, Marshall said that two attempts to publish the fact had been thwarted. The information would be allowed to leak out, but it had to be done privately and from the White House or the State Department to Japanese officials. If the information became public knowledge, fanatics in the Japanese army would demand war before the Philippines were better fortified. But if the Japanese officials knew first, Marshall explained, they could tell their cabinet, "[the Americans] really mean to bomb our cities, and they have the equipment with which to do it. We'd better go slow." This approach would make any public face-saving unnecessary and might avert a war. America wanted to avert a war with Japan because it would divert supplies from the British. Yet, should war be unavoidable, the United States would fight "mercilessly." Flying Fortresses, said the general, would be dispatched immediately to set the paper cities of Japan on fire, and there would be no hesitation about bombing civilians—it would be all-out. The B-17s could not make the round-trip to Japan from the Philippines, but arrangements were being made to provide landing fields in Vladivostok. Safe landing fields could be provided in China. The new B-24s could make the round-trip, and they would be dispatched to the Philippines as soon as they came off the assembly line.

Marshall demonstrated his great faith in the Army Air Forces and its bombers by saying that the United States Navy would not play much of a role in a war with Japan. The army bombers could take care of the Japanese navy and cities without the use of the navy. As evidence, he displayed a map with concentric circles marking the range of American bombers. It showed that the Army Air Forces could fight throughout the entire western Pacific, from Australia to Alaska. Looking at the map, the correspondents saw that Japanese naval bases in the mandated islands were within range of the bombers and highly vulnerable, but Marshall emphasized that Japan was the main target. Flying weather over Japan was "propitious" at that time because the rainy season had ended, and with such good weather the high flying bombers could wreak havoc, unmolested by Japanese fighters. Repeating a mistaken belief held by most Americans, Marshall claimed that the Japanese had no fighters that could reach the B-24s. Marshall emphasized the need for secrecy, but he should have known that military secrets are the most difficult to keep. Only four days later, Arthur Krock exposed in the *New York Times* almost everything that Marshall had asked to be kept secret.[51] However, the Krock article might have been a carefully planned leak emanating from the White House. Arthur Krock was one of the best-known, most prestigious journalists in the nation. Although proud of his scoops, Krock was not likely to participate in a serious security breach.[52]

Krock's article had little effect on Japanese-American relations. On November 7, Roosevelt had told Secretary Hull to do everything possible to keep negotiations with Japan from collapsing, but the Japanese were moving toward their decision for war. Early in November, after six months' work, the Japanese completed their plans to attack the United States, Great Britain, and the Dutch East Indies. They made only minor changes in the plan before implementing it on December 7. Tokyo told Ambassador Kichisaburo Nomura on November 5 that a peace agreement had to be reached by November 25 or Japanese-American relations would go into a "chaotic condition." Through "Magic," President Roosevelt knew of Tokyo's order, but he rejected two more Japanese peace plans as unacceptable to the United States. From another intercepted message, Roosevelt learned that the Japanese would extend the deadline for successful talks from November 25 to November 29 and that after that date, "things are automatically going to happen." On November 22, Roosevelt pessimistically offered Japan a counter proposal. FDR feared that the Japanese would place him in a difficult situation by attacking British or Dutch territory but not American territory. If the United States responded militarily without having been attacked, it would share the blame for war with Japan. The president wanted Japan to be recognized as the aggressor. He told Hull, Knox, Marshall, Stark, and Stimson on November 25 that the question was "how we should maneuver them into the position of firing the first shot without allowing too much danger to ourselves." The next day, Roosevelt was told that ships carrying five divisions of Japanese soldiers had been sighted south of Formosa. Believing that the Japanese had tried to dupe him by negotiating for a truce and a withdrawal from Indochina while sending this expedition south, Roosevelt became enraged. Roosevelt and Hull sent another proposal to Tokyo on November 26, but they both knew that negotiations with Japan were over.

On December 1, Lord Halifax, the British ambassador, suggested issuing parallel warnings to Japan. Roosevelt wanted to ask the Japanese about their troop movements first, but he gave Halifax the impression that the United States would support any British response to a Japanese reinforcement of Indochina or an attack on Thailand. More importantly, Roosevelt spoke to Halifax about using the air force in the Philippines and a long-distance naval blockade. The Japanese gave him an evasive answer about their troop movements on December 6, and Roosevelt decided to ask the emperor to remove the troops from Indochina as the only way to have peace in the South Pacific. That night, FDR received thirteen parts of the fourteen-part Japanese answer to his latest proposal. After reading them, he told Harry Hopkins that the answer meant war. Hopkins suggested a first strike, but Roosevelt refused to fire the first shot and ruin America's record of being a peaceful nation.[53]

President Roosevelt had not maneuvered the Japanese into beginning hostilities in order to get America into the war through a back door. He wanted to avoid becoming embroiled in a Pacific war because it would drain supplies from the Atlantic war. But if war had to come, FDR wanted a clear case of Japanese aggression to unite the American people in a common cause. Yet, by yielding the initiative to the Japanese, Roosevelt had displayed neither a callous disregard for the lives of American servicemen nor a naive belief that a democracy should not strike the first blow in a fight. Rather, as his discussion with Halifax showed, Roosevelt's decision was proof of his confidence in the Army Air Forces.

Frank Andrews, Oscar Westover, and Hap Arnold had proved throughout the Roosevelt presidency that the Army Air Corps could fulfill its promises. The corps had won the confidence of the War Department and General Staff by turning from the antagonistic methods used by Billy Mitchell and working within the system. As the bitterness between the airmen and the General Staff subsided, the General Staff became more receptive to the airmen's needs and gave them greater responsibility. Through hard work and careful planning, the GHQ Air Force added validity to the claims of air power with a record of successful bombing tests and long-range flights. By the time the Munich Crisis forced Roosevelt to give up hope of eliminating bombers, the Army Air Corps had proven itself a capable and efficient organization. After the war in Europe demonstrated that unopposed air power could defeat naval power, the Roosevelt administration became confident that the Army Air Forces could do to the Japanese navy what the Luftwaffe had done to the Royal Navy off Norway and Crete.

On the eve of Pearl Harbor, Roosevelt believed he had found a way to maneuver the Japanese into attacking without endangering American defenses. Expecting the Japanese to attack Malaya, the Dutch East Indies, or the Philippines, Roosevelt believed the Army Air Forces would destroy the invasion fleet before much damage could be done.

Unfortunately, the Japanese devastated the United States Pacific fleet's battleship forces at Pearl Harbor and the Army Air Forces' aircraft at Hickam Field on December 7, 1941. In the Philippines, despite knowledge of the attack on Pearl Harbor, Japanese planes from Formosa caught the Far East Air Force on the ground and destroyed eighteen of its thirty-five B-17s and fifty-three of 107 P-40s on the first day. With counter air activities that Spaatz had warned of much earlier, the Japanese made the American air fields untenable.[54] Japanese pilots won complete mastery of the skies over the Philippines and saved their navy and cities, but their victory was temporary. All too soon, Curtis LeMay's B-29s would bring to life Japan's greatest fear: the burning of their cities.

> The best-laid schemes o' mice an' men
> Gang aft agley,
> An' lea'e us nought but grief an' pain,
> For promis'd joy!

ROBERT BURNS[55]

Commentary on Giulio Douhet and the Army Air Corps

Assessing the influence of Giulio Douhet, the Italian air power advocate, on Army Air Corps officers presents a difficult problem. Those men must have discussed Douhet's most famous work, *Command of the Air*, which was available to them. Published in Italian in 1921, the Air Service Tactical School had a translation of *Command of the Air* by 1923, and extracts of his other works found their way around the Air Corps Tactical School by the early 1930s. In 1933, Major General Foulois, chief of the Air Corps, sent thirty mimeographed copies of an article about Douhet's theories to the chair of the House Committee on Military Affairs. Foulois called the article "an excellent exposition of certain principles of air war."[1] However, comments about Douhet did not find expression in the personal or official correspondence of the most important army fliers of the 1930s and World War II. The papers of Benjamin Foulois, Hap Arnold, Frank M. Andrews, Ira Eaker, and Carl Spaatz in the Library of Congress carry only fleeting, if any, mention of the Italian's theories about air power. Douhet's influence, therefore, might be best measured by comparing the theories expounded in *Command of the Air* against Billy Mitchell's *Winged Defense* and the actions of the Army Air Corps officers before and during the Second World War.

Douhet concerned himself with only one type of war, one in which "the entire population and all the resources of a nation are sucked into the maw of war." All future wars, he believed, would be "total in character and scope."[2] Using this reasoning to justify the rejection of any limitations on military activities, Douhet pointed to the recent World War to prove his points. Modern warfare required the support of an industrial base, but the civilian populations had been left "in safety and comparative peace" to produce the necessary war materiel because neither side could invade the other's territory.[3] Defensive weapons, he explained, had become too strong, and armies could no longer break through defenses without paying a staggering cost in lives and national wealth. Air power, Douhet argued, offered the solution: airplanes could bypass the ground defenses simply by flying over them. Therefore, no area could exist "in which life can be lived in safety and tranquillity, nor can the battlefield be limited to actual combatants. . . . all citizens will be come combatants, since all of them will be exposed to the enemy."[4]

Certain that aerial assaults posed the greatest danger to his homeland, Douhet wrote to demonstrate how Italy could defend itself through the proper application of air power. Italy could not be protected by scattering anti-aircraft guns or defensive fighter planes across the countryside, "but by preventing the enemy from flying." In other words, by "conquering the command of the air" through "offensive and not defensive action, the very action best suited to air power."[5] For him, the only effective aerial defense consisted of destroying the enemy's air force at its bases, on the ground and not through aerial combat.[6]

Like Douhet, the American army fliers believed that air attacks presented the greatest threat to their nation, and they also saw air power as the essential element for national security. In his book, *Winged Defense* (1925), Billy Mitchell echoed Douhet, writing that the only defense against aircraft was to strike the enemy first and as far away from home as possible. Like Douhet, he believed that anti-aircraft fire could not thwart an air attack.[7] However, Mitchell thought that pursuit aircraft could intercept and severely damage an attacking force of bombers.[8]

Douhet and Mitchell shared a common belief that only independent air forces, carrying out offensive aerial actions, could protect their respective homelands. Nevertheless, geography dictated differences in their approaches toward the application of air power. The Alps separated Italy from its potential enemies, but Douhet recognized that airplanes could easily span that natural barrier. To prevent enemy aircraft from crossing the Alps, he called for an initial assault on the enemy's air force. Once command of the air had been gained, stated Douhet, the independent air force would be free to conduct other offensive operations against "railroad junctions and depots, population centers at road junctions, military depots, and other vital objectives" to prevent the enemy from mobilizing his army. Air attacks on naval facilities would neutralize the opposing fleet. And finally, bombing "the most vital civilian centers" could spread terror through the nation and quickly break down the enemy's "material and moral resistance."[9] Powerless to resist further onslaughts, the enemy would have been defeated before the armies could meet on the battlefield.

For the United States, separated from any potential adversary by two oceans, Billy Mitchell suggested a different offensive strategy. Assuming that America would go to war only if attacked by an invasion force, Mitchell advocated a four-phased strategy, initially based upon defensive measures. Obviously referring to labor unrest experienced during the World War and the postwar Red Scare, he stated that the ground army would first ensure "domestic tranquility in the country itself" so that the preparation for war could proceed unhindered. Second, the air force would defend the coasts by defeating hostile aircraft or invasion fleets. Mitchell of course believed that battleships were helpless against airplanes, but he also assumed that carrier planes were no match for land-based airplanes. Third, the air force, in conjunction with submarines, would win control of the sea lanes. The fourth step was conducting an offensive war across the seas. It required land troops, under the protection of air power, to occupy a succession of land bases, until the enemy could "be attacked directly through the air." Only after "complete dominion of the air had been established," he argued, could an invasion be successfully prosecuted.[10] In his next book, *Skyways* (1930), Mitchell's thinking moved toward Douhet and advocated the bombing of civilian populations.[11]

The Army Air Corps's officers agreed with Douhet about the importance of air power, and they also wanted an independent air force. However, *Command of the Air* contained very little practical information for them. Air Corps planners had to consider America's geographic position, and Douhet's strategy for Italy was not applicable. Mitchell's four-phased plan, however, gave the Air Corps planners something they could use. Fourteen years after the publication of *Winged Defense*, the influence of Mitchell could still be seen in Air Corps plans. The report issued by the air board on May 7, 1939, contained elements reminiscent of *Winged Defense*. Stating that the primary function of the armed services was to defend United States territory by deterring or defeating an invasion force, the air board's report adapted Mitchell's discussion of conducting transoceanic invasions. It assumed that an enemy would establish a series of ever-closer bases from which air attacks would be made upon America's vital centers. Offensive in nature, the mission of American air power would be to defeat the enemy's air force by destroying its air bases. At this point, the air board, wavering from Mitchell and toward Douhet, called for aircraft factories to emphasize the building of bombers.[12] Mitchell, on the other hand, had believed that efficient reconnaissance and an adequate force of pursuit planes could inflict prohibitive losses on an attacking formation of bombers.[13]

Douhet had said that the independent air force should comprise bombers and "units of combat," by which he meant pursuit planes used to clear the way for the bombers.[14] But Douhet was not speaking of speedy, maneuverable pursuit planes. Rather, he wanted the units of combat to be a "slower, heavily armed plane, able to clear its way with its own armament. . . ."[15] They only had to be faster than the bombers. Once the enemy's air force had been destroyed, the units of combat would be converted into bombers to further the bombing campaign.[16]

Although they wanted the aircraft industry to center on the production of bombers, the Army Air Corps leaders of the late 1930s viewed the bomber differently than Douhet had. While commanding the 1933 maneuvers, Oscar Westover had concluded that pursuit planes could not stop a force of fast bombers.[17] These maneuvers were conducted before the advent of radar, and combat experience later proved the fallacy of this notion. In contradiction to Douhet, the Army Air Forces' leaders went to war believing in a doctrine that held that tight formations of well-armed bombers could get through pursuit defenses without any escort.

The army fliers also differed from Douhet over the employment of bombers. Douhet never expected bombers to achieve the accuracy of artillery. Therefore, he saw no reason for bombers to attack small targets: "Bombing objectives should always be large; small targets are unimportant. . . ."[18] He wanted the bomber pilots to be trained for flying in loose formations and spreading their loads over targets as "uniformly as possible." This tactic would methodically destroy large areas, like cities.[19] During the Second World War, both sides employed this method known as "carpet bombing." But throughout the 1930s and World War II, American army fliers emphasized flying tight formations and using precision bombing to destroy small targets, such as specific factories. The numerous efforts of Frank Andrews and the GHQ Air Force to prove how accurately they could deliver concentrated bomb loads from high altitude demonstrated their rejection of Douhet's dictum that "since by their very nature bombing operations are characterized by dispersion rather than concentration of fire, bombing raids can be carried out effectively at very high altitudes."[20]

Finally, one would be mistaken to conclude from their preparations made in 1941 to firebomb Tokyo that the army aviators had adopted this method because of Douhet's influence. The diligence with which they carried out the daylight, precision bombing raids over Europe and Japan clearly demonstrated their adherence to the idea of stopping an enemy's industrial production by destroying carefully chosen targets. Their belief in daylight bombing found its clearest exposition with the raids on the Schweinfurt ball bearing plants in 1943. Also, the first B-29 raids over Japan showed the army fliers' continued faith in precision bombing. However, these men also recognized the potential military value of destroying Tokyo. For years, the city's susceptibility to fire had been widely known, and the bomber force deployed to the Philippines fell far short of the six groups of heavy bombers Spaatz had called for in his report in September of 1939, "Strategically Offensive Operations in the Far East." The limited number of bombers available approached the number Spaatz stated would be necessary just to defend the islands.[21] Conducting an aerial bombing campaign, like the army fliers would have preferred, would have been impossible with such a small number of bombers.

After Chennault's visit of December, 1940, the idea of dropping incendiaries on Japanese cities had taken hold within the Roosevelt administration, but this idea did not appear among the army fliers until six or seven months later. As the decision to send bombers to the Philippines took shape in late July, 1941, Spaatz ordered conventional bombs, not incendiaries, sent to the Philippines.[22] Afterward, military events around the world influenced the hurried efforts to provide the Far East Air Force with incendiaries. The Japanese had used incendiaries in China for years, and the Roosevelt administration had already started thinking about their employment against Japanese cities. However, Hap Arnold's trip to Great Britain in April, 1941, seems to have been the turning point among the army fliers. After the war, he wrote: "One of my chief interests when I returned to the U.S. was the development of incendiary bombs. We had made little advance in this field, although the British and Germans, whose incendiaries were different from ours, had used them very effectively." With samples of the British and German bombs as guides, Arnold directed the development of American incendiary bombs. He then learned from Dr. Vannevar Bush about napalm. Arnold called this invention "the start of a new era in incendiary bomb construction" for the Army Air Forces.[23]

Like Giulio Douhet who had witnessed air raids during the First World War, Arnold had seen the results of German bombs dropped on British cities, and it became apparent to him that incendiary bombs were effective weapons already being employed by the warring powers. Once that mental transition had been made, Arnold became willing to use incendiaries as well. With Tokyo particularly vulnerable to fire, Arnold and the other Army Air Forces officers undoubtedly viewed its reduction to ashes as the best way to destroy a major segment of Japan's industrial capability with the small number of bombers available. This military expedient came not from the writings of Giulio Douhet, but from current practices around the globe. Firebombing had gained a dubious validity through its application by other nations.

List of Army Airfields Mentioned[1]

Airfield	*Location*
Albrook Field	Corozal, Canal Zone
Barksdale Field	Shreveport, Louisiana
Bolling Field	Anacostia, District of Columbia
Brooks Field	San Antonio, Texas
Chanute Field	Rantoul, Illinois
Clark Field	Fort Stotsenburg, Philippine Islands
Hickam Field	Oahu, Territory of Hawaii
Kelly Field	San Antonio, Texas
Langley Field	Hampton, Virginia
McCook Field	Dayton, Ohio
March Field	Riverside, California
Maxwell Field	Montgomery, Alabama
Mitchel Field	Garden City, Long Island, New York
Muroc Bombing Field	Muroc, California
Randolph Field	San Antonio, Texas
Roosevelt Field	Mineola, Long Island, New York
Selfridge Field	Mount Clemens, Michigan

Key Civilian and Military Officials

PRESIDENTS OF THE UNITED STATES

Woodrow Wilson (March, 1913–March, 1921)
Warren G. Harding (March, 1921–August, 1923)
Calvin Coolidge (August, 1923–March, 1929)
Herbert Hoover (March, 1929–March, 1933)
Franklin D. Roosevelt (March, 1933–April, 1945)

SECRETARIES OF WAR

Newton D. Baker (March, 1916–March, 1921)
John W. Weeks (March, 1921–October, 1925)
Dwight F. Davis (October, 1925–March, 1929)
James W. Good (March, 1929–November, 1929)
Patrick J. Hurley (December, 1929–March, 1933)
George H. Dern (March, 1933–August, 1936)
Harry H. Woodring (September, 1936–June, 1940)
Henry L. Stimson (July, 1940–September, 1945)

CHIEFS OF STAFF, UNITED STATES ARMY

Maj. Gen. Peyton C. March (May, 1918–June, 1921)
General of the Armies John J. Pershing (July, 1921–September, 1924)
Maj. Gen. John L. Hines (September, 1924–November, 1926)
Gen. Charles P. Summerall (November, 1926–November, 1930)
Gen. Douglas MacArthur (November, 1930–October, 1935)

Gen. Malin Craig (October, 1935–August, 1935)

General of the Army George C. Marshall (Acting Chief of Staff, August, 1935–September, 1939)

General of the Army George C. Marshall (September, 1939–November, 1945)

HEADS OF ARMY AVIATION

Directors of Air Service
John D. Ryan (August, 1918–November, 1918)
Maj. Gen. Charles T. Menoher (December, 1918–June, 1920)

Chiefs of the Air Service
Maj. Gen. Charles T. Menoher (June, 1920–October, 1921)
Maj. Gen. Mason M. Patrick (October, 1921–July, 1926)

Chiefs of the Air Corps
Maj. Gen. Mason M. Patrick (July, 1926–December, 1927)
Maj. Gen. James E. Fechet (December, 1927–December, 1931)
Maj. Gen. Benjamin D. Foulois (December, 1931–December, 1935)
Maj. Gen. Oscar Westover (December, 1935–September, 1938)
Maj. Gen. Henry H. Arnold (September, 1938–June, 1941)

Commanding Generals, GHQ Air Force
Maj. Gen. Frank M. Andrews (March, 1935–March, 1939)
Maj. Gen. Delos C. Emmons (March, 1939–June, 1941)

Chief, Army Air Forces
Maj. Gen./Gen. Henry H. Arnold (June, 1941–March, 1942)

Commanding General, Army Air Forces
Lt. Gen./Gen./General of the Army Henry H. Arnold (March, 1942–February, 1946)

Notes

INTRODUCTION

1. John F. Shiner, *Foulois and the U.S. Army Air Corps, 1931–1935* (Washington, D.C.: Office of Air Force History, United States Air Force, 1983), p. 81.

2. Hanson W. Baldwin, *United We Stand! Defense of the Western Hemisphere* (New York: Whittlesey House, 1941), p. 220.

CHAPTER I. THE BILLY MITCHELL YEARS

1. This illustration can be found in Ezra Bowen, *Knights of the Air: The Epic of Flight* (Alexandria, Virginia: Time Life Books, 1980), p. 146.

2. Wesley Frank Craven and James Lea Cate, eds., *The Army Air Forces in World War II* (Chicago: University of Chicago Press, 1948–55), vol. 1, *Plans and Early Operations, January 1939 to August 1942,* pp. 5–10.

3. Lee Kennett, *A History of Strategic Bombing* (New York: Charles Scribner's Sons, 1982), pp. 60–61; Craven and Cate, *Army Air Forces,* vol. 1, p. 15.

4. Craven and Cate, *Army Air Forces,* vol. 1, pp. 12–15.

5. Alfred F. Hurley, *Billy Mitchell: Crusader for Air Power* (New York: Franklin Watts, 1964; Bloomington: Indiana University Press, 1974), p. 37; Daniel R. Beaver, *Newton D. Baker and the American War Effort, 1917–1919* (Lincoln: University of Nebraska Press, 1966), p. 169.

6. Robin Higham, *Air Power: A Concise History* (New York: St. Martin's Press, 1972), pp. 68–69.

7. H. H. Arnold, *Global Mission* (New York: Harper and Brothers, 1949), p. 91; William Mitchell, *Winged Defense: The Development and Possibilities of Modern Air Power—Economic and Military* (New York: G. P. Putnam's

Sons, 1925), pp. 101–102; Russell F. Weigley, *The American Way of War: A History of United States Military Strategy and Policy,* The Wars of the United States (New York: Macmillan Publishing Co., 1977), pp. 234–35.

8. Arnold, *Global Mission,* pp. 95–97; Thomas M. Coffey, *Hap: The Story of the U.S. Air Force and the Man Who Built It, General Henry H. "Hap" Arnold* (New York: Viking Press, 1982), pp. 102–103.

9. Benjamin D. Foulois with C. V. Glines, *From the Wright Brothers to the Astronauts: The Memoirs of Major General Benjamin D. Foulois* (New York: McGraw-Hill Book Company, 1968), pp. 186–88.

10. Foulois and Glines, *Memoirs,* pp. 185–86; Arnold, *Global Mission,* p. 97.

11. Frank Freidel, *Franklin D. Roosevelt: The Apprenticeship* (Boston: Little, Brown and Co., 1952), pp. 364–65; Frank Freidel, *Franklin D. Roosevelt: The Ordeal* (Boston: Little, Brown and Co., 1954), pp. 26–27.

12. Russell F. Weigley, *History of the United States Army* (New York: Macmillan Publishing Co., 1967), pp. 396–400; Craven and Cate, *Army Air Forces,* vol. 1, p. 24.

13. Arnold, *Global Mission,* pp. 102–105. For the navy's interpretation of the bombing tests and for an explanation as to why the navy aviators did not align themselves with the army fliers in seeking independence, see Archibald D. Turnbull and Clifford L. Lord, *History of United States Naval Aviation* (New Haven: Yale University Press, 1949), pp. 193–204, 238–40.

14. Craven and Cate, *Army Air Forces,* vol. 1, pp. 25–26; Arnold, *Global Mission,* p. 111.

15. Craven and Cate, *Army Air Forces,* vol. 1, p. 27; Weigley, *The American Way of War,* pp. 230–31.

16. Hurley, *Billy Mitchell,* pp. 79–80, 92–93.

17. William Mitchell, "How Should We Organize Our National Air Power?" pp. 6–7, Mitchell, "American Leadership in Aeronautics," p. 18, cartoon, p. 20, all in *Saturday Evening Post,* Mar. 14, 1925; Curtis D. Wilbur, "A Balanced Navy," p. 10, *Saturday Evening Post,* Jan. 10, 1925.

18. Hurley, *Billy Mitchell,* pp. 97–98; Craven and Cate, *Army Air Forces,* vol. 1, p. 27.

19. Ironically, the first of the series of articles that Mitchell published in the *Saturday Evening Post* was printed alongside one about the *Shenandoah.* Stanford E. Moses, "Life on the Shenandoah," *Saturday Evening Post,* Dec. 20, 1924, p. 5; Hurley, *Billy Mitchell,* pp. 101–102; Craven and Cate, *Army Air Forces,* vol. 1, p. 28.

20. Burl Noggle, *Teapot Dome: Oil and Politics in the 1920's* (Baton Rouge: Louisiana State University Press, 1962; New York: W. W. Norton and Co., 1965), p. 175; Hurley, *Billy Mitchell,* pp. 101–102.

21. Arnold, *Global Mission,* pp. 119–21; Craven and Cate, *Army Air Forces,* vol. 1, pp. 27–28.

22. Arnold, *Global Mission,* pp. 121–22.

23. Craven and Cate, *Army Air Forces,* vol. 1, pp. 28–29; Edwin H. Rutkowsky, *The Politics of Military Aviation Procurement, 1926–1934: A Study*

in the Political Assertion of Consensual Values (Columbus: Ohio State University Press, 1966), pp. 20, 59–61.

24. John W. Killigrew, *The Impact of the Great Depression on the Army* (New York: Garland Publishing, 1979), pp. III-18–III-23.

25. John F. Shiner, *Foulois and the U.S. Army Air Corps, 1931–1935* (Washington, D.C.: Office of Air Force History, United States Air Force, 1983), pp. 43–45.

26. *New York Times*, Jan. 2, Jan. 21, 1932.

27. Killigrew, *Impact of the Great Depression on the Army*, pp. V-5–V-7, V-21.

28. Foulois, *Memoirs*, pp. 221–24; Shiner, *Foulois and the U.S. Army Air Corps*, pp. 76–78; *New York Times*, Feb. 5, 1932.

29. Foulois, *Memoirs*, p. 225; Shiner, *Foulois*, pp. 41–48; Weigley, *The American Way of War*, pp. 234–36.

30. Thomas H. Greer, *The Development of Air Doctrine in the Army Air Arm, 1917–1941* (Maxwell Air Force Base, Alabama: USAF Historical Division, Research Studies Institute, Air University, 1955; Washington, D.C.: Office of Air Force History, United States Air Force, 1985), pp. 52–57, 66–67. Even though Chennault advocated a strong pursuit arm, he too believed in the importance of bombardment planes. In an article for the *Infantry Journal*, he wrote about the importance of bombardment. Claire L. Chennault, "Some Facts about Bombardment Aviation," *Infantry Journal* 42 (Sept.–Oct., 1935): 387–93.

31. Shiner, *Foulois*, pp. 52–54, 72; Craven and Cate, *Army Air Forces*, vol. 1, pp. 30, 62.

32. Shiner, *Foulois*, pp. 56–59; Andrews to Arnold, Aug. 17, Aug. 27, 1931, Frank M. Andrews Papers, General Correspondence, Box 1, Personal Correspondence, "A" 1930–42, Library of Congress, Washington, D.C.

CHAPTER II. THE ARMY AIR CORPS AND THE NEW DEAL

1. James MacGregor Burns, *Roosevelt: The Lion and the Fox, 1882–1940* (New York: Harcourt, Brace and World, 1956), p. 139.

2. Coffey, *Hap*, p. 172; telegram from R. H. Fleet to Roosevelt, Oct. 15, 1932, Benjamin F. Foulois Papers, Correspondence, Box 5, File Number 3, 1931–35, Library of Congress, Washington, D.C.

3. Telegram from R. H. Fleet to Hoover, Oct. 18, 1932, telegram from Fleet to Foulois, Oct. 18, 1932, and telegram from Foulois to Fleet, Oct. 19, 1932, all in Foulois Papers, Correspondence, Box 5, File Number 3, 1931–35.

4. *New York Times*, Nov. 9, 1932.

5. *New York Times*, Feb. 19, Mar. 5, Mar. 6, 1933.

6. William E. Leuchtenburg, *Franklin D. Roosevelt and the New Deal, 1932–1940*, The New American Nation Series, ed. Henry Steele Commager and Richard B. Morris (New York: Harper and Row, 1963), p. 11.

7. Burns, *The Lion and the Fox*, pp. 166–71.

8. Shiner, *Foulois*, pp. 113–17; *New York Times*, May 7, 1933.

9. Douglas MacArthur, *Reminiscences* (New York: McGraw Hill Book Co., 1964), pp. 100–101.

10. MacArthur, *Reminiscences*, pp. 100–101; Robert Dallek, *Franklin D. Roosevelt and American Foreign Policy, 1932–1945* (New York: Oxford University Press, 1979), p. 36; Shiner, *Foulois*, p. 115.

11. Hurley, *Billy Mitchell*, pp. 122–26; *New York Times*, Mar. 25, Apr. 9, 1933.

12. Killigrew, *Impact of the Great Depression*, pp. IV-13–IV-14; *New York Times*, June 8, 1933.

13. Carl Spaatz to Hap Arnold, Sept. 29, 1933, Carl Spaatz Papers, Diaries, Box 6, Aug. 3–Oct. 3, 1933, Library of Congress, Washington, D.C.

14. Kennett, *Strategic Bombing*, pp. 68–70. For an example of how people expected a war would be conducted, see Hanson W. Baldwin, "If War Should Again Assail the World," *New York Times Magazine*, June 4, 1932, pp. 8–9. Also see the photograph of Parisians being taught how to use gas masks by the prefect of police in the same day's photograph section of the *New York Times*.

15. William Phillips to Assistant Secretary to the President Marvin H. McIntyre, Apr. 28, 1933, in Edgar B. Nixon, ed., *Franklin D. Roosevelt and Foreign Affairs* (Cambridge, Mass.: Belknap Press, 1969), vol. 1, *January 1933–February 1934*, p. 91.

16. Memorandum from Roosevelt to Secretary of State Cordell Hull, May 6, 1933, and Presidential Press Conference, May 10, 1933, both in Nixon, *FDR and Foreign Affairs*, vol. 1, pp. 91, 107–109.

17. Roosevelt to the Heads of Nations Represented at the London and Geneva Conferences, May 16, 1933, in Nixon, *FDR and Foreign Affairs*, vol. 1, pp. 125–28.

18. Memorandum from Brig. Gen. Charles Kilbourne to Lt. Col. George V. Strong with the American delegation at Geneva, May 3, 1933, Record Group 165, WPD, 599-169, National Archives, Washington, D.C.; William Phillips to Roosevelt, May 27, 1933, in Nixon, *FDR and Foreign Affairs*, vol. 1, pp. 185–86; *New York Times*, May 28, 1933.

19. Memorandum from Roosevelt to Cordell Hull, May 27, 1933, memorandum from Hull to Roosevelt, May 27, 1933, both in Nixon, *FDR and Foreign Affairs*, vol. 1, pp. 172–76.

20. Dallek, *FDR and American Foreign Policy*, p. 75.

21. *New York Times*, Aug. 20, 1933.

22. Roosevelt to Malcolm E. Peabody, Aug. 19, 1933, in Nixon, *FDR and Foreign Affairs*, vol. 1, p. 370.

23. Shiner, *Foulois*, pp. 118–23.

24. Craven and Cate, *Army Air Forces*, vol. 1, pp. 63–64; Shiner, *Foulois*, pp. 59–65; Foulois, *Memoirs*, p. 227.

25. Foulois, *Memoirs*, p. 227; Arnold, *Global Mission*, pp. 140–41.

26. Craven and Cate, *Army Air Forces*, vol. 1, pp. 64–66; Foulois, *Memoirs*, pp. 227–30.

27. Kennett, *Strategic Bombing*, pp. 70–71.

28. William E. Dodd to Roosevelt, Oct. 13, 1933, Dodd to Roosevelt,

Oct. 28, 1933, and Roosevelt to Dodd, Nov. 13, 1933, all in Nixon, *FDR and Foreign Affairs*, vol. 1, pp. 424–25, 442–43, 484–85.

29. Speech by Roosevelt at the Woodrow Wilson Foundation dinner, Dec. 28, 1933, in Nixon, *FDR and Foreign Affairs*, vol. 1, pp. 558–63.

30. *New York Times*, Jan. 12, Jan. 13, 1934.

31. *Washington Post*, Jan. 13, 1934.

32. Chicago *Daily Tribune*, Jan. 12, 1934.

33. *New York Times*, Jan. 13, 1934.

34. *New York Times*, Jan. 24, 1934.

35. Shiner, *Foulois*, pp. 125–27; Foulois, *Memoirs*, pp. 236–37.

36. Ibid.

37. Norman E. Borden, Jr., *Air Mail Emergency, 1934: An Account of Seventy-Eight Tense Days in the Winter of 1934 When the Army Flew the United States Mail* (Freeport, Maine: Bond Wheelwright Co., 1968), pp. 14–20; Shiner, *Foulois*, pp. 134–37.

38. Foulois, *Memoirs*, pp. 241–45; Shiner, *Foulois*, pp. 135–37; Eddie Rickenbacker, "Army Planes Unfit, the Boys Are Sacrificed!" *Washington Post*, Feb. 25, 1934, p. 5.

39. *New York Times*, Feb. 24, Feb. 26, 1934; *Washington Post*, Feb. 25, 1934; John Boettiger, "Flying of Mail by Army Seen as Big Blunder," Chicago *Daily Tribune*, Feb. 25, 1934.

40. Chicago *Daily Tribune*, "Gen. Foulois Comes to Defense of Army Pilot's Mail Record," Feb. 25, 1934.

41. *New York Times*, Mar. 2, Mar. 11, 1934. I am not suggesting that Foulois had callously risked the lives of his men to win independence or appropriations for better aircraft. He always showed great concern for the safety of his men.

42. Shiner, *Foulois*, pp. 140–48; Foulois, *Memoirs*, pp. 253–58.

43. Dallek, *FDR and American Foreign Policy*, p. 75.

44. Eaker to Col. Walter R. Weaver, Mar. 14, 1934, Ira C. Eaker Papers, Correspondence, Box 3, 1934 Air Mail File, Library of Congress, Washington, D.C.

45. Eaker to Arnold, Apr. 5, 1934, and Arnold to Eaker, Apr. 6, 1934, both in Eaker Papers, Correspondence, Box 3, 1934 Air Mail File.

46. Foulois, *Memoirs*, pp. 236–37.

47. *New York Times*, Apr. 1, 1934.

48. *New York Times*, May 6, 1934.

49. *New York Times*, Apr. 1, May 6, May 7, 1934.

50. Foulois, *Memoirs*, p. 259; *New York Times*, May 8, 1934.

51. Shiner, *Foulois*, p. 51.

52. Arnold, *Global Mission*, p. 122.

CHAPTER III. A NEW ARMY AIR ARM

1. United States Army regulations concerning exceptions to competitive bidding are reprinted in Rutkowski, *Politics of Military Aviation Procurement*, p. 259.

2. Shiner, *Foulois*, pp. 150–66.

3. Rutkowski, *Politics of Military Aviation Procurement*, pp. 257–58.

4. Shiner, *Foulois*, pp. 150–66.

5. Keith McFarland, *Harry H. Woodring: A Political Biography of FDR's Controversial Secretary of War* (Lawrence: University of Kansas Press, 1975), pp. 92–96.

6. Shiner, *Foulois*, pp. 150–66; *New York Times*, Apr. 4, May 8, 1934.

7. *New York Times*, June 18, June 19, 1934. For examples of Foulois's turning down small gifts, see his letters to Glenn Martin, Aug. 28, 1934, and Congressman A. C. Willford, Feb. 23, 1934, Foulois Papers, Correspondence, File 3, 1931–35.

8. Shiner, *Foulois*, pp. 188–92. For detailed information on the procurement provisions of the Air Corps Act of 1926 and Foulois's dealings with Congress, see Rutkowski, *Politics of Military Aviation Procurement*.

9. Craven and Cate, *Army Air Forces*, vol. 1, pp. 29–30; Shiner, *Foulois*, pp. 94–99.

10. Memorandum from Kilbourne to deputy chief of staff, Nov. 17, 1933, RG 165, WPD, 888-81.

11. Shiner, *Foulois*, pp. 94–99; Brig. Gen. Kilbourne, "General Staff Supervision of the Air Corps," Feb. 19, 1934, Foulois Papers, Subject File, Box 16, Administration-C, General Staff Supervision of the Air Corps. Around the time of the Drum Board, Foulois had told the army leaders that if the GHQ Air Force were created, campaigns for independence would probably cease. The failure of the General Staff to create the GHQ Air Force convinced Foulois that the new organization would not be forthcoming soon and pushed him into working with McSwain on an independent air force bill. Letter from John F. Shiner to the author, Jan. 10, 1989.

12. Beaver, *Newton D. Baker and the American War Effort*, p. 169.

13. Shiner, *Foulois*, pp. 94–100 and 193–98.

14. Memorandum from Kilbourne to Foulois, "Remarks of General Kilbourne before Board Investigating Air Matters," Foulois Papers, Subject File, Box 28, Statements and Recommendations, Baker Board, "Air Corps Relations with War Department General Staff," S and R-g.

15. *New York Times*, July 28, 1934. The text of the final report of the War Department Special Committee on Army Air Corps (the official title of the Baker Board) final report is printed in the *New York Times*, July 23, 1934.

16. Shiner, *Foulois*, pp. 199–201.

17. Arnold, *Global Mission*, pp. 145–46; *New York Times*, July 18, Aug. 21, 1934; *Washington Post*, July 18–20, July 22, Aug. 21, 1934.

18. In February, Foulois had approved the blue-and-yellow color scheme to simplify logistics. The repainting of all tactical aircraft took some time, and many Air Corps planes still carried the duller markings for months afterward. Dana Bell, *Air Force Colors* (Carrollton, Texas: Squadron/Signal Publications, 1979), vol. 1, *1926–1942*, p. 23.

19. *New York Times*, July 19, 1934.

20. Arnold, *Global Mission*, p. 146; Shiner, *Foulois*, pp. 216–17; *New York Times*, Aug. 21, 1934.

21. Foulois, *Memoirs*, pp. 270–71.

22. Shiner, *Foulois*, pp. 200–201.

23. *Washington Post*, Oct. 3, 1934; *New York Times*, Oct. 7, Oct. 30, 1934.

24. Dallek, *FDR and American Foreign Policy*, pp. 87–88.

25. Roosevelt to Norman H. Davis, Oct. 5, 1934, press conference on Oct. 5, 1934, both in Nixon, *FDR and Foreign Affairs*, vol. 2, *March 1934–August 1935*, pp. 225–29.

26. Memorandum from Roosevelt to Swanson, Dec. 17, 1934, in Nixon, *FDR and Foreign Affairs*, vol. 2, pp. 322–23.

27. *New York Times*, Feb. 12, 1935; *Washington Post*, Feb. 12, 1935; Shiner, *Foulois*, pp. 250–51.

28. *New York Times*, Feb. 12, 1935. For a full, if implausible, discussion of Mitchell's ideas about the patent monopoly, see Emile Gauvreau, *The Wild Blue Yonder: Sons of the Prophet Carry On* (New York: E. P. Dutton Co., 1944).

29. Roosevelt to the Congress, Jan. 4, 1935, in Nixon, *FDR and Foreign Affairs*, vol. 2, p. 334.

30. *New York Times*, Jan. 1, Jan. 8, 1935.

31. *New York Times*, Feb. 9, Feb. 10, 1935; *Washington Post*, Feb. 9, 1935.

32. Mitchell, *Skyways: A Book on Modern Aeronautics* (Philadelphia: J. B. Lippincott, 1930), pp. 257–58.

33. Edwin L. James, "Oil Is the Weak Point in Tokyo's Strategy," *New York Times*, Feb. 3, 1935.

34. Raymond J. Sontag, *A Broken World, 1919–1939*, The Rise of Modern Europe, ed. William L. Langer (New York: Harper and Row, 1971), pp. 280–85.

35. Breckinridge Long to Roosevelt, Feb. 3, 1935, in Nixon, *FDR and Foreign Affairs*, vol. 2, pp. 386–87.

36. Craven and Cate, *Army Air Forces*, vol. 1, pp. 86–87; Arnold, *Global Mission*, p. 148.

37. Shiner, *Foulois*, pp. 203–207.

38. Maurer Maurer, *Aviation in the U.S. Army, 1919–1939* (Washington, D.C.: Office of Air Force History, United States Air Force, 1987), pp. 325–33.

39. Shiner, *Foulois*, pp. 203–207; Craven and Cate, *Army Air Forces*, vol. 1, pp. 31–32; *New York Times*, Dec. 27, 1934. To avoid confusion, I shall try to refer to all army aviation as the Army Air Corps, the combat section as the GHQ Air Force, and the supply and training section as the Air Corps.

40. Arnold, *Global Mission*, pp. 148–49; Shiner, *Foulois*, pp. 207–208; it is postulated that the airmen compromised on the new organization for a long-range bomber program, Craven and Cate, *Army Air Forces*, vol. 1, pp. 66–67.

41. *Washington Post*, Feb. 9, 1935; *New York Times*, Feb. 26, 1935.

42. Carl Spaatz to Arnold, Feb. 5, 1935, Spaatz Papers, Diaries, Box 7, Jan. 2–Aug. 27, 1935.

43. *New York Times*, Mar. 2, Mar. 3, 1935.

44. Andrews to Arnold, Mar. 23, 1935, Andrews Papers, General Correspondence, Box 1, Personal Correspondence, "A" 1935–37. Officially, the flight was cancelled due to lack of funds. See Maurer, *Aviation in the U.S. Army*, p. 326.

45. "Notes on Propaganda Talk," Mar. 12, 1935, Andrews Papers, Official Papers, Box 9, GHQ Air Force Directives, 1930–37.

46. Andrews to Arnold, Aug. 27, 1931, and Mar. 23, 1935, Andrews Papers, General Correspondence, Box 1, Personal Correspondence, "A" 1930–42.

47. For details of the formation of Pan American and its relationship to American foreign policy, see Arnold, *Global Mission*, pp. 114–15.

48. *New York Times*, Mar. 12, Mar. 14, 1935.

49. Harris Hull, "China's Gilded Door May Be Held Ajar by an Airplane Propeller," *Washington Post*, Oct. 21, 1934.

50. *Washington Post*, Nov. 26, 1934, Mar. 2, 1935; *New York Times*, Mar. 12, 14, 15, 1935.

51. *New York Times*, Mar. 15, 1935.

52. John Powell, "Japanese Fight U.S. Schemes for Pacific Airline," Chicago *Daily Tribune*, Mar. 15, 1935.

53. Hugh Byas, "Most of All Japan Fears an Air Attack," *New York Times Magazine*, Aug. 4, 1935, pp. 6–7.

54. Memorandum from Hull to Roosevelt, Apr. 16, 1935, and memorandum from Roosevelt to Swanson, May 3, 1935, both in Nixon, *FDR and Foreign Affairs*, vol. 2, pp. 495–96.

55. Memorandum from Roosevelt to Swanson, May 30, 1935, fn 1, both in Nixon, *FDR and Foreign Affairs*, vol. 2, p. 523.

56. *New York Times*, Apr. 24, 28, 29, 30, May 2, 1935; *Washington Post*, Apr. 28, Apr. 29, 1935.

57. Andrews to Westover, May 28, 1935, Andrews Papers, General Correspondence, Box 7, Personal Correspondence, Westover, 1935–38.

58. Peter M. Bowers, *Fortress in the Sky* (Granada Hills, California: Sentry Books, 1967), pp. 9–27; *New York Times*, July 6, 1935. The Chicago *Daily Tribune*, July 30, 1935, carried a photograph of the new bomber, but it expressed more excitement over the potential commercial offshoots than the military capacities of the plane. To see how excited Air Corps flyers were about the new B-15 and B-17, see letters from Spaatz to Arnold, Feb. 5, 1935, and McClelland to Spaatz, Mar. 6, 1935, Spaatz Papers, Diaries, Box 7, Jan. 2–Aug. 27, 1935. After seeing the still secret Project A bomber, Spaatz told Arnold, "Air power is going to be an entirely different thing than what we have visualized it in the distant past and the future is going to justify our most rosy dreams."

59. Bowers, *Fortress in the Sky*, pp. 10, 31–37; *New York Times*, Aug. 21, 1935.

60. *New York Times*, June 6, July 17, 24, 25, 30, 31, Aug. 10, 1935; *Washington Post*, June 3, June 6, July 11, 17, 25, 30, 1935.

61. *New York Times*, Aug. 20, Aug. 25, 1935.

62. Andrews to Arnold, Oct. 23, 1935, Andrews Papers, General Correspondence, Box 1, Personal Correspondence, "A" 1935–37.

63. *New York Times*, Nov. 7, 1935.

64. Weigley, *History of the United States Army*, pp. 415–16; Andrews to Arnold, Nov. 23, 1935, Andrews Papers, General Correspondence, Box 1, Personal Correspondence, "A" 1935–37.

65. Memorandum from Craig to Westover, Nov. 6, 1935, Foulois Papers, Subject File, Box 16, Administration, Policy of Air Corps (General O. Westover —1935).

66. Oscar Westover, "Air Corps Policies," Nov. 6, 1935, Foulois Papers, Subject File, Box 16, Administration, Policy of Air Corps (Gen. O. Westover —1935).

67. Memorandum from Andrews to Craig, Nov. 23, 1935, Andrews Papers, General Correspondence, Box 2, Personal Correspondence, Craig File.

68. Coffey, Hap, pp. 168–69; New York Times, Dec. 12, 1935.

69. Arnold, Global Mission, pp. 150–53; Coffey, Hap, pp. 168–69.

70. Col. G. C. Brant to Andrews, Jan. 6, 1936, Andrews Papers, General Correspondence, Box 1, Personal Correspondence, "B" 1934–36.

71. Arnold, Global Mission, pp. 153–54.

CHAPTER IV. EARLY ATTEMPTS TO SHAPE PUBLIC OPINION

1. New York Times Dec. 26, 1935.

2. New York Times Dec. 18, 22, 26, 1935; Washington Post Dec. 17, 18, 19, 22, 1935; James Trapier Lowe, A Philosophy of Air Power (Lanham, Md.: University Press of America, 1984), p. 112; Williamson Murray, Strategy for Defeat: The Luftwaffe, 1933–1945 (Maxwell Air Force Base, Ala.: Air University Press, 1983), pp. 3–19.

3. Dallek, FDR and American Foreign Policy, pp. 101–102.

4. Ibid., pp. 103–108.

5. Craven and Cate, Army Air Forces, vol. 1, pp. 83–84.

6. Memorandum from Dern to Roosevelt, Aug. 22, 1935, Franklin D. Roosevelt Papers, President's Secretary's File, Confidential File, Box 14, War Department, 1931–41, Franklin D. Roosevelt Library, Hyde Park, New York.

7. Ambassador Breckinridge Long to Roosevelt, Sept. 6, 1935, Ambassador John Cudahy to Roosevelt, Oct. 11, 1935, both in Nixon, FDR and Foreign Affairs, vol. 3, September 1935–January 1937, pp. 3–4, 21–22.

8. Sontag, A Broken World, pp. 287–90.

9. Washington Post, Dec. 21, 1935.

10. New York Times, Jan. 1, 1936. For an example of the negative sort of article, see Maj. Gen. Foulois's review, in which he wrote, "Due to budgetary limitations, no combined Air Corps manoeuvres were held during the year." In contrast, Rear Adm. Ernest J. King, chief of the Bureau of Aeronautics, wrote, "The successful participation of patrol squadrons in all fleet exercises demonstrated their value as a patrol and striking force, and in consequence they are now considered to be an essential part of the United States fleet." New York Times, Jan. 1, 1935.

11. Maxwell rewrote his lecture as an article, and the New York Times published it on Jan. 26, 1936.

12. Memorandum from Maxwell to the assistant chief of staff, G-2, Mar. 27, 1936, Maxwell to Ira Eaker, Mar. 28, 1936, both in Eaker Papers, Correspondence 1931, 1934–39, Box 3, 1936 File.

13. The Washington Post carried photographs of the maneuvers on

February 4, 5, 9, and 16, 1936, and photographs appeared in the Chicago *Daily Tribune* on February 3, 1936.

14. *New York Times,* Feb. 15, June 26, 1936; *Washington Post,* Feb. 15, Feb. 16, 1936.

15. Dallek, *FDR and American Foreign Policy,* pp. 89–90.

16. Roosevelt to the Reverend G. Ashton Oldham, Mar. 3, 1936, in Nixon, *FDR and Foreign Affairs,* vol. 3, pp. 228–29.

17. Roosevelt to the People's Mandate to End War Committee, Mar. 12, 1936, in Nixon, *FDR and Foreign Affairs,* vol. 3, pp. 248–51. Roosevelt mistakenly reported the numbers of aircraft possessed by the army, but he correctly stated that the Army Air Corps was considerably smaller than the other nations' air arms.

18. Augur, "British Navy Looks to a Wider Domain," *New York Times,* Mar. 22, 1936.

19. Memorandum from Andrews to Westover, Apr. 18, 1936, Andrews Papers, General Correspondence, Box 7, Personal Correspondence, Westover 1935–38.

20. Andrews to Brig. Gen. Harry B. Clagett, Apr. 29, 1936, Andrews Papers, General Correspondence, Box 2, Personal Correspondence, "C" 1934–37; Westover to Andrews, May 12, 1936, Andrews Papers, General Correspondence, Box 7, Personal Correspondence, Westover 1935–38.

21. *New York Times,* May 6, 1936.

22. Andrews's flight to Puerto Rico established a new world record for non-stop distance for amphibious planes. *Washington Post,* June 30, 1936.

23. Andrews to Boake Carter, July 7, 1935, Andrews Papers, General Correspondence, Box 2, Personal Correspondence, "C" 1934–37.

24. Memorandum from Maj. Robert Olds to Andrews, Aug. 5, 1936, memorandum from Andrews to Westover, Aug. 14, 1936, both in Andrews Papers, General Correspondence, Box 7, Personal Correspondence, Westover 1935–38.

25. *Air Corps News Letter,* Sept. 1, 1936, pp. 12–13. Published by the Air Corps Information Division, the *Air Corps News Letter* disseminated official information to the army fliers. The foreign policy of the United States contemplated defense only, stated the *Air Corps News Letter,* and the policy of the Army Air Corps was "to organize, train, and equip military aviation in time of peace as to permit it in time of war to be employed immediately in defense of our territory." *Air Corps News Letter,* July 15, 1936, p. 19.

26. Speech written by George C. Kenney for Andrews to deliver to the Air Corps Tactical School, dated Aug. 25, 1936, Andrews Papers, General Correspondence, Box 5, Personal Correspondence, "K" 1929–41.

27. Memorandum from Andrews to Craig, Sept. 29, 1936, Andrews Papers, General Correspondence, Box 2, Personal Correspondence, Craig File.

28. Andrews, "Critique—Joint Coastal Frontier Defense Air Exercise No. 1," Oct. 21, 1936, Record Group 18, Army Air Forces, Box 24, 354.2, National Archives, Washington, D.C.

29. Andrews to Maj. Gen. Hugh A. Drum, Sept. 12, 1936, Drum to Andrews, Dec. 14, 1936, both in Andrews Papers, General Correspondence, Box

3, Personal Correspondence, "D" 1930-42. For Drum's views on Hawaii, see his interview with Lauren D. Lyman, *New York Times*, Oct. 25, 1936.

30. William Bullitt to Roosevelt, Nov. 24, 1936, in Nixon, *FDR and Foreign Affairs*, vol. 3, 499-502.

31. R. Walton Moore to Roosevelt, Nov. 27, 1936, in Nixon, *FDR and Foreign Affairs*, vol. 3, p. 512.

32. Speech by Roosevelt to the Inter-American Conference for the Maintenance of Peace, Dec. 1, 1936, in Nixon, *FDR and Foreign Affairs*, vol. 3, p. 517.

33. Lauren D. Lyman, "Huge Boats for Defense," *New York Times*, Nov. 15, 1936; *New York Times*, Dec. 1, Dec. 3, 1936. The Chicago *Daily Tribune* ran the Associated Press story with a photograph on December 2 and December 4, 1936.

34. Mark J. Ginsbourg, "Transpacific Flights Stimulate Far East," *Washington Post*, Jan. 5, 1936.

35. See the Associated Press photograph of a Japanese poster with menacing Soviet tanks and airplanes in the *Washington Post*, Feb. 29, 1936.

36. Coffey, *Hap*, pp. 174-75; Bowers, *Fortress in the Sky*, pp. 39-40.

CHAPTER V. ARRIVAL OF THE FLYING FORTRESS

1. Arnold, *Global Mission*, pp. 161-62.

2. *New York Times*, Jan. 19, 1937.

3. DeWitt S. Copp, "Frank M. Andrews: Marshall's Airman," in *Makers of the United States Air Force*, ed. John L. Frisbee (Washington, D.C.: Office of Air Force History, United States Air Force, 1987), pp. 56-57. Copp attributes Andrews's actions to a desire for a better air force and for advancement of his career.

4. John Jouett to Swanee Taylor, Mar. 30, 1937, Arnold to Jouett, Apr. 1, 1937, both in Arnold Papers, Box 15, File 234, General Correspondence, Manuscript Division, Library of Congress, Washington, D.C.

5. Ira Eaker to Arnold, Apr. 7, 1937, Arnold to Eaker, Apr. 13, 1937, both in Arnold Papers, Box 12, File 152, General Correspondence. Before the Second World War, Eaker and Arnold coauthored books and articles.

6. Reed G. Landis to Arnold, Mar. 29, 1937, Arnold to Landis, Apr. 1, 1937, Landis to Arnold, Apr. 16, 1937, Arnold to Landis, Apr. 24, 1937, all in Arnold Papers, General Correspondence, Box 16, File 261.

7. Memorandum from Woodring to Roosevelt, June 9, 1937, FDR Papers, Official File, War Department, Box 32, OF 25-U, Chief of Air Corps, 1937-39. By then, General Westover had convinced Craig of his loyalty, because Craig specifically excluded him from the group of dissatisfied officers. By not mentioning Andrews, Craig implied that he was one of the dissatisfied officers.

8. *Air Corps News Letter*, Mar. 15, 1937, pp. 4, 7-8; Apr. 1, 1937, pp. 8-9; May 15, 1937, p. 13; Apr. 15, 1937, p. 9.

9. Arnold's entry for June 16, 1937, Arnold Papers, Official File 1932-46, Box 55, Daily Record of Events 1932-39.

10. Arnold, *Global Mission*, pp. 110, 128-29; Coffey, *Hap*, pp. 175-76;

Arnold to Reed Landis, Apr. 24, 1937, Arnold Papers, General Correspondence, Box 16, File 261. After their flight to Alaska, Knerr mistakenly believed that Arnold had tried to take all the credit for himself, and for years afterward, Knerr believed that Arnold was motivated by self-interest. Not until many years latter did Knerr discover his error. For further information, see Murray Green, "Major General Hugh J. Knerr, Hard Campaigner for Air Power," *Air Force Magazine* 61, Oct., 1978, pp. 90-92.

11. Spaatz to Arnold, Feb. 5, 1935, H. M. McClelland to Spaatz, Mar. 6, 1935, both in Spaatz Papers, Diaries, Box 7, Jan. 2-Aug. 27, 1935.

12. *New York Times,* Apr. 17, 1937.

13. "Purchase of New Experimental Boeing Bombardment Plane," *Air Corps News Letter,* May 1, 1937, pp. 5-6.

14. Andrews's fear was justified; the XB-15 never went into production. Not until Boeing produced the B-29 during World War II did Arnold receive the long-range bomber he wanted.

15. Memorandum from Andrews to Adj. Gen., May 1, 1937, RG 165, WPD, 3774-11; memorandum from Brig. Gen. George P. Tyner to assistant chief of staff WPD, May 13, 1937; memorandum from Brig. Gen. W. Kruger to assistant chief of staff, G-3, June 8, 1937, RG 165, WPD, 4002.

16. Reference to memorandum from the president's naval aide to the secretary of the navy on May 17, 1937, in a joint memorandum from Secretary of War Woodring and Secretary of the Navy Swanson, Oct. 19, 1937, RG 18, Army Air Forces, Box 26, 354.2 Maneuvers (Joint Army and Navy).

17. Andrews to Brig. Gen. A. W. Robins, June 1, June 22, 1937, Robins to Andrews, July 10, 1937, Andrews to Robins, July 13, 1937, all in Andrews Papers, General Correspondence, Box 6, Personal Correspondence, File "R" 1937-39; Curtis E. LeMay with MacKinlay Kantor, *Mission with LeMay: My Story* (Garden City, N.Y.: Doubleday, 1965), pp. 142-43; Andrews to Westover, July 30, 1937, Andrews Papers, General Correspondence, Box 7, Personal Correspondence, Oscar Westover, 1935-38.

18. Craig to Andrews, Aug. 4, 1937, Andrews Papers, General Correspondence, Box 2, Personal Correspondence, Craig File.

19. Details of the exercise are found in LeMay, *Mission with LeMay,* pp. 142-52.

20. Andrews to Craig, Aug. 6, 1937, memorandum from Craig to Andrews, Aug. 27, 1937, both in Andrews Papers, General Correspondence, Box 2, Personal Correspondence, Craig File.

21. Joint memorandum from Woodring and Swanson to Roosevelt, Oct. 19, 1937, RG 18, AAF, Box 26, 354.2 Maneuvers (Joint Army and Navy).

22. Arnold to Andrews, Sept. 8, 1937, Andrews Papers, General Correspondence, Box 1, Personal Correspondence, "A" 1935-37.

23. Andrews to Arnold, Sept. 13, 1937, Andrews Papers, General Correspondence, Box 1, Personal Correspondence, "A" 1935-37.

24. *Air Corps News Letter,* Sept. 15, 1937, pp. 1-2.

25. Capt. Wendell G. Johnson expressed this view in the *Infantry Journal.* In the Spanish Civil War, aviation had "only *contributed* to successes, as one of the combined arms." "Men, *Not Machines,* Win Wars," *Infantry Jour-*

nal 45 (Jan.–Feb. 1938): 59. In a review of books and articles by European military writers, Johnson quoted Dr. Helmut Klotz as saying, "The Spanish civil war has conclusively shown that the final decision of the war takes place on the ground and not in the sky. . . . Aviation, and even bombing aviation must be associated (with infantry) as an auxiliary and subordinate arm. An arm, important, irreplaceable, extremely efficacious, but nevertheless, an auxiliary arm and nothing more." "The Spanish War: A Review of the Best Foreign Opinion," *Infantry Journal* 45 (July–Aug., 1938): 353.

26. Memorandum from Knerr to Andrews, Sept. 20, 1937, Andrews Papers, General Correspondence, Box 5, Personal Correspondence, "K" 1929–41.

27. Speech by Westover to the reserve officers convention at Oakland, California, titled "An Adequate Air Arm for the Nation's Defense," in *Air Corps News Letter*, Oct. 15, 1937, pp. 7–10.

28. Johnson quoted Dr. Klotz as saying that "because modern planes go so fast, bombing small objectives, such as bridges and cross-roads, is largely a matter of chance," in "The Spanish War," p. 352; "The Air Corps," speech by Arnold, Oct. 7, 1937, Foulois Papers, Subject File, Box 37, General Reports and Papers, 4-B.

29. *New York Times*, Dec. 6, 1937.

30. Charles McLean, "Big Planes in Air Corps," *New York Times*, Dec. 5, 1937.

31. Andrews, "The General Headquarters Air Force: A Review of 1937 and New Year's Message," *Air Corps News Letter*, Jan. 1, 1938, pp. 3–4; Westover, "Army Air Corps Accomplishments for 1937 and Plans for 1938," *Air Corps News Letter*, Jan. 1, 1938, pp. 12–13.

32. Speech by Westover to the National Aviation Planning Conference, Jan. 11, 1938, the *Air Corps News Letter*, Jan. 15, 1938, pp. 3–5.

33. Memorandum from Andrews to Col. Edwin M. Watson, Jan. 4, 1938, RG 18, AAF, Box 27, 354.2, Joint Army and Navy Exercises (General), Folder No. 2.

34. Memorandum from Adm. William D. Leahy to Roosevelt, Nov. 8, 1937, in Donald B. Schewe, ed., *Franklin D. Roosevelt and Foreign Affairs* (New York: Garland, 1979), vol. 3, *August 1937–November 1937.*

35. Adm. Harry E. Yarnell to Admiral Leahy, Oct. 15, 1937, in Schewe, *FDR and Foreign Affairs*, vol. 3.

36. Ibid.

37. Memorandum from Roosevelt to Leahy, Nov. 10, 1937, in Schewe, *FDR and Foreign Affairs*, vol. 3.

38. For a discussion of responses and interpretations of the President's Quarantine Address, see Dallek, *FDR and American Foreign Policy,* pp. 148–51.

39. Memorandum from Roosevelt to Leahy, Nov. 10, 1937, in Schewe, *FDR and Foreign Affairs*, vol. 3.

40. Ibid.

41. Dallek, *FDR and American Foreign Policy,* pp. 153–55; Harold L. Ickes, *The Secret Diary of Harold L. Ickes*, vol. 2, *The Inside Struggle, 1936–1939* (New York: Simon and Schuster, 1954), pp. 274–75.

42. A year earlier, Roosevelt had watched a reenactment of the burning of the frigate U.S.S. *Philadelphia* in the Harbor of Tripoli. *Washington Post*, May 31, 1936.

43. *New York Times*, Dec. 29, 1937, and Jan. 28, 1938.

44. Knerr to Andrews, undated but probably from early Feb., 1938, Andrews Papers, Official Papers, Box 9, Organization and Operation of G.H.Q. Air Force, 1938.

CHAPTER VI. THE WINGS OF DEMOCRACY

1. William H. Hornibrook to Roosevelt, Jan. 4, 1938, in Schewe, *FDR and Foreign Affairs*, vol. 4, *December 1937–February 1938*.

2. John W. White, "Italy Sways South America," *New York Times*, Jan. 30, 1938.

3. *Washington Post*, Nov. 14, Nov. 16, 1937.

4. See *American Aviation*, "Fascist Aviation Inroads in S. A.," Mar. 15, 1938, p. 11. *American Aviation* was a trade journal for the aviation industry.

5. *Washington Post*, Feb. 3, Feb. 4, 1938.

6. LeMay, *Mission with LeMay*, p. 153; William A. Wieland to Louis Johnson, Jan. 25, 1938, memorandum from Johnson to Stephen T. Early, Jan. 25, 1938, both in Schewe, *FDR and Foreign Affairs*, vol 4.

7. McFarland, *Woodring*, pp. 160–63; Arnold, *Global Mission*, p. 167.

8. *Washington Post*, Nov. 5, 1937.

9. Memorandum from Marvin H. McIntyre to Roosevelt, Feb. 4, 1938, in Schewe, *FDR and Foreign Affairs*, vol. 4.

10. Memorandum from Craig to Andrews, Feb. 5, 1938, RG 18, AAF, Secret Correspondence, 373, "Airplane Flights, Buenos Aires."

11. Memorandum from Col. W. H. Franks to the commanding general, Second Wing, GHQ Air Force, Feb. 9, 1938, RG 18, AAF, Secret Correspondence, 373, "Airplane Flights, Buenos Aires."

12. LeMay, *Mission with LeMay*, pp. 152–66; Roosevelt to Roberto Ortiz, Feb. 15, 1938, in Schewe, *FDR and Foreign Affairs*, vol. 4; *Washington Post*, Feb. 19, 1938. In its front-page story on the flight, the *Post* reported that the sixth B-17 landed in a rainstorm. The Chicago *Daily Tribune* correctly reported that the flight was privately acknowledged in Washington, D.C., as an exhibition of the United States' might and to give answer to Bruno Mussolini's flight. Chicago *Daily Tribune*, Feb. 19, 1938.

13. *Time*, Feb. 28, 1938, p. 18; "U.S. Bombers Make History for Aviation and Argentina," *Newsweek*, Feb. 28, 1938, p. 20.

14. Los Angeles *Times*, Feb. 22, 1938.

15. *New York Times*, Feb. 22, 1938.

16. Chicago *Daily Tribune*, Feb. 16, 1938.

17. Barry Sullivan, "'Flying Fortresses' Carry New Message of Goodwill to South America on Argentine Visit," *Washington Post*, Feb. 20, 1938.

18. Dow W. Barter to Andrews, Feb. 19, 1938, Andrews to Barter, Feb. 21, 1938, both in Andrews Papers, General Correspondence, Box 4, Personal Correspondence, "H" 1929–40.

19. Andrews to Brig. Gen. Delos C. Emmons, Feb. 9, Feb. 21, 1938, Andrews Papers, General Correspondence, Box 3, Personal Correspondence, "E" 1930–43.

20. Craig to Andrews, Feb. 23, 1938, Andrews to Craig, Feb. 24, 1938, both in Andrews Papers, General Correspondence, Box 2, Personal Correspondence, "Craig, Malin File."

21. "The Argentine Flight" and "Argentine Flight Proves Excellent State of Training in the GHQ Air Force," both in *Air Corps News Letter*, Mar. 1, 1938, pp. 1, 4.

22. Sidney Olson, "Flight to Buenos Aires Likened to Fleet's World Tour," *Washington Post*, Feb. 19, 1938, p. 1.

23. Andrews to George Brett, Mar. 17, 1938, Andrews Papers, General Correspondence, Box 1, Personal Correspondence, "B" 1924–39.

24. White House press conference, Feb. 15, 1938, in Schewe, *FDR and Foreign Affairs*, vol. 4.

25. *New York Times*, Mar. 1, 1938.

26. For an example of the assumptions most airmen held about Roosevelt, see the comments Mitchell made just before his death, Emile Gauvreau, *The Wild Blue Yonder: Sons of the Prophet Carry On* (New York: E.P. Dutton and Co., 1944), pp. 169–71.

27. *New York Times*, Feb. 26, 1938.

28. Arnold, *Global Mission*, p. 97.

29. McFarland, *Woodring*, pp. 160–63.

30. *Time*, Mar. 7, 1938, pp. 44–45.

31. Memorandum from Arnold to Johnson (original draft by Eaker also in files), Mar. 9, 1938, Arnold Papers, Box 15, File 228, General Correspondence.

32. "Address of Brigadier General H. H. Arnold, over Station KFI, Los Angeles, April 21st, 1938," Eaker Papers, Speech, Book, Article File 1934–54 + Undated, Box 38, Speeches — Gen. Arnold (prepared by I.C.E) 1937–39.

33. "Speech for General Westover for Delivery at Montgomery, Alabama, before the Southeastern Aviation Conference on April 15, 1938," Eaker Papers, Speech, Book, and Article File, Box 39, Speeches — General Westover (prepared by I.C.E.?) 1937–38.

34. Telford Taylor, *Munich: The Price of Peace* (Garden City, New York: Doubleday, 1979), pp. 754–64.

35. Maj. Truman Smith, "An American Estimate of the German Air Force, November 1, 1937," reprinted in *The Airpower Historian*, vol. 10, no. 2, Apr. 1963, pp. 54–56.

36. Joseph P. Kennedy to Roosevelt, Feb. 9, 1938, in Schewe, *FDR and Foreign Affairs*, vol. 4.

37. George Norton Northrop to Roosevelt, Apr. 15, 1938, Roosevelt to Northrop, Apr. 20, 1938, both in Schewe, *FDR and Foreign Affairs*, vol. 5, *March 1938–April 1938*.

38. Charles A Lindbergh, *The Wartime Journals of Charles A. Lindbergh* (New York: Harcourt Brace Jovanovich, 1970), pp. 25–26.

39. President Roosevelt quoted the wrong distance between Venezuela and the United States. Caracas and Miami, Florida, are approximately fifteen

hundred miles apart. Whether he committed an eleven-hundred-mile mistake or stated a smaller number to make a point is uncertain. It seems doubtful that he would have made such an error. Some aircraft were capable of flying at speeds in excess of three hundred miles an hour, but planes could not fly from Venezuela to America in just one and a half hours in 1938, as Roosevelt commented. White House press conference, Apr. 20, 1938, in Schewe, *FDR and Foreign Affairs*, vol. 5.

40. Flint O. DuPre, *U.S. Air Force Biographical Dictionary* (New York: Franklin Watts, 1965), pp. 61–62; Lt. Col. H. H. C. Richards, Chief of the Information Division, to Prof. Albert A. Sutton, Apr. 4, 1938, and Westover to W. B. Bizzell, President of the University of Oklahoma, Apr. 4, 1938, both in Eaker Papers, Correspondence, Box 3, 1938 File.

41. Memorandum from Eaker to chief of staff, GHQ Air Force, Apr. 20, 1938, Eaker Papers, Subject File, Miscellaneous 1929–39, Box 36, GHQ Air Force Maneuvers, May, 1938.

42. LeMay, *Mission with LeMay*, pp. 183–93; Los Angeles *Times*, May 11, 1938; George W. Goddard with Dewitt S. Copp, *Overview: A Life-Long Adventure in Aerial Photography* (Garden City, New York: Doubleday, 1969), pp. 254–60; Maurer, *Aviation in the U.S. Army*, pp. 406–408; *New York Times*, May 12, May 13, 1938; "The GHQ Air Force Maneuvers," *Air Corps News Letter*, June 1, 1938, p. 3; Harris B. Hull, "The GHQ Air Force Maneuvers," *Air Corps News Letter*, June 1, 1938, pp. 9–11.

43. Hanson W. Baldwin "'Flying Fortresses' Meet Liner at Sea," *New York Times*, May 13, 1938. Goddard's photograph of the *Rex* also appeared in the Los Angeles *Times*, May 14, 1938. *Time* magazine carried a two-page article on the maneuvers and a map showing where the bombers met the *Rex* (*Time*, "Soldiers in the Sky," May 23, 1938, pp. 10–11).

44. Chicago *Daily Tribune*, May 13, 1938.

45. *New York Times*, May 14, May 15, 1938.

46. Radio address by Arnold, May 16, 1938, Eaker Papers, Subject File, Miscellaneous 1929–39, Box 36, GHQ Air Force Maneuvers, May, 1938.

47. "Enemy Bombers 'Destroy' Farmingdale, L.I., in First U.S. Black-Out Test," and "These Chinese Are Watching Two Air Armadas Battle in Clouds over Hankow," both in *Life*, May 30, 1938, vol. 4, pp. 15–17, 18–19. The Los Angeles *Times* ran a photograph of a frightened six-year old boy in Farmingdale hiding under some bushes while the army bombers made a "mass attack" on his home town. He wore a coal scuttle for a helmet "to keep him from harm" (Los Angeles *Times*, May 18, 1938, p. 3).

48. Hull, "The GHQ Air Force Maneuvers," *Air Corps News Letter*, June 1, 1938, p. 10–11.

49. Rep. Maury Maverick of Texas had announced his opposition to the naval expansion bill. He had threatened to use information, given to him by "regular and retired flying officers," about bombing tests that had proved the vulnerability of ships to air attack. Hanson W. Baldwin, "Naval Plans Spur Army Air Backers," *New York Times*, Mar. 14, 1938; Arnold, *Global Mission*, pp. 176–77; LeMay, *Mission with LeMay*, pp. 192–93; Coffey, *Hap*, p. 177; Maurer, *Aviation in the U.S. Army*, pp. 408–12.

50. For a discussion of the importance of radio and photography in America, see William Stott, *Documentary Expression and Thirties America* (New York: Oxford University Press, 1973); *New York Times*, May 14, 1938. The hysterical response to Orson Welles's broadcast of H. G. Wells's *The War of the Worlds* that Halloween also suggests the influence of radio.

51. LeMay, *Mission with LeMay*, pp. 169–73.

52. Eaker to Col. Walter H. Frank, July 11, 1938, Eaker to Andrews, July 20, 1938, Eaker to Frank, July 21, 1938, Eaker to Col. W. G. Kilner, Aug. 25, 1938, Eaker Papers, Correspondence, Box 3, 1938. Eaker had good reason to recommend Beirne Lay, Jr. He had already won a reputation as a writer with his book, *I Wanted Wings* (New York: Harper and Brothers, 1937), about his experiences during flight training at Randolph Field. After World War II, Lay became better known as the coauthor of *Twelve O'Clock High!* (New York: Harper, 1948), which was later made into the classic aviation movie.

53. Col. Lewis Brereton to Eaker, Oct. 4, 1938, Eaker to Brereton, Mar. 16, 1939, both in Eaker Papers, Correspondence, Box 3, 1939 File.

54. Mark S. Watson, *Chief of Staff: Prewar Plans and Preparations* (Washington, D.C.: Historical Division, Department of the Army, 1950), pp. 35–36; Coffey, *Hap*, pp. 177–78.

55. Forrest C. Pogue, *George C. Marshall: Education of a General, 1880–1939* (New York: Viking Press, 1963), pp. 314–19.

56. Larry I. Bland and Sharon R. Ritenour, eds., *The Papers of George Catlett Marshall*, (Baltimore: Johns Hopkins University Press, 1981), vol. 1, "The Soldierly Spirit," *December 1880–June 1939*, pp. 50, 53–54, 545–547; Anderton, *History of the U.S. Air Force* (New York: Crescent Books, 1981), pp. 15–17.

57. Arnold, *Global Mission*, pp. 44, 163–64; Coffey, *Hap*, pp. 77–80; Pogue, *Marshall: Education of a General*, pp. 119–24.

58. Marshall to Rear Adm. Walter S. Anderson, Aug. 8, 1938, Marshall to Gen. John J. Pershing, Aug. 22, 1938, Marshall to Maj. Gen. Ewing E. Booth, Aug. 26, 1938, interview with Marshall, Jan. 22, 1957, all in Bland and Ritenour, "The Soldierly Spirit," pp. 616–19.

59. Andrews to George Brett, Aug. 19, 1938, and Andrews to Claire Egtvedt, Aug. 22, 1938, both in Andrews Papers, General Correspondence, Box 1, Personal Correspondence, "B" 1924–39.

60. Interview with Marshall, Jan. 22, 1957, memorandum for Deputy Chief of Staff Gen. Embick, Aug. 22, 1938, both in Bland and Ritenour, "The Soldierly Spirit," pp. 617–18.

61. Pogue, *Education of a General*, pp. 319–20; speech by Marshall to the American Legion Convention at Clarksburg, West Virginia, Sept. 4, 1938, speech by Marshall to the Air Corps Tactical School at Maxwell Field, Alabama, Sept. 19, 1938, both in Bland and Ritenour, "The Soldierly Spirit," pp. 620–26, 631–35.

CHAPTER VII. ROOSEVELT AND THE MUNICH CRISIS

1. Samuel I. Rosenman, ed., *The Public Papers and Addresses of Franklin D. Roosevelt* (New York: Macmillan, 1938–50), vol. 8, *War—and Neutrality*, p. 463.

2. Rosenman, *Public Papers and Addresses of FDR*, vol. 9, *War—and Aid to Democracies*, p. 643.

3. Foster Rhea Dulles, *America's Rise to World Power, 1898–1954*, The New American Nation Series, ed. Henry Steele Commager and Richard B. Morris (New York: Harper and Row, 1954; New York: Harper and Row, 1963), p. 195.

4. Dallek, *FDR and American Foreign Policy*, pp. 158–61; Burns, *Lion and the Fox*, pp. 352–57.

5. McFarland, *Woodring*, pp. 182–83.

6. John McVickar Haight, Jr., "France's First War Mission to the United States," *Air Power Historian* 11 (Jan., 1964): 11; McFarland, *Woodring*, pp. 183–84.

7. William C. Bullitt to Roosevelt, May 12, 1938, Roosevelt to Bullitt, June 5, 1938, both in Schewe, *FDR and Foreign Affairs*, vol. 6, *May 1938–August 1938*.

8. William C. Bullitt to Roosevelt, June 13, 1938, in Schewe, *FDR and Foreign Affairs*, vol. 6.

9. Roosevelt to Bullitt, June 25, 1938, in Schewe, *FDR and Foreign Affairs*, vol. 6.

10. Hugh R. Wilson to Roosevelt, July 11, 1938, in Schewe, *FDR and Foreign Affairs*, vol. 6.

11. Dallek, *FDR and American Foreign Policy*, pp. 162–65.

12. Roosevelt to William Phillips, Sept. 15, 1938, in Schewe, *FDR and Foreign Affairs*, vol. 7, *September 1938–November 1938*.

13. *New York Times*, Sept. 17, 1938.

14. Ickes, *Secret Diary*, vol. 2, pp. 467–69.

15. Mitchell, *Skyways*, pp. 255–56; Weigley, *American Way of War*, pp. 233–35; Craven and Cate, *Army Air Forces*, vol. 1, pp. 41–42.

16. Ickes, *Secret Diary*, vol. 2, pp. 472–76; Dallek, *FDR and American Foreign Policy*, pp. 164–66; Bullitt to Roosevelt, Sept. 20, 1938, in Schewe, *FDR and Foreign Affairs*, vol. 7.

17. Bullitt to Roosevelt, Sept. 28, 1938, in Schewe, *FDR and Foreign Affairs*, vol. 7.

18. Memorandum from Cordell Hull to Roosevelt, Sept. 27, 1938, in Schewe, *FDR and Foreign Affairs*, vol. 7.

19. Memorandum from Adm. William D. Leahy to Roosevelt, Sept. 29, 1938, in Schewe, *FDR and Foreign Affairs*, vol. 7.

20. Memorandum from Hull to Leahy, Oct. 8, 1938, in Schewe, *FDR and Foreign Affairs*, vol. 7.

21. Robert Sherwood, *Roosevelt and Hopkins: An Intimate History* (1948; rev. ed., New York: Harper and Brothers, 1950), pp. 99–102; Pogue, *Marshall: Education of a General*, pp. 325–26.

22. Arnold, *Global Mission*, pp. 171–75.

23. Ibid.

24. Arnold, *Global Mission*, pp. 171–75; McFarland, *Woodring*, pp. 164–65.

25. Watson, *Chief of Staff*, pp. 131–32; *New York Times*, Oct. 15, 1938.

26. Memorandum from Assistant Secretary of War Louis Johnson to Roosevelt, Oct. 15, 1938, FDR Papers, PSF, Departmental, Box 105, War Department, Louis Johnson.

27. Andrews to Marshall, Oct. 18, 1938, Marshall to Andrews, Oct. 25, 1938, both in Andrews Papers, General Correspondence, Box 5, Personal Correspondence, "M" 1929-39.

28. McFarland, *Woodring*, pp. 165, 182-84.

29. Memorandum from Arnold to Johnson, Mar. 9, 1938, Arnold Papers, Box 15, File 228, General Correspondence; Arthur Krock, "In the Nation," *New York Times*, Dec. 9, 1938; Leuchtenburg, *FDR and the New Deal*, pp. 244-45, 256-57.

30. Notes taken by Arnold, Nov. 14, 1938, FDR Papers, OF, War Department, Box 30, OF 25, Chief of Staff, 1935-39; Arnold, *Global Mission*, pp. 177-80; Watson, *Chief of Staff*, pp. 136-39; McFarland, *Woodring*, pp. 165-66; interview with Marshall, Mar. 6, 1957, in Bland and Ritenour, *"The Soldierly Spirit,"* pp. 650-51.

31. Arnold, *Global Mission*, pp. 179-80.

32. Burns, *Lion and the Fox*, pp. 166-71.

33. *New Republic*, Jan. 4, 1939.

34. McFarland, *Woodring*, pp. 166-67; Watson, *Chief of Staff*, p. 138.

35. White House Press Conference, Nov. 15, 1938, in Schewe, *FDR and Foreign Affairs*, vol. 7.

36. Arthur Murray to Roosevelt, Dec. 15, 1938, Roosevelt to Murray, Jan. 19, 1939, both in Schewe, *FDR and Foreign Affairs*, vol. 8, *December 1938-February 1939*.

37. Orders relieving Eaker of duty in the information division and transferring him to duty as the executive of the executive division, Eaker Papers, Correspondence Box 3, 1939 File.

38. Watson, *Chief of Staff*, pp. 139-40; McFarland, *Woodring*, pp. 167-71; Marshall to John J. Pershing, Nov. 23, Dec. 20, 1938, in Bland and Ritenour, *"The Soldierly Spirit,"* pp. 652-53 and 654-55.

39. Watson, *Chief of Staff*, pp. 137-43; McFarland, *Woodring*, pp. 167-71; "Statement to the Assistant Chiefs of Staff" by Marshall, Nov. 17, 1938, in Bland and Ritenour, *"The Soldierly Spirit,"* p. 680; Acting Secretary of War Louis Johnson to General Craig, Dec. 10, 1938, letter and memorandum entitled "Army Two-year Augmentation Program," Dec. 19, 1938, FDR Papers, PSF, Subject Box 116, Aviation; Dallek, *FDR and American Foreign Policy*, pp. 171-74; Roosevelt's address to Congress, Jan. 12, 1939, in Rosenman, *Public Papers and Addresses of FDR*, vol. 8, pp. 70-74.

40. "Flying Range of the 'Flying Fortress' Bombers," *New York Times*, Jan. 15, 1939.

41. Andrews to Lt. Col. Clinton W. Howard, Jan. 13, 1939, Andrews Papers, General Correspondence, Box 4, Personal Correspondence, "H" 1929-40; *New York Times*, Jan. 17, 1939.

42. McFarland, *Woodring*, pp. 182-85.

43. Conference with the Senate Military Affairs Committee in the White House, Jan. 31, 1939, press conferences on Feb. 3, Feb. 17, 1939 [Roosevelt

repeated much of what he told the senators to the press on February 17, 1939], all in Schewe, *FDR and Foreign Affairs*, vol. 8; Arnold, *Global Mission*, pp. 184–86; Coffey, *Hap*, pp. 192–95; McFarland, *Woodring*, pp. 185–91; Arthur Krock, "Foreign Policy Mix-up Follows Secret Moves," *New York Times*, Feb. 5, 1939.

44. There are other possible reasons for the president's compromise: FDR might have agreed to a smaller number after the public responded negatively to Louis Johnson's call for a large air force; he may have spoken about such a large number to appear judicious when he accepted a smaller number; or, he may have hoped to jar the Army Air Corps into thinking and planning in large numbers. For further information, see Irving Brinton Holley, *Buying Aircraft: Materiel Procurement for the Army Air Forces* United States Army in World War II: Special Studies (Washington: Office of the Chief of Military History, Department of the Army, 1964), pp. 172–73.

45. Bullitt to Roosevelt, Sept. 28, 1938, in Schewe, *FDR and Foreign Affairs*, vol. 7.

46. For an example of how Roosevelt's reduced request made him appear moderate, see the *New York Times*, Jan. 13, 1939.

47. Memorandum from Roosevelt to Under Secretary of State Sumner Welles, Dec. 10, 1938, Welles to Roosevelt, Dec. 15, 1938, with enclosure from Joseph C. Green, Chief, Office of Arms and Munitions Control, Department of State, July 1, 1938, both in Schewe, *FDR and Foreign Affairs*, vol. 8.

48. Rosenman, *Public Papers and Addresses of FDR*, vol. 8, p. 589.

49. *New York Times*, Jan. 11, 1939.

50. Memorandum from Adm. William Leahy to Roosevelt, Dec. 15, 1938, in Schewe, *FDR and Foreign Affairs*, vol. 8.

51. Hanson Baldwin, "Vast Defense Plans Are Started on Their Way," *New York Times*, Jan. 9, 1939; Hanson Baldwin, "Island Defense Plans Alter Pacific Picture," *New York Times*, Feb. 12, 1939; Hanson Baldwin, "Navy Still Presses for Fund for Guam," *New York Times*, Mar. 12, 1939; *New York Times*, Jan. 15, Jan. 17–20, 1939; White House Press Conference, Jan. 17, 1938, in Schewe, *FDR and Foreign Affairs*, vol. 8.

CHAPTER VIII. STRATEGIC PLANNING AND THE ARMY AIR CORPS

1. Watson, *Chief of Staff*, pp. 284–86; Craven and Cate, *Army Air Forces*, vol. 1, p. 114.

2. Paraphrase of memorandum from Lt. Col. Russell L. Maxwell to Marshall, Feb. 13, 1939, memorandum from Marshall to Gen. Robert Beck, Feb. 15, 1939, both in Bland and Ritenour, *"The Soldierly Spirit,"* pp. 698–700.

3. Watson, *Chief of Staff*, pp. 284–86; Craven and Cate, *Army Air Forces*, vol. 1, p. 114.

4. Andrews to Marshall, Oct. 18, 1938, Andrews Papers, General Correspondence, Box 5, Personal Correspondence, "M" 1929–39; DuPre, *U.S. Air Force Biographical Dictionary*, pp. 6, 67–68; Coffey, *Hap*, pp. 234–35.

5. Letter and paper entitled "Air Power for the United States" from Knerr to Andrews, May 14, 1939, Andrews Papers, General Correspondence, Box 5,

Personal Correspondence, "K" 1929–41; DuPre, *U.S. Air Force Biographical Dictionary,* p. 6; Coffey, *Hap,* pp. 234–36.

6. In his biography of Hap Arnold, Thomas M. Coffey relates the incident without commenting upon the reason why Arnold became so upset over Knerr's actions. He also fails to note how worried Knerr was that Arnold would find out from Andrews the source of the paper (Coffey, *Hap,* pp. 235–36).

7. Hanson Baldwin, "Army Corps Sends 1,500 Planes in Air," *New York Times,* Aug. 3, 1939.

8. White House press conference, Apr. 20, 1939, in Schewe, *FDR and Foreign Affairs,* vol. 9, *March 1939–May 1939.*

9. Memorandum from Roosevelt to Cordell Hull, July 7, 1939, memorandum of conversation between Kensuke Horinouchi and Hull, July 10, 1939, memorandum from Hull to Roosevelt, July 25, 1939, all in Schewe, *FDR and Foreign Affairs,* vol. 10, *June 1939–August 1939;* Dallek, *FDR and American Foreign Policy,* pp. 193–96; William L. Langer and S. Everett Gleason, *The Challenge to Isolation: 1937–1940* (New York: Harper and Brothers, 1952), pp. 150–59.

10. Roosevelt to Arthur Murray, July 10, 1939, Prime Minister A. Neville Chamberlain to Roosevelt, Aug. 25, 1939, Roosevelt to Chamberlain, Aug. 31, 1939, all in Schewe, *FDR and Foreign Affairs,* vol. 10; memorandum from Watson to Roosevelt, Sept. 25, 1939, FDR Papers, Departmental, Box 103, PSF, War Department 1939.

11. General Marshall understood how to impress important points on President Roosevelt. Thinking that the president might visit Fort Benning, Georgia, on a trip to Warm Springs, Marshall told the commandant of the infantry school how Roosevelt's interest in the practical side of training might be awakened. No one should "press him to see this or that or understand this or that: that whatever is furnished him in the way of data be on one sheet of paper, with all high-sounding language eliminated, and with very pertinent paragraphed under-lined headings; that a little sketch of ordinary page size is probably the most effective method, as he is quickly bored by papers, by lengthy discussions, and by anything short of a few pungent sentences of description. You have to intrigue his interest, and then it knows no limit." Marshall recommended using "a good sergeant with the gift of restrained gab" to deal with Roosevelt. "I have found," said Marshall, "that the ordinary Army method of presenting things to the President gets us nowhere and rather irritates him." Marshall to Brig. Gen. Asa L. Singleton, Nov. 22, 1939, in Larry I. Bland, *The Papers of George Catlett Marshall,* vol. 2, *"We Cannot Delay," July 1, 1939–December 6, 1941* (Baltimore: Johns Hopkins Press, 1986), pp. 107–108.

12. Watson, *Chief of Staff,* pp. 100–101; Robert F. Futrell, *Ideas, Concepts, Doctrine: A History of Basic Thinking in the United States Air Force, 1907–1964* (Maxwell Air Force Base, Ala.: Air University, 1974; Maxwell Air Force Base, Ala.: Air University, 1979), pp. 49–51.

13. "Memorandum for Brigadier General Edwin M. Watson, Secretary to the President," Oct. 10, 1939, RG 165, WPD, Box 75, 888-106.

14. Note the similarities between this plan and Knerr's paper. Lt. Col.

Carl Spaatz, "Strategically Offensive Operations in the Far East," Sept. 1, 1939, and Arnold, "Implementation of Air Board Report," Oct. 19, 1939, RG 165, WPD, Box 187, 3747.

15. For a discussion of War Plan ORANGE, see Weigley, *The American Way of War*, pp. 245–46. Langer and Gleason, *Challenge to Isolation*, pp. 149–50; Maurice Matloff and Edwin M. Snell, *Strategic Planning for Coalition Warfare, 1941–1942* (Washington, D.C.: Office of the Chief of Military History, Department of the Army, 1953), pp. 1–10. For an example of the public expression of the army's belief in the indefensibility of the Philippines, see Maj. Gen. (Ret.) William C. Rivers's letter to the editor in the *New York Times*, Nov. 26, 1939.

16. Notes of the meeting on October 30 were reconstructed from memory and brief notes taken by H. S. Hansell (memorandum from H. S. Hansell to Eaker, Oct. 31, 1939, Spaatz Papers, Diaries, Box 7, Apr. 24–Dec., 1939).

17. *New York Times*, Nov. 27, 1939.

18. McFarland, *Woodring*, pp. 192–93, 210–18; Arnold, *Global Mission*, pp. 186–87.

19. Memorandum from Marshall to Stark, Nov. 7, 1939, quoted in editor's note and letter from Marshall to Lt. Gen. Albert J. Bowley, Nov. 9, 1939, in Bland, *"We Cannot Delay,"* pp. 100–102; *New York Times*, Jan. 7, 1940.

20. *New York Times*, Feb. 25, 1940.

21. Marshall to Maj. Gen. Charles D. Herron, Feb. 14, 1940, in Bland, *"We Cannot Delay,"* pp. 157–58.

22. Haywood S. Hansell, Jr., "Harold L. George: Apostle of Air Power," in *Makers of the United States Air Force*, ed. John L. Frisbee (Washington, D.C.: Office of Air Force History, United States Air Force, 1987), pp. 81–82; Marshall to Maj. Gen. Edmund L. Daley, Feb. 14, 1940, Marshall to Maj. Gen. Charles D. Herron, Feb. 14, 1940, Marshall to Brazilian Army Chief of Staff Goes Monteiro, Mar. 18, 1940, Marshall to Maj. Gen. Daniel Van Voorhis, Apr. 2, 1940, all in Bland, *"We Cannot Delay,"* pp. 156–58, 175, 186–87.

23. Langer and Gleason, *The Challenge to Isolation*, pp. 419–26; *New York Times*, May 2, 3, 5, 6, 1940. On May 6, a *Times* editorial called for yet another advisory commission appointed by the president to consider "every aspect of our defense problem."

24. *New Republic*, Apr. 29, May 13, 1940.

25. George Fielding Eliot, "Three Thousand More Airplanes?: The President's Proposals for National Defense," *New Republic*, Jan. 29, 1939, pp. 334–35.

26. Dallek, *FDR and American Foreign Policy*, p. 238; Samuel Eliot Morison, *History of United States Naval Operations in World War II*, vol. 3, *The Rising Sun in the Pacific, 1931–April 1942* (Boston: Little, Brown and Company, 1948), pp. 42–43; *New York Times*, May 8, May 9, 1940.

27. Langer and Gleason, *The Challenge to Isolation*, pp. 436–68; Matloff and Snell, *Strategic Planning for Coalition Warfare*, pp. 11–12.

28. Marshall to Bernard M. Baruch, May 14, 1940, editor's note, both in Bland, *"We Cannot Delay,"* pp. 212–13; Langer and Gleason, pp. 472–75; Watson, pp. 166–68; president's message to the Congress, May 16, 1940, in Rosenman, *Public Papers and Addresses of FDR*, vol. 9, pp. 198–205.

29. Matloff and Snell, *Strategic Planning for Coalition Warfare*, pp. 12–21; memorandum entitled "National Strategic Decisions," May 22, 1940, memorandum from Marshall to WPD, May 23, 1940, both in Bland, *"We Cannot Delay,"* pp. 218–21.

30. Watson, *Chief of Staff*, pp. 305–306.

31. *New York Times*, Sept. 13, Sept. 17, 1940; memorandum from Marshall to Roosevelt, Nov. 13, 1940, in Bland, *"We Cannot Delay,"* pp. 348–49; Watson, *Chief of Staff*, pp. 305–309.

32. Langer and Gleason, *The Challenge to Isolation*, pp. 193–94, 291–95, 597–98; Dallek, *FDR and American Foreign Policy*, pp. 238–40.

33. Matloff and Snell, *Strategic Planning for Coalition Warfare*, pp. 24–29; memorandum from Stark to Secretary of the Navy Knox, Nov. 12, 1940, FDR Papers, PSF Safe File Box 5, Navy Department "Plan Dog;" memorandum from Marshall to General Gerow, Jan. 17, 1941, in Bland, *"We Cannot Delay,"* pp. 391–92.

34. Michael Schaller, "American Air Strategy in China, 1939–1940: The Origins of Clandestine Air Warfare," *American Quarterly*, vol. 28, Spring, 1976, pp. 3–12; William L. Langer and S. Everett Gleason, *The Undeclared War, 1940–1941* (New York: Harper and Brothers, 1953), pp. 302–304; Duane Schultz, *The Maverick War: Chennault and the Flying Tigers* (New York: St. Martin's Press, 1987), pp. 1–15.

35. "Uproar over War Control Bill Halts Diet in Air-Scared Tokyo," *Washington Post*, Feb. 25, 1938. The Chicago *Daily Tribune* carried a front-page article on February 24, 1938, about the Chinese raid along with an article about the B-17 flight to Argentina. The Los Angeles *Times*, on February 24, 1938, reported the incident on its front page as well. On February 25, an editorial cartoon in the *Times* showed a Chinese dragoon dropping bombs on Formosa and looking angrily toward Japan. Two days later the *Times* presented a map showing where the air raids took place with the comment, "Terror was spread in the southern islands of Japan proper. . . ."

36. Schaller, "American Air Strategy in China," pp. 3–12; Langer and Gleason, *The Undeclared War*, pp. 302–304; Schultz, *The Maverick War*, pp 1–15.

CHAPTER IX. THE BEST-LAID SCHEMES OF MICE AND MEN

1. McFarland, *Woodring*, pp. 223–34; Burns, *Lion and the Fox*, p. 424; Bruce Allen Murphy, *The Brandeis/Frankfurter Connection: The Secret Political Activities of Two Supreme Court Justices* (New York: Oxford University Press, 1982), pp. 195–200.

2. Watson, *Chief of Staff*, pp. 286–95; Craven and Cate, *Army Air Forces*, vol. 1, pp. 114–16; Arnold, *Global Mission*, p. 194; Coffey, *Hap*, pp. 219–20.

3. Knerr to Andrews, June 18, 1941, Andrews to Knerr, June 23, 1941, Andrews to Knerr, July 1, 1941, all in Andrews Papers, General Correspondence, Box 5, Personal Correspondence, "K" 1929–41; Andrews to Alexander de Seversky, July 30, 1941, Andrews Papers, General Correspondence, Box 6, Personal Correspondence, "S" 1930–42; Coffey, *Hap*, pp. 234–37.

4. Matloff and Snell, *Strategic Planning for Coalition Warfare*, pp. 32–48, 65–67; Watson, *Chief of Staff*, pp. 423–25; Arnold, *Global Mission*, p. 209.

5. Watson, *Chief of Staff*, pp. 425–32.

6. Memorandum from Marshall to Gerow, Feb. 10, 1941, extract of memorandum from Gerow to Marshall, Feb. 11, 1941, both in Bland, *"We Cannot Delay,"* pp. 416–18.

7. *New York Times*, Feb. 21, Feb. 22, 1941.

8. Memorandum from Marshall to Gerow, Feb. 26, 1941, in Bland, *"We Cannot Delay,"* pp. 430–33.

9. *New York Times*, Feb. 28, 1941.

10. Watson, *Chief of Staff*, pp. 331–43; Matloff and Snell, *Strategic Planning for Coalition Warfare*, pp. 58–62.

11. *New York Times*, May 6, 1941.

12. Stimson included Roosevelt's directive in a letter to Rep. Carl Vinson, chairman of the House Naval Affairs Committee, July 24, 1941, RG 107, Secretary of War (Safe File), Box 2, "Big Bomber Project," National Archives, Washington, D.C.

13. Memorandum from Brig. Gen. Sherman Miles to Marshall, "Information from Cairo, Egypt," May 29, 1941, paraphrase of code cablegram sent from Cairo, May 27, 1941, both in FDR Papers, PSF Departmental, Box 103, War Department 1941.

14. James MacGregor Burns, *Roosevelt: The Soldier of Freedom, 1940–1945* (New York: Harcourt Brace Jovanovich, 1970), p. 76; Russell Grenfell, *The "Bismarck" Episode* (New York: Macmillan, 1948), reprinted in *Reader's Digest: Illustrated Story of World War II* (Pleasantville, N.Y.: Reader's Digest Association, 1969), pp. 136–42.

15. *New York Times*, May 26, 1941; Alexander P. de Seversky, "The Twilight of Sea Power," *American Mercury* (June, 1941), pp. 647–58.

16. Abstract of a memorandum for the president's information, May 26, 1941, FDR Papers, Official File, OF 25-U, War Department Box 32, Chief of the Air Corps, Abstracts.

17. Dallek, *FDR and American Foreign Policy*, pp. 261–65; Morison, *The Rising Sun in the Pacific*, pp. 56–58; Undated Aide-Memoire, "Defense of Hawaii," FDR Papers, PSF Departmental, Box 103, War Department 1941. The aide-memoire was undated and unsigned, but an office note stated that it was added to President Roosevelt's files on May 3, 1941. Also, somebody (possibly General Marshall) added a handwritten footnote that a mass flight of B-17s from the mainland to Hawaii was scheduled for May 20 and that a number "of this type of plane could be dispatched immediately if the situation grew critical." Since planning for this flight started in early April, the paper appeared while Roosevelt was still considering transferring the ships to the Atlantic. Written by a third person at the top of the document is the statement, "Modern Planes have completely changed the situation as to defensibility."

18. Craven and Cate, *Army Air Forces*, vol. 1, pp. 172–73.

19. Hanson Baldwin, "The Atlantic Fleet Grows," *New York Times*, May 30, 1941.

20. *New York Times*, June 12, 18, 19, 1941.

21. Henry N. Dorris, "Philippines Arm as Key in Defense," *New York Times*, June 22, 1941.

22. Burns, *Soldier of Freedom*, pp. 106–10; Watson, *Chief of Staff*, pp. 434–38; telegram from Marshall to MacArthur, July 26, 1941, in Bland, "*We Cannot Delay*," p. 577.

23. Watson, *Chief of Staff*, pp. 436–40.

24. Stimson to Vinson, July 24, 1941, RG 107, Secretary of War (Safe File), Box 2, "Big Bomber Project." The terms *long-range* and *heavy* referred to four-engine bombers. The army referred to the B-17s and B-24s as heavy bombers. Twin-engine B-18s and B-25s were called medium bombers.

25. Ickes, *Secret Diary*, vol. 2, pp. 467–70.

26. *New York Times*, Aug. 22, 1941.

27. Craven and Cate, *Army Air Forces*, vol. 1, pp. 177–78; statement by Former Secretary of War Henry L. Stimson to the Joint Committee on the Investigation of the Pearl Harbor Attack, 79th Cong., 2d sess., Apr. 9, Apr. 11, May 23, May 31, 1946, p. 5417; memorandum from Marshall to Arnold, July 16, 1941, in Bland, "*We Cannot Delay*", pp. 567–68; memorandum from Arnold to Marshall, "Status of Airplanes and Pilots in the Philippine Islands," July 18, 1941, Arnold Papers, Official File, 1932–46, Box 51, Philippine File No. 254; memorandum from Assistant Chief of Staff Brig. Gen. L. T. Gerow to assistant chief of Staff, G-3: "Deterrent to Japan's Move South," July 25, 1941, RG 165, WPD, 4544-2.

28. Memorandum from Marshall to Stark, Sept. 12, 1941, in Bland, "*We Cannot Delay*," pp. 605–606.

29. Arnold's notes on the Argentia Conference for Aug. 7, 1941, Arnold Papers, Conference File 1941–45, Box 181, "Argentia" Conference.

30. Haywood S. Hansell, Jr., *The Air Plan that Defeated Hitler* (Atlanta: Higgins-McArthur/Longino and Porter, 1972), pp. 57–67; Craven and Cate, *Army Air Forces*, vol. 1, pp. 146–48.

31. Memorandum from Spaatz to Arnold, "Strategically Offensive Operations in the Far East," Sept. 1, 1939, RG 165, WPD, Box 187, 3748-18.

32. Craven and Cate, *Army Air Forces*, vol. 1, pp. 178–81; Arnold to MacArthur, Oct. 7, Oct. 14, 1941, Arnold Papers, Official Decimal File 1938–46, 686 Far East File.

33. Lewis H. Brereton, *The Brereton Diaries: The War in the Air in the Pacific, Middle East and Europe, 3 October 1941–8 May 1945* (New York: William Morrow and Company, 1946), pp. 3–11; rough draft of Brereton's book, pp. 2–5, Arnold Papers, Subject File, 1918–49, Box 225, Philippine Islands Defense.

34. Arnold to MacArthur, Oct. 7, Oct. 14, 1941, Arnold Papers, Official Decimal File, 1938–46, 686 Far East File.

35. Rough draft of Brereton's book, p. 4, Arnold Papers, Subject File, 1918–49, Box 225, Philippine Islands Defense. Mention of Vladivostok and Russia in the rough draft was marked for exclusion and left out of the published book.

36. Memorandum from Gerow to Stimson, "Strategic Concept of the Philippine Islands," Oct. 8, 1941, RG 107, Secretary of War (Safe File), Box 11, "Philippines."

37. Memorandum and map of the western Pacific from Stimson to Hull, Oct. 4, 1941, RG 107, Secretary of War (Safe File), Box 11, "Philippines."

38. Memorandum of conversation between Secretary Hull and Soviet Ambassador Maxim Litvinov, Dec. 11, 1941, FDR Papers, PSF, Diplomatic Correspondence, Box 68, Russia 1941.

39. Stimson to Roosevelt, Sept. 22, 1941, and Roosevelt to Stimson, Oct. 14, 1941, FDR Papers, PSF Departmental, Box 103, War Department, 1941.

40. Memorandum from Arnold to Stimson, "Diversion of Additional Heavy Bombers," Oct. 16, 1941, RG 107, Secretary of War (Safe File), "Big Bomber Project"; Stimson to Roosevelt, Oct. 21, 1941, RG 107, Secretary of War (Safe File) Stimson, Box 15, "White House Correspondence."

41. Memorandum from Spaatz to the assistant chief of staff, G-4, "Bombs and Fuses, Philippine Department," July 31, 1941, Arnold Papers, Official Decimal File, 1938–46, Box 136, SAS 471.6 (4) File.

42. Arnold, *Global Mission*, p. 243; Arnold to Vannevar Bush, September 24, 1941, Bush to Arnold, Sept. 29, 1941, memorandum from Col. Edgar P. Sorensen, chief of A-4 Division, to Arnold, Oct. 13, 1941, all in Arnold Papers, Official File, 1932–46, Box 41, File No. 39, "Bombs."

43. Dr. Roger Adams to Lt. Col. Max Schneider, Oct. 14, 1941, Schneider to Adams, Oct. 24, 1941, both in Arnold Papers, Official Decimal File, 1938–46, Box 136, File No. 471.6 (52).

44. Memorandum from Marshall to Stark, Sept. 12, 1941, in Bland, *"We Cannot Delay,"* pp. 605–606.

45. Memorandum from the Adj. Gen. to the chief of Chemical Warfare Service, "Shipment of Air Corps Bombs to the Philippines," Nov. 4, 1941, Arnold Papers, Official Decimal File, Box 136, File 471.6 (26); memorandum from Arnold to Marshall, "Bomb Situation in the Philippines," Dec. 1, 1941, Arnold Papers, Official File, 1932–46, Box 51, Philippine File No. 254.

46. Telegram from Grew to Secretary of State Hull, Nov. 3, 1941, FDR Papers, PSF, Confidential, Box 30, Japan, 8 May 1939–17 Nov. 1941.

47. E. Ruffcorn Armstrong to Sen. Arthur Capper, Nov. 15, 1941, Capper to Arnold, Nov. 25, 1941, and Lt. Col. William W. Dick to Capper, Dec. 4, 1941, all in Arnold Papers, Official File, 1932–46, Box 51, Philippine File No. 254.

48. Speech delivered by General Arnold at West Point, Oct. 10, 1941, Eaker Papers, Speech Article Book File Box 38, Speeches by General Arnold prepared by Ira C. Eaker.

49. Memorandum from Stimson to Marshall, "Proposed Announcement as to the Rearmament of the Philippines," Oct. 31, 1941, RG 107, Secretary of War (Safe File), Box 11, "Philippines."

50. Memorandum by Col. Charles W. Bundy of his conversation with Marshall, Nov. 1, 1941, editor's note, both in Bland, *"We Cannot Delay,"* pp. 657–60.

51. Memorandum from Robert L. Sherrod to David W. Hulburd, Jr.,

Nov. 15, 1941, in Bland, *"We Cannot Delay,"* pp. 676–81. The Americans believed that the Japanese fighters had a ceiling of only 15,000 feet, which is half that of the B-24. Walter D. Edmonds, *They Fought with What They Had* (Boston: Little, Brown and Company, 1951), pp. 5–6; Arthur Krock, "Philippines as a Fortress: New Air Power Gives Islands Offensive Strength, Changing Strategy in Pacific," *New York Times*, Nov. 19, 1941.

52. This possibility was suggested by Frank Freidel (letter to the author, July 27, 1988).

53. Dallek, *FDR and American Foreign Policy*, pp. 305–10; memorandum for the president, "Japanese Convoy Movement towards Indo-China," Nov. 26, 1941, in Bland, *"We Cannot Delay,"* p. 686.

54. Louis Morton, *The War in the Pacific: The Fall of the Philippines*, *United States Army in World War II* (Washington, D.C.: Office of the Chief of Military History, Department of the Army, 1953), pp. 77–88; "Telephone Conversation between General Arnold and General Brereton, Manila, 12-8-41," Arnold Papers, Miscellaneous Official Records 1941–46, Box 185.

55. Robert Burns, "To a Mouse," *The Complete Works of Burns* (Boston: Houghton Mifflin Co., 1897), pp. 31–32.

APPENDIX I

1. Giulio Douhet, *Command of the Air*, trans. Dino Ferrari (New York: Coward-McCann, 1942; Washington, D.C.: Office of Air Force History, 1983), pp. viii–ix.

2. Douhet, *Command of the Air*, pp. 5–6.

3. Ibid., p. 9.

4. Ibid., pp. 9–10.

5. Ibid., p. 19.

6. Ibid., pp. 52–54.

7. William Mitchell, *Winged Defense: The Development and Possibilities of Modern Air Power — Economic and Military* (New York: G. P. Putnam's Sons, 1925), p. 213.

8. Mitchell, *Winged Defense*, pp. 101–102.

9. Douhet, *Command of the Air*, pp. 55–58.

10. Mitchell, *Winged Defense*, pp. 101–102.

11. Weigley, *The American Way of War*, pp. 234–36.

12. Watson, *Chief of Staff*, pp. 100–101.

13. Weigley, *The American Way of War*, pp. 226–27.

14. Douhet, *Command of the Air*, pp. 34–35.

15. Ibid., pp. 44–45.

16. Ibid., p. 57.

17. Craven and Cate, *Army Air Forces*, vol. 1, pp. 64–66.

18. Douhet, *Command of the Air*, pp. 19–20.

19. Ibid., p. 21.

20. Ibid., p. 39.

21. Lt. Col. Carl Spaatz, "Strategically Offensive Operations in the Far East," Sept. 1, 1939, RG 165, WPD, Box 187, 3747.

22. Memorandum from Spaatz to the assistant chief of staff, G-4, "Bombs and Fuses, Philippine Department," July 31, 1941, Arnold Papers, Official Decimal File, 1938–46, Box 136, SAS 471.6 (4) File.

23. Arnold, *Global Mission*, p. 242.

APPENDIX II

1. Maurer, *Aviation in the U.S. Army*, pp. 451–53; Robert Mueller, *Air Force Bases*, vol. 1, *Active Air Force Bases within the United States of America on 1 January 1974* (Maxwell AFB, Montgomery, Ala.: Research Division, Albert F. Simpson Historical Research Center, 1982), pp. 7, 18, 21, 34, 154, 168, 199, 206, 267.

Bibliographic Essay

This essay does not list all the sources I looked at while researching and writing this book. It includes only the most significant. I hope my comments will facilitate further research on the Army Air Corps.

Joseph J. Corn, *The Winged Gospel: America's Romance with Aviation, 1900–1950* (New York: Oxford University Press, 1983), helped me understand the importance of aviation to Americans in the years between the world wars. Amid wild schemes to build landing fields over cities and at sea, the proclamations of the supporters of air power seemed tame. William Stott, *Documentary Expression and Thirties America* (New York: Oxford University Press, 1973), demonstrated the importance of radio and photography during the period.

For the political life of Franklin D. Roosevelt, I have used Frank Freidel's *Franklin D. Roosevelt: The Apprenticeship* and *Franklin D. Roosevelt: The Ordeal* (Boston: Little, Brown and Co., 1952, 1954); James MacGregor Burns's two-volume study, *Roosevelt: The Lion and the Fox, 1882–1940* and *Roosevelt: The Soldier of Freedom, 1940–1945* (New York: Harcourt, Brace and World, 1965; Harcourt Brace Jovanovich, 1970), and William E. Leuchtenburg's *Franklin D. Roosevelt and the New Deal, 1932–1940* (New York: Harper and Row, 1963). The influence of Felix Frankfurter on FDR is discussed in Bruce Allen Murphy, *The Brandeis/Frankfurter Connection: The Secret Political Activities of Two Supreme Court Justices* (New York: Oxford University Press, 1982). The internal workings of the Roosevelt presidency and the president's private conversations are found in Harold L. Ickes, *The Secret Diary of Harold L. Ickes,* vol. 2, *The Inside Struggle, 1936–1939* (New York: Simon and Schuster, 1954), and Robert E.

Sherwood, *Roosevelt and Hopkins: An Intimate History*, rev. ed. (New York: Harper and Brothers, 1950). Although I believe he places too much importance on influence of public opinion, I have turned to Robert Dallek, *Franklin D. Roosevelt and American Foreign Policy, 1932–1945* (New York: Oxford University Press, 1979), for information concerning FDR's foreign policy. I also found in William L. Langer and S. Everett Gleason, *The Challenge to Isolation: 1937–1940* (New York: Harper and Brothers, 1952) and *The Undeclared War, 1940–1941* (New York: Harper and Brothers, 1953), important information about FDR's reactions to air attacks in Europe. Douglas MacArthur, *Reminiscences* (New York: McGraw Hill, 1964), describes his dealings with President Roosevelt.

The public papers of Franklin Roosevelt are available to scholars in Samuel I. Rosenman, ed., *The Public Papers and Addresses of Franklin D. Roosevelt*, 13 volumes (New York: Macmillan, 1938–50). More recently, Roosevelt's papers dealing with foreign affairs have been published by Edgar B. Nixon, ed. *Franklin D. Roosevelt and Foreign Affairs*, 3 volumes, *January 1933–February 1934* (Cambridge, Massachusetts: Belknap Press, 1969), and Donald B. Schewe, ed., *Franklin D. Roosevelt and Foreign Affairs*, 10 volumes, *January 1937–August 1939* (New York: Garland, 1979).

Russell F. Weigley provides a short discussion of the United States Army between the wars in *History of the United States Army* (New York: Macmillan, 1967). The budgetary problems of the War Department under Presidents Hoover and Roosevelt are discussed in John W. Killigrew's *The Impact of the Great Depression on the Army* (New York: Garland, 1979). Important insights into the political workings within the War Department under Roosevelt can be found in Keith D. McFarland's *Harry H. Woodring: A Political Biography of FDR's Controversial Secretary of War* (Lawrence: University of Kansas Press, 1975). American military planning for the First World War is discussed in Daniel R. Beaver's *Newton D. Baker and the American War Effort, 1917–1919* (Lincoln: University of Nebraska Press, 1966).

Forest C. Pogue, *George C. Marshall*, 3 volumes (New York: Viking, 1963–73), is the best biography of the wartime chief of staff. Larry I. Bland and Sharon R. Ritenour, *The Papers of George Catlett Marshall*, 2 volumes (Baltimore: Johns Hopkins University Press, 1981, 1986), have done an excellent job in editing the general's papers through December 6, 1941.

Telford Taylor, *Munich: The Price of Peace* (Garden City, N.Y.: Doubleday, 1979), is the best source for information about the Munich Crisis. Taylor deals primarily with the crisis from a European perspective, but he presents important commentary on Charles A. Lindbergh's role in shaping British and French impressions of the Luftwaffe. The importance of Lindbergh on Ambassador Joseph Kennedy may be seen in Charles A. Lindbergh, *The Wartime Journals of Charles A. Lindbergh* (New York: Harcourt Brace Jovanovich, 1970). Lindbergh and Maj. Truman Smith's warning about the Luftwaffe has been published in *The Airpower Historian* 10 (Apr., 1963), pp. 54–56. For the general history of Europe, I used Raymond J. Sontag, *A Broken World, 1919–1939*, vol. 19 of *The Rise of Modern Europe*, ed. by William L. Langer, (New York: Harper and Row, 1971).

The sections written about the Army Air Corps and the United States Air Force by Robert R. Futrell and Robert T. Finney in Robin Higham, *A Guide to the Sources of United States Military History* and *Supplement* (Hamden, Conn.: Archon Books, 1975, 1981), pp. 404–29 and 106–15 respectively, indicate an increased interest in American military aviation. A majority of the works they list deal with tactics or the technical aspects of airplanes. Good introductions to the concepts of air power are found in Robin Higham, *Air Power: A Concise History* (London: Macdonald, 1972), and Lee Kennett, *A History of Strategic Bombing* (New York: Charles Scribner's Sons, 1982). Another source is James Trapier Lowe, *A Philosophy of Air Power* (Lanham, N.Y.: University Press of America, 1984). The formulation of air power doctrines in the Army Air Corps is discussed in Robert R. Futrell, *Ideas, Concepts, Doctrine: A History of Basic Thinking in the United States Air Force, 1907–1964* (Maxwell Air Force Base, Ala.: Air University, 1974), and Thomas H. Greer, *The Development of Air Doctrine in the Army Air Arm, 1917–1941* (Washington, D.C.: Office of Air Force History, 1955). An interesting discussion of Billy Mitchell is found in Russell Weigley, *The American Way of War: A History of United States Military Strategy and Policy* (Bloomington: Indiana University Press, 1977), pp. 223–41. To see how British planning differed from American, one might read Malcolm Smith, *British Air Strategy Between the Wars* (Oxford: Clarendon Press, 1984).

A good history of the United States Air Force is not available. Carrol V. Glines, *The Compact History of the United States Air Force* (New York: Hawthorn Books, 1963), and Monro MacCloskey, *The United States Air Force* (New York: Frederick A. Praeger, 1967), have written popular histories. David A. Anderton, *The History of the U.S. Air Force* (New York: Crescent Books, 1981), at least includes colorful photographs and drawings.

Generally, discussion of the interwar army air force is relegated to introductions in works dealing with wartime activities. The one great exception, however, is Maurer Maurer's *Aviation in the U.S. Army: 1919–1939* (Washington, D.C.: Office of Air Force History, 1987).

Descriptive rather than analytical, which Maurer freely admits (p. viii), this is the starting place for any research on interwar army aviation. Wesley Frank Craven and James Lee Cate, eds., *The Army Air Forces in World War II*, 6 volumes (Chicago: University of Chicago Press, 1948–1955), provide the next best source for detailed information. President Roosevelt's expansion of the Army Air Corps is described in Irving B. Holley, Jr., *Buying Aircraft: Materiel Procurement for the Army Air Forces* (Washington, D.C.: Office of the Chief of Military History, Department of the Army, 1964). Specific information about aircraft design and production may be found in Benjamin S. Kelsey, *The Dragon's Teeth: The Creation of United States Air Power for World War II* (Washington, D.C.: Smithsonian Institution Press, 1982). American aircraft sales to France are discussed in John McVickar Haight, Jr., "France's First War Mission to the United States," *Airpower Historian* 11 (Jan., 1964): 11–15. Haight argues that the French were not dilatory in their efforts to purchase American-built airplanes.

Peter M. Bowers, *Fortress in the Sky* (Granada Hills, Calif.: Sentry Books, 1976), provides technical details and many photographs of the Boeing B-17. Color drawings and information on the markings of the various planes and units of the Army Air Corps are found in Dana Bell, *Air Force Colors*, vol. 1, *1926–1942* (Carrollton, Tex.: Squadron/ Signal Publications, 1979).

Biographies of army aviators are lacking. William Mitchell has received the most attention, but biographies of the vocal airman pay scant attention to the years after his court-martial in 1926. Alfred F. Hurley, *Billy Mitchell: Crusader for Air Power* (New York: Franklin Watts, 1964; Bloomington: Indiana University Press, 1975), and Isaac D. Levine, *Mitchell: Pioneer of Air Power* (New York: Duell, Sloan and Pearce, 1943), are the best. Mitchell expressed his thoughts in books and articles, such as *Winged Defense: The Development and Possibilities of Modern Air Power—Economic and Military* (New York: G. P. Putnam's Sons, 1925), *Skyways: A Book on Modern Aeronautics* (Philadelphia: J. B. Lippincott, 1930), and "How Should We Organize Our National Air Power?" *Saturday Evening Post*, Mar. 14, 1925, pp. 6–7. A selected bibliography of Mitchell's writings may be found in Raymond R. Flugel, "United States Air Power Doctrine: A Study of the Influence of William Mitchell and Giulio Douhet at the Air Corps Tactical School, 1921–1935" (Ph.D diss., University of Oklahoma, 1965). Emile Gauvreau, *The Wild Blue Yonder: Sons of the Prophet Carry On* (New York: E.P. Dutton, 1944), zealously describes Mitchell's attempts to ferret out conspiracies. Examples of Mitchell's public debates with the navy about air power versus battleships may be found in articles by Mitchell, "How Should We Organize Our National

Air Power?" *Saturday Evening Post,* Mar. 14, 1925, pp. 6–7, and Curtis D. Wilbur, "A Balanced Navy," *Saturday Evening Post,* Jan. 10, 1925, p. 10. The Office of Air Force History has reissued Guilio Douhet's *Command of the Air,* translated by Dino Ferrari (New York: Coward-McCann, 1942) as part of the United States Air Force Project Warrior Studies Series, Richard H. Kohn and Joseph P. Harahan, general eds., (Washington, D.C.: New Imprint by the Office of Air Force History, 1983).

Few other army airmen have received attention. Although he leaves out important army fliers like Hugh Knerr, Flint O. DuPre, *U.S. Air Force Biographical Dictionary* (New York: Franklin Watts, 1965), provides brief sketches. John L. Frisbee, *Makers of the United States Air Force* (Washington, D.C.: Office Air Force History, 1987), has compiled article length biographies of twelve key air force officers.

Benjamin D. Foulois with C. V. Glines, *From the Wright Brothers to the Astronauts: The Memoirs of Major General Benjamin D. Foulois* (New York: McGraw-Hill, 1968), is the only work that encompasses this airman's entire life. Understandably, Foulois is biased against Roosevelt, and he takes great pains to clear his name of the air mail and aircraft purchasing scandals. Norman E. Borden, Jr., *Air Mail Emergency, 1934: An Account of Seventy-Eight Tense Days in the Winter of 1934 When the Army Flew the United States Mail* (Freeport, Maine: Bond Wheelwright, 1968), provides a detailed narrative of the air mail episode with little analysis. John F. Shiner, *Foulois and the U.S. Army Air Corps, 1931–1935* (Washington, D.C.: Office of Air Force History, 1983), fills an important gap in the years between Mitchell and Pearl Harbor. Foulois' troubles with Congress are detailed in Edwin H. Rutkowsky, *The Politics of Military Aviation Procurement, 1926–1934: A Study in the Political Assertion of Consensual Values* (Columbus: Ohio State University Press, 1966).

Although sometimes confused about the date of events, Henry H. "Hap" Arnold's memoirs, *Global Mission* (New York: Harper and Brothers, 1949), give valuable information on army aviation to the end of the Second World War. Thomas M. Coffey, *Hap: the Story of the U.S. Air Force and the Man Who Built It, General Henry H. "Hap" Arnold* (New York: Viking Press, 1982), is the only biography available. Arnold and Ira C. Eaker coauthored two books before the Second World War, *This Flying Game* (New York: Funk and Wagnalls, 1936) and *Winged Warfare* (New York: Harper and Brothers, 1941). Written for a general audience, these two books provide a view of prewar military and general aviation.

The other commanders of the army air arm have been neglected. For information on the *Utah* and *Rex* episodes and the South American flights, see Curtis E. LeMay and MacKinlay Kantor, *Mission with LeMay: My Story* (Garden City, New York: Doubleday, 1965) and George W. Goddard with DeWitt S. Copp, *Overview: A Life-Long Adventure in Aerial Photography* (Garden City, New York: Doubleday, 1969). Thomas M. Coffey, *Iron Eagle: The Turbulent Life of General Curtis LeMay* (New York: Crown, 1986), deals mainly with LeMay's career after 1941. James Parton's biography of Ira Eaker, *"Air Force Spoken Here": General Ira Eaker and the Command of the Air* (Bethesda, Md.: Adler and Adler, 1986) is too episodic. A brief sketch of Hugh Knerr is found in Murray Green, "Major General Hugh J. Knerr, Hard Campaigner for Air Power," *Air Force Magazine* 61 (Oct., 1978): 90–92. Biographies of Claire Chennault include Marth Byrd, *Chennault: Giving Wings to the Tiger* (Tuscaloosa: University of Alabama Press, 1987) and Duane Schultz, *The Maverick War: Chennault and the Flying Tigers* (New York: St. Martin's Press, 1987). David R. Mets has written a biography of Carl Spaatz, *Master of Airpower: General Carl A. Spaatz* (Novato, Calif.: Presidio Press, 1988). Byrd and Mets have produced the best biographies of the air force commanders.

America's strategic planning before World War II is described in Mark S. Watson, *Chief of Staff: Prewar Plans and Preparations* (Washington, D.C.: Historical Division, Department of the Army, 1950), and Maurice Matloff and Edwin M. Snell, *Strategic Planning for Coalition Warfare, 1941–1942* (Washington, D.C.: Office of the Chief of Military History, Department of the Army, 1953). Haywood S. Hansell, *The Air Plan that Defeated Hitler* (Atlanta: Higgins-McArthur/Longino and Porter, 1972), offers an inside look at the Air War Plans Division and AWPD/1. Problems encountered by the United States in the Pacific are described in Samuel Eliot Morison, *History of the United States Naval Operations in World War II,* volume 3, *The Rising Sun in the Pacific, 1931–April 1942* (Boston: Little, Brown and Co., 1948).

Information on the Philippines may be found in Louis Morton, *The War in the Pacific: The Fall of the Philippines* (Washington, D.C.: Office of the Chief of Military History, Department of the Army, 1953), and Walter D. Edmonds, *They Fought with What They Had: The Story of the Army Air Forces in The Southwest Pacific, 1941–1942* (Boston: Little, Brown and Co., 1951). The firsthand account of the commander of the Far East Air Force is in Lewis H. Brereton, *The Brereton Diaries: The War in the Air in the Pacific, Middle East and Europe, 3 October 1941–8 May 1945* (New York: William Morrow and Co., 1946). A draft of Brereton's book with editorial suggestions is in the H. H. "Hap" Arnold Papers.

Most of the works I consulted have a conservative slant and point to the past as proof that more tax dollars should be spent on the air force. Recently, however, historians have turned away from the traditional studies to investigate the motives behind the use of bombing. Ronald Schaffer has looked at the ethical considerations of America's military aviators in "American Military Ethics in World War II: The Bombing of German Civilians," *Journal of American History* (Dec., 1980) and *Wings of Judgement: American Bombing in World War II* (New York: Oxford University Press, 1985). Michael Sherry has studied how perceptions of air power, racism, and bureaucracy influenced American bombing campaigns in *The Rise of American Air Power: The Creation of Armageddon* (New York: Yale University Press, 1987).

During the 1930s, the *New York Times* printed notices of its commitment to aviation, and every Sunday it devoted a page to aviation news. The editors often objected to spending more money on the Army Air Corps and supported battleships over airplanes for defense. At the same time, the aviation correspondents were writing articles that supported the Army Air Corps. Fliers are not very good at leaving documents, but they love to tell stories. Taking advantage of that quirk, correspondents from the *Times* would report what the army fliers at Mitchel Field, Long Island, said, which left a written record. As the *Times*'s military affairs correspondent, Hanson Baldwin exhibited a pro-navy bias. A pro-battleship viewpoint was also expressed by the *Washington Post*. Isolationist leanings will be found in the Chicago *Daily Tribune,* and West Coast attitudes were expressed in the Los Angeles *Times.* The *New Republic* voiced a liberal interpretation of military affairs and military spending. *Time, Newsweek,* and *Life* magazines also carried articles and photographs of the army air arm during the interwar years.

The official organ of the Army Air Corps was the *Air Corps News Letter.* Published intermittently by the Office of the Chief of the Air Corps, the *News Letter* contained notices of transfers, deaths, retirements, and pilots' anecdotes. However, it also contained speeches and articles by the commanders of the Army Air Corps. The General Staff's ideas on military subjects may be found in *Infantry Journal,* published by the United States Infantry Association. *American Aviation,* a business journal, presented the aircraft industry's views. Originally critical of Roosevelt, *American Aviation* became more favorable to the president's policies once they included the expansion of America's military and naval aviation.

Before starting any research project on the United States Air Force or its predecessors, one should consult Lawrence J. Paszek, *United States Air Force History: A Guide to Documentary Sources* (Washington, D.C.: Office of Air Force History, 1973). Although dated, this guide describes collections pertaining to the air force at air force depositories, the National Archives, presidential libraries, the Library of Congress, and university libraries around the nation.

I consulted the Franklin D. Roosevelt Papers at the Franklin D. Roosevelt Library, Hyde Park, New York. Most of those records pertaining to the military deal with the war years, but the Official File (OF 25-U), the President's Secretary's File (PSF), and the President's Personal File (PPF) proved useful. The cross reference sheets for 1933–41 in OF 25-U were helpful.

At the Manuscript Division, Library of Congress, Washington, D.C., I used the papers of Frank M. Andrews, Henry H. Arnold, Ira C. Eaker, Benjamin D. Foulois, and Carl Spaatz. Finding aids for all but the Foulois Papers have been reproduced in the microfiche publication *National Inventory of Documentary Sources in the United States: Manuscript Division, Library of Congress* (Teaneck, N.J.: Chadwyck-Healey, 1983). A draft inventory of the Foulois Papers is in the Manuscript Division, and a photocopy may be purchased for a small fee. The Andrews, Arnold, and Foulois Papers are the most useful for the interwar years.

For research in the National Archives and Records Service, Washington, D.C., the *Guide to the National Archives of the United States* (Washington, D.C.: National Archives and Records Service, General Services Administration, 1974) is helpful, but Paszek's guide is more useful. At the National Archives, Military Archives Division, I used Record Group 18 (Army Air Forces), Record Group 107 (Secretary of War), and Record Group 165 (General and Special Staffs). I found the manuscript collections at the Library of Congress more useful than the records at the National Archives. For an organizational history, the reverse was true. Preliminary inventories of these three record groups are available in the Military Archives Division.

Before traveling to Washington, D.C., I recommend contacting the staff of Manuscript Division of the Library of Congress and the Military Archives Division of the National Archives. Their recommendations allowed me to make a thorough search of the large volume of material available and avoid unprofitable avenues.

Although the congressional hearings on Pearl Harbor were concerned with the Japanese attack on the American fleet, the published records reveal how the army intended to employ its bombers in the Philippines. Particularly important are the comments by Secretary of War Henry Stimson, U.S. Congress, Joint Committee on the Investigation of the Pearl Harbor Attack, *Pearl Harbor Attack, Hearings before the Joint Committee on the Investigation of the Pearl Harbor Attack Pursuant to S. Con. Res. 27,* 79th Cong., 2d sess., Apr. 9, Apr. 11, May 23, May 31, 1946.

Index

The Wings of Democracy was composed into type on a Compugraphic digital phototypesetter in ten point Trump Medieval with two points of spacing between the lines. Trump Medieval was also selected for display. The book was designed by Jim Billingsley, typeset by Metricomp, Inc., printed offset by Thomson-Shore, Inc., and bound by John H. Dekker & Sons, Inc. The paper on which this book is printed carries acid-free characteristics for an effective life of at least three hundred years.

TEXAS A&M UNIVERSITY PRESS : COLLEGE STATION